BHAKT

A NECKLACE OF DEVOTIONAL GEMS

An Anthology from Bhagavata

by

VISHNU PURI

with English Translation, Introduction
and Commentary

by

SWAMI TAPASYANANDA

SRI RAMAKRISHNA MATH

MADRAS-600 004 : India

Published by
Adhyaksha
Sri Ramakrishna Math
Mylapore, Chennai-4

IV-2M 3C-8-2009
ISBN 81-7120-224-1

Printed in India at
Sri Ramakrishna Math Printing Press
Mylapore, Chennai-4

PREFACE

An Anthology is certainly no original work, but the four hundred and odd verses comprising the **Bhakti Ratnavali** is something more than a mere selection based on the **Bhagavata**. The methodical way adopted in selection and the systematic treatment of the theme make the work as significant as an original writing itself. As the author has pointed out, its object is to give a person who cannot go through the whole of the **Bhagavata** Text, an idea of the central theme treated therein in a nutshell. The luxuriant foliage of the **Bhagavata** narrative is necessarily omitted, but the main principles of the theme of Bhakti are delineated in it in terms of the original Text of the **Bhagavata**.

According to a prevailing tradition, Vishnu Puri had cultivated the acquintance of Sri Chaitanya during the latter's visit to Banares. Sometime later, a group of Vishnu Puri's devotees went to Jagannath Puri to pay homage to Sri Chaitanya. On the eve of their return, these devotees asked Sri Chaitanya for some message to their teacher, Vishnu Puri. To their utter surprise he asked them to report to Vishnu Puri that he wants from him a necklace of jems. When this message was carried to him, Vishnu Puri understood its real meaning. Subsequently he selected from the Bhagavata this devotional necklace of thirteen strands and sent the same to Sri Chaitanya, who offered it to Jagannath and through Him, to mankind. The verse 7 of the first strand and verse 11 of the 13th strand may be taken as references to this tradition.

In the Introduction and the comments an attempt has been made to present the outlines of the philosophy of Bhakti in a systematic way, besides expounding the significance of the verses selected. The English translation is free, without being unfaithful to the original.

It is hoped that the study of it will interest the readers in the **Bhagavata** Text as a whole.

SRI RAMAKRISHNA MATH
MADRAS
SNANA PURNIMA
JUNE 10, 1979.

PUBLISHER

CONTENTS

GENERAL INTRODUCTION

I

Origin of the Puranas

Srimad *Bhagavata*, which forms the source book for this Anthology called *Bhakti Ratnavali*, belongs to the class of Hindu religious literature known as the Puranas. The word Purana literally means 'narratives of ancient time'. Though the Puranic literature began to take their present shape only from the 5th century B.C., the nucleus from which it developed existed much earlier, and was as old as the Vedic Samhitas themselves. The earliest mention of Purana is in the *Atharva Veda* (XI. 7.24), where it is said to have originated from the residue (Ucchishta) of sacrifice along with Rks (verses), Samans (songs) and Chandas (metres). *Sathapatha Brahmana, Gopatha Brahmana* and *Brihadaranyaka Upanishad* mention this, the last of them stating it to have sprung along with the Vedas and the Itihasas from the breath of the Mahabhuta (Paramatman).

It is, however, to be noted that only the singular noun Purana is used in all these references. We have to infer from this that the Purana was a branch of Vedic learning and not a separate and diversified religious literature that it came to be in later days. The recital of the Purana, consisting of traditional lore about creation, ancient histories and anecdotes, proverbial sayings and genealogies of kings and Rishis, traditions about the origin of Vedic Mantras, and sacrifices etc., was a regular practice during periods of interval between rites and ceremonies of protracted Vedic sacrifices. Especially at the royal sacrifices like Aswamedha and Rajasuya, the recitals of what are called Pāriplava Ākhyānas or recurring narrations, commemorating the genealogies of great kingly lines and their pious liberality towards the sacrificial cult, formed an important part of the rites. The earliest beginnings of the Purana literature are to be traced to these narrative portions (Ākhyāna-bhāga) of Vedic rites.

Purana-samhita separates from the Veda

In the earliest stages, the recital of the Purana at the sacrificial rites must have been the function of the Brahmana priests themselves; but as time went on, it gradually came to be relegated to a mixed caste called the Suta, probably because its relation with the sacrificial rite was not integral. This bifurcation is indicated by the tradition supported in common by the *Vayu, Brahmanda* and *Vishnu Puranas* that the great sage Vyasa, after compiling the original Purana Samhita, entrusted it to his Suta disciple, Lomaharsha, who, in turn, made it into six versions and taught them to his six disciples. Of these disciples, three made separate Samhitas, and these together with the original of Lomaharsha became the source for all the Purana literature.

This tradition helps us to understand many of the important features of the Purana literature. It proves that there was an original Purana prevalent and that it was very closely associated with Vedic rites under the custody of Brahmana priests. Vyasa, to whom the codification of the Veda is attributed, systematised the original Purana Samhita also, separated it from its identification with Vedic rites, entrusted it to Sutas, who were not Brahmanas, and authorised its elaboration for catering to the changing needs of man from age to age. By the time of the *Apastambha Dharma Sutras* (600-300 B. C.), Puranas had become a specialised literature, as we find Apastambha citing three passages from an unspecified Purana and one passage from a *Bhavishya Purana*. So the Vedic revelation remained fixed and unalterable, while the Puranas, which embody the philosophy of the Vedas cast in a form and against a background that are their own, multiplied into a huge body of literature during a period extending at least from the 6th century B. C. to the 12th century A.D., embodying the devotional teachings of numerous cults and saintly teachers that came up from time to time, as also much available information on a variety of scientific, occult, social and historical themes.

Maha-puranas and Upa-puranas

The Puranas recognised as ancient and comprehensive, and distinguished therefore as Maha-puranas, are eighteen in number*.

---

* The order in which these eighteen Puranas are listed is as follows: Brahma; Padma; Vishnu: Vayu; Bhagavata; Naradiya; Markandeya; Varaha; Agni ;

The number eighteen was fixed rigidly by the 7th century A.D, probably because this number was considered sacred and because the names of the Puranas included in the list were cited in most of these older works. But the tendency to multiply the Puranas did not stop with this. Revelation had to be an ever-renewing process, as the needs and ideas of new cults and of new peoples, consisting both of foreign invaders and indigenous aboriginals, pressed for accommodation within the pale of the unalterable Vedic revelation, until another eighteen texts classed as Upa-puranas came to be formed between 650 and 800 A.D.

If a Mahapurana can be described as a 'Major Purana', an Upapurana may, in contrast to it, be described as a 'Subsidiary Purana'. Though many of these texts do not recognise any such subordinate status for themselves, the *Vayupurana* interprets the name Upapurana to mean a 'sub-division' (*upa-bheda*), and the *Saura Purana* a 'supplement' (*khila*), in respect of its relation to the major Puranas. Thus the accepted theory is that all the Puranas other than the recognised eighteen Mahapuranas are to be affiliated with one or another of them as a sub-division or a supplement.

II
Their Principal Features and Contents

All the Puranas, with the exception of a few like the *Markandeya Purana,* are more or less sectarian in nature, exalting as they do, some one or another of the Cult–Gods like Vishnu, Siva, or Sakti. This exaltation of one aspect of the Deity and the subordination of the others to it, is often wrongly interpreted to mean narrow sectarian rivalry among these cults, by people who do not understand the genius of the Vedic religion. In the Vedas themselves we find the tendency to exalt one or another of the gods to the status of the supreme Godhead by turn, as it were, thus displaying the understanding of the Vedic Rishis that the one Being can be adored under different names and forms. It is this very

Bhavishya ; Brahma-vaivarta ; Linga; Skanda; Vamana; Kumara; Matsya ; Garuda; and Brahmanda. The order does not indicate antiquity or importance.

insight and breadth of vision that assert themselves in the Puranas when they exalt the God of a particular cult as the Supreme Being and subordinate the others to Him. The intention is to strengthen the faith of the follower of a particular cult in its Deity and not to disparage the faith of others. Each Purana glorifies its own Cult-Deity by a vivid portrayal, often in the language of imaginative idealisation and symbology, of His form, attributes, abode, paraphernalia and doings in the worlds of men, gods and demons, and thus provides the votary with a very realistic and personalised conception of the Deity for centring his heart's devotion.

Apart from this, a Purana is expected to deal with the following five subjects according to Amarasimha, the author of the *Amarakosa* (6th Century A.D.) : Sarga (primary creation or evolution), Pratisarga (secondary creation or re-creation from the elements into which the universe is dissolved at the end of a cosmic cycle or Kalpa), Vamsa (genealogies of gods, demons, Manus, Rishis and kings), Manvantara (cosmic cycle ruled over by a Manu or Father of Mankind) and Vamsanucharita (accounts of royal dynasties). This restricted scope of the Puranas was probably the early tradition when the Purana was meant for recital during the intervals of elaborate rites at Vedic sacrifices. But as it became a separate body of religious literature meant to convey the techings of the Veda and the message of personalised devotional cults for the religious instruction of vast bodies of men, the concept of the Mahapurana evolved to meet these needs. The scope of the Puranas was widened and five more topics were added, as given in the *Bhagavata* and the *Brahma-vaivarta Puranas*. A theory also was propounded that the original five characteristics are applicable to Upa-Puranas and the ten characteristics to Mahapuranas, although this contention will not stand close scrutiny. We have to take that these characteristics were added as the scope of the Purana literature widened.

The ten topics that form the subject matter of a Mahapurana according to the *Bhagavata* (12.7.9-10) are as follows : (1) Sarga or Primary Creation is the evolution of undifferentiated Prakriti (root matter) into Ahamkara (ego) and all subsequent categories ending with gross elements. (2) Visarga or Secondary Creation consists in the latent tendencies of creatures becoming manifest, just as trees come out of the seed, under the influence of time, and as a result, all embodied beings, sentient and insentient, getting formed by the combination of the categories evolved out of Prakriti, through the creative activity of Brahma. (3) Vritti or Means of Sustenance is the description of the system by which the more evolved beings are ordained to subsist on less evolved species as prompted by Nature and enjoined by scriptures. (4) Raksha or Protection includes the accounts of all the Incarnations of the Lord in various species of beings wherein His sportive actions for the establishment of spirituality and the salvation of devotees are described, besides His bestowal of unconditioned grace even on unworthy men. (5) Manvantara or Epoch of Manus consists in the description of the combined activities of Manus, Devas, sons of Manus, Indra, Rishis and specially endowed souls for the promotion of life and the well-being of all creatures. (6) Vamsa or Genealogy gives descriptive lists of great royal and priestly lines descended from Brahma. (7) Vamsanucharita or Dynastic History deals with rule of distinguished kings and their dynasties that served the cause of devotion to God and well-being of the universe. (8) Samstha or Dissolution is the description of the four kinds of dissolution of the manifested universe into a finer condition brought about by the influence of Time, Karma, and Gunas. These dissolutions or Pralayas are the total dissolution of the manifested universe (Prakrita-pralaya), partial dissolution (Naimittika-pralaya), and daily dissolution in sleep (Nitya-pralaya), besides salvation of man (Ātyantika-pralaya) which implies the dissolution (Pralaya) of all his gross and subtle bodies. (9) Hetu or Purpose is the discussion of the root cause and significance of all creative activity. It is the Jiva (the individual soul), the product of Avidya (ignorance) and its ensuing effects of desire and Karma. All creative activity is to confer on Jivas the fruits of their Karmas and ultimately redeem them from ignorance and rebirth. So subjects like the nature of the Jiva, of the ways of his redemption, the purpose of creation etc., will come under this topic. (10) Apāsraya or Ultimate Support. This is God who is the ultimate Being and the Support of all relative supports. In Him and by His will all the above–mentioned events and processes of the relative world take place. It is to bring man into an adequate conception of His excellences and to generate in him devotion to the Lord, that all the other themes mentioned before are discussed in the Puranas. There will be found scattered all over the Puranas considerable matter relating to history, geography, astronomy, natural sciences, sociology etc., as understood in ancient days. The object of such accounts is not to give us some information claiming to be factual as in the case of the modern studies of such subjects, but to engender in us a feeling that all functions of Nature and of human and divine agencies are to proclaim the glory of the Supreme and thus generate in us a sense of His omnipotence, omniscience and redeeming love.

The *Brahma-vaivarta Purana*, a much later work, recast the list as follows : Srishti (primary creation); Visrishti (secondary creation ; Sthiti (maintenance of the worlds); Palana (protection and redemption of Jivas); Karma Vasana (latent tendencies of work); Manvantara (accounts of the Manus); Pralaya-varnana (accounts of final dissolution of the worlds); Mokshanirupana (dissertation on Moksha or liberation); Hari-kirtana (discourses on Hari or God); and Deva-kirtana (discourses on gods).

The *Brahma-vaivarta* is one of the latest Puranas, having evolved from the 8th century A.D. to 1600 A.D., and its elimination of genealogies of Rishis and kings and addition of novel features are the result of the changed times in which Rishis and ancient dynasties of kings had ceased to be of importance.

III

The Place of the Bhagavata among the Puranas

What exactly is the place of the *Bhagavata Purana* in this vast body of religious literature? It will be noted that it is included in the traditional list of eighteen Mahapuranas, but this has been questioned by the *Devi Bhagavata*, which claims to be the *Bhaga-vata-mahapurana*, thus relegating the *Vishnu Bhagavata* to the position of an Upa-purana. According to Prof. Hazra (*Cultural*

Heritage of India Vol. II, Pp. 281) the *Devi Bhagavata* is only a very late production of the 12th century and it has carefully incorporated the features of the description of the *Bhagavata* as found in the *Matsya, Skanda* and *Agni Puranas* in order to claim itself to be the *Bhagavata* and thus gain the required prestige for infusing its Sākta ideas among men. If for any reason the claim of the *Devi Bhagavata* is accepted, then the place of the *Vishnu Bhagavata* can only be that of a Super-Purana and not that of an Upa-Purana. For its excellences are of such a transcending nature that it has practically eliminated all the other Puranas from the minds of men and become the one book of its kind that is widely studied by all devotees, commented upon by scholars of all schools of thought, and translated into several Indian languages, besides English. Though it is Vaishnava, and therefore sectarian in a way, its sectarianism is not one of narrowness and exclusion but only its way of eliciting the undivided attention and devotion of men to the Deity of their choice. In the sublimity, fervour and comprehensiveness of the pattern of devotion it inculcates, in the dignity, elevation and terseness of its Sanskrit diction, and in the lyrical beauty and wealth of imagery of its poetry, there is no Purana that comes anywhere near it. It is undoubtedly one of the greatest productions of the literary and spiritual genius of India.

IV

The Date of the Bhagavata

On the date and the present textual form of the *Bhagavata*, modern scholarship is not yet in a position to give a firm answer. According to Prof. Hazra[1] the present text of the *Bhagavata* must have taken shape in the early half of the 6th century A.D. It is however admitted by him that there was an earlier text of it differing very much from the present, as could be found from the description of it given in the *Matsya Purana* (of early 4th century A.D.). In the Introduction to his exhaustive research work entitled the *Philosophy of the Bhagavata Vol. 1*, Prof. Siddheswara Bhattacharya writes : "The conclusion therefore seems to emerge

1 *Cultural Heritage of India II,* Pp. 259.

that Srimad *Bhagavata* has three phases of development. In its earliest form it consists of very old material; it was given the shape of a Maha-purana, and this is the second phase in the early Christian era; and its last and final phase represents the contribution of the Tamil saints. Viewed from this point of view the extant Srimad *Bhagavata* may be said to be contemporaneous with the Tamil saints".[1]

This last conclusion is supported by the highly complementary reference of Srimad *Bhagavata* to the great Bhakti movement inaugurated by the Alwars in the following passage (11.5.38-40): "Men of the Krita and other ages desire to be born in the so called degenerate age of Kali. For in Kali age are surely born many devotees of Lord Narayana in several parts of Dravida country through which holy rivers like the Tamraparni, the Kritamala, the Payasvini and the Cauveri flow. Those who drink the water of these rivers become pure in heart and develop devotion to Vasudeva." It is evident from this that the *Bhagavata*, as it exists today, has been thoroughly revised by some unknown great man of South India imbued with the devotional fervour of the Alwars. Though versions of the *Bhagavata* might have been in existence earlier, the last editor of it must have recast it radically. For, throughout, it maintains the same highly elevating style which is so different from that of every other Purana. Besides, in the general presentation of its very extensive theme, which comprises all the ten subjects mentioned before as coming within the scope of a Maha-purana, it displays a rough unity of treatment in subordinating them all to its devotional purpose. Of the ten subjects, the last one Apāsraya, the Supreme Being who is the final stay of all, and man's duty of cultivating devotion to Him, form the one theme with which the *Bhagavata* is primarily concerned, and all the other subjects are subordinated to it. For the *Bhagavata*, the Supreme Being, Maha Vishnu, is essentially His complete Incarnation Sri Krishna, and the elaborate treatment of His life and message is given in the last three Cantos, the earlier nine Cantos

---

1 The reference is to the great movement inaugurated by the Alwars, all of whom are supposed to have lived between 5th and 8th century A.D.

being the preparation for the advent of Krishna and the message of Bhakti in all its phases that He preached. Behind this unity of style and theme, the hand of a master mind is clearly visible, and from the familiarity it shows with the renaissance of Vaishnavism in the South under the Alwars, it will be safe to infer that much of the original text of the *Bhagavata* was rewritten into its present form by an un-known Vaishnava scholar-devotee of the South. The time of the Alwar movement is between the 5th and the 8th century A.D., and so it will be safe to say that it was produced somewhere during or shortly after this period. Though Prof. Hazra assigns it to the early part of the 6th century, it is safe to push it even to a little later date in view of its acquaintance with the full impact of the Alwar movement.

There is a view that attributes the authorship of the *Bhagavata* to Vopadeva (12th century). But this theory falls when it is noted that Albaruni, the celebrated Arab scholar (1030 A.D.), refers to '*Vaishnava Bhagavata*'[1] in his book on India.

There is, however, an anomalous circumstance to the acceptance of this or an earlier date to Bhagavata in so far as no quotation from it has been given by Sri Ramanuja, born in 1017 A.D., in his extensive writings. He has taken his quotations only from the *Vishnu Purana* (4th century A.D.) which is much earlier to the *Bhagavata* and in many respects parallel, but much inferior to it as a sacred text. Such a great Vaishnava scripture like the *Bhagavata*, produced most probably in the South and extolling the Vaishnavism of the Alwars for which Ramanuja stood, should have been known to him if it had taken shape between the 5th and the 8th century. There are two possible explanations for his silence : 1. The hypothesis that the *Bhagavata* was produced in the South between the 5th and the 8th century is wrong. It must have been produced in the North and had not yet become known

1 Sachaw: *Albaruni's India* Pp. 131, referred to in the Introduction (XII) of Prof. Siddheswar Bhattacharya's *Philosophy of the Bhagavata*, It is as follows: "The question of its composition by Vopadeva melts away by Albaruni's (about 1030 A.D.) reference to the *Bhagavata* in which, according to his view, Vasudeva has been extolled."

in the South by the time of Albaruni (1030). 2. Or, Ramanuja
avoided reference to it because of doctrinal reasons.

The second alternative is the more probable one. Ramanuja
was a great propagandist of the Pāncharatra Agama and did not
like, as some scholars think, the leanings of the *Bhagavata* towards
the Vaikhanasa Agama, as also its acceptance of Siva almost on a
par with Vishnu. Next, in Ramanuja's system Sriman Narayana in
Vaikuntha is the highest form of Brahman, whereas the *Bhagavata*
seems to accept—and it has been so interpreted by Vaishnava
sects like those of Chaitanya and Vallabha—that Sri Krishna is
the Supreme form of Brahman (Bhagavan Svayam)[1]. Vasudeva,
a name which primarily indicates Sri Krishna, is the most sacred
name for God in the *Bhagavata*, whereas Narayana is the most
important and sacred one for the Pāncharatrins. The Bhagavatas
and the Pancharatrins, though always devoted to Vishnu, seemed
to have been distinct sectaries at an earlier date, and Ramanuja's
preference for *Vishnu Purana*, which has admittedly more of Pāncharatra leanings than the *Bhagavata*, might have been due to
this.[2] Further, *Bhagavata* is non-dualistic in its trend, although
what brand of non-dualism it represents is disputable. Saktimat
and Sakti (Power-holder and Power) rather than Sariri-sarira
(soul and body) seems to be the relationship envisaged by the
Bhagavata between God and the world. Ramanuja, however, is
committed to the latter view. For these reasons Ramanuja might
have ignored the *Bhagavata*, although it became the main text of
most of the Vaishnava schools like those of Nimbarka, Chaitanya,
Vallabha and Sankara Deva in later times. Even Ramanuja's
junior contemporary, Parasara Bhatta, is said to refer to it.

V

Sri Krishna and the Bhagavata: His Dominance in it

The main thesis of the *Bhagavata* is to inculcate the glory and
greatness of Bhagavan Sri Krishna and the necessity of cultivating

---

1. This is a much disputed point, which is discussed in a succeeding section
   of this Introduction.
2. The *Bhagavata* apparently downgrades Rama, saying in a place that the

devotion to Him. The rest of the subject matter, including the accounts of other Incarnations, is made subordinate to it. It is an accepted principle of interpretation that the subject matter of a book will be reflected in its introduction and conclusion. Judged from this point of view, the whole of the 1st Canto of the *Bhagavata* deals with Sri Krishna and the bestowal of His grace on the Pandavas, and the three concluding Cantos deal directly with Him and His teachings and the times that follow His demise.

The question of the Rishis of Naimisaranya, in answer to which Suta recites the *Bhagavata*, is almost exclusively related to Krishna. They ask him, "O Suta, tell us what was the purpose for which the Bhagavan was born in Devaki as the son of Vasudeva? Tell us, who are endowed with spiritual zeal, about the noble and sportive activities of His, of which sages have sung. Tell us about the incidents of the Incarnation of Hari, wherein He manifested His sportive nature through His own mysterious power. We are never satisfied with hearing the glorious activities of the Lord, the descriptions of which appear so sweet to true connoisseurs at every stage. What superhuman acts did the Bhagavan perform along with Rama, having adopted the mask of a human body?" (1.1.12, 17-20). The whole of the *Bhagavata* is an answer to these questions.

Further, the very reason which prompted Vyasa to compose the *Bhagavata* was the urge to produce a devotional work exclusively devoted to the glorification of Vasudeva. It is stated in the *Bhagavata* that when Vyasa was sitting in a mood of depression and dissatisfaction, and worrying himself to know the cause of it, the great Rishi Narada approached him and informed him that the cause of this depression was the fact that in all the works he had written, he had dealt only with human values, at best with slight touches of devotional element. He said: "You have not, O sage, described the transcendent glory of Vasudeva in an exhaus-

---

Rama Incarnation is to show man that too much attachment to one's near and dear ones as also adherence to the letter of the law is often likely to bring on one great sorrow and affliction. This probably militates against the view of Ramanuja's sect.

tive manner as you have done with regard to Dharma (morality)
and Artha (power) [1.5.9.]'' And the consequence of this advice
was the production of the *Bhagavata* which describes itself as
follows : "In other works the Supreme Lord Hari who destroys all
the evils of Iron Age of Kali has not been praised in all their
parts, but in this narrative the Bhagavan has been glorified in
every word of it" (12.12.65). Further, "When Krishna disappeared
from the world, and along with Him, Dharma and Jnana, there
arose this sun of the *Bhagavata Purana* as a guide to men caught
in the darkness of Kali (1.1 13) If a person hears or studies this
text, describing the activities of the Lord, the Bhagavan will very
soon become manifest in his heart. Having entered the heart
through the ear, Krishna purifies the mind as the spring season
clarifies all the rivers. One whose mind has thus been purified,
finds eternal rest at the feet of Krishna, as a traveller does on
reaching home after passing through ever so many troubles and
tribulations" (2.8.4-6).

Not only in its purport, but even structurally, the *Bhagavata*
is dominated by the personality of Sri Krishna. Of its twelve
Cantos, the tenth and the eleventh, covering about one third of the
whole text, deal with Krishna's life and teachings, while the first
two Cantos stem directly from His life, and the third is a conversation between Vidura and Uddhava, two great contemporaries
and devotees of Sri Krishna.

VI

Sri Krishna in relation to the Mahavishnu Conception

Taking all this into consideration, the *Bhagavata* is undis-
putedly a text of the Krishna cult and of the Bhagavata Dharma
propounded by Him. But the conception of Krishna in the *Bhagavata* has been complicated by the attempts made by Krishna
devotees to push the matter further and contend that Krishna is
not an Incarnation of Vishnu, the Godhead, as ordinarily understood, but the Godhead(Bhagavan)Himself, and that Vishnu is only
an emanation of Krishna. For a liberal-minded devotee, this dispute is of little interest or significance, but as it has been foisted
upon a great text like the *Bhagavata*, it requires some considera-

tion. This theory is a special contention of the Bengal (Chaitanya) School of Vaishnavism, but what is of special significance is that it has found support in a recent very thorough-going research work entitled The *Philosophy of the Bhagavata* by Dr. Sidhheswar Battacharya. The main basis of this theory, in addition to what has been pointed out above about the obvious dominance of Krishna's personality in the *Bhagavata,* is the famous verse "All the above are Amsa-Kalas (partial expressions) of the Purusha (Supreme Being), but Krishna is Bhagavan (God) Himself" (1.3.28). This is no doubt a puzzling verse in the context in which it appears. It is given at the end of a dozen or so of verses citing twentyfour incarnations of Vishnu, in which Krishna also is included as one without any distinctive status over others. Then this verse, a solitary verse, with this purport in the whole of the *Bhagavata,* occurs in contradiction to the spirit in which the foregoing list of Incarnations is given, as also of several other verses in other places in which Krishna is expressly declared as an Amsa or Kala (part) of Mahavishnu, the Supreme Being, as conceived in the *Bhagavata.* At birth what Krishna reveals to his mother and father, Devaki and Vasudeva, is the Divine form of Mahavishnu as described everywhere in Vaishnava Puranas, and when Krishna finally passes away, being struck by the arrow of a hunter, he is seen to abandon his earthly body and merge into Mahavishnu. In the light of all the express statements of the *Bhagavata* to the effect that Krishna is a descent of Mahavishnu, one can consider the contrary statement that Mahavishnu is an emanation of Krishna as only an attempt to accommodate the *Bhagavata* to the peculiar doctrine of a sect. The verse concerning Sri Krishna that 'He is Bhagavan Himself' is to be intrepreted in subservience to other statements about him in the text, and then it can only mean that in the view of the *Bhagavata* there was a fuller manifestation of Divine excellences in Krishna than in any other Incarnation. It discovers all the majesties of God in Sri Krishna the Incarnate, and therefore equates Him with the Bhagavan Himself in the sense of 'fulness of manifestation'—not in the sense that Krishna becomes the Godhead and Vishnu an emanation of His. In fact every Incarnation is hypostatic with the Divine, and if Krishna is to be distinguished from among them, it is only in point of manifestation of Divine powers and attributes. This is quite natural in a text devoted to the exposition Sri Krishna's life and greatness. The *Ramayana*, which expounds the life and excellences of Rama, would say the same of Rama. Every devotee will find the highest expression of the Divine in his own Chosen Ideal.

Further, in order to raise Sri Krishna from an Incarnation to Godhead, a new heavenly abode called Goloka, different from Vaikuntha Dhama, the highest state of Vishnu according to Vaishnava sects in general, is foisted on the *Bhagavata*. But unfortunately for this theory, there is not even mention of a Goloka in the *Bhagavata* text, and to make up for this deficiency, it is claimed that the description of Gokula, the cowherd settlement where Sri Krishna spent his boyhood and revealed His Vrindavana majesties, is to be taken as that of Goloka. It is maintained that the heavenly Goloka manifested as Gokula for a time in an earthly setting along with Sri Krishna and His attendants, and it is the description of it that is given in what appears to be a description of Nanda's Gokula, its inhabitants and their relation-ship with Sri Krishna. Nothing can be said of these assertions except that they are assumptions unwarranted by the text of the *Bhagavata*.

Historicity of Krishna

What the *Bhagavata* seeks to do is to stress the superb glory and significance of the Krishna Incarnation by subordinating the whole of its contents to this one theme and expounding the Gospel of Bhakti Yoga centring upon His life and teachings. It is doubtful whether it lends support to the sectarian feat of converting an emanation into the Godhead and the Godhead into an emanation. In the process of the treatment of the personality of Krishna, the *Bhagavata Purana* no doubt idealises Him. While His humanity is not lost sight of, His transcendent divine glory is expressed through every incident of His life. While the orthodox Hindu in the past had taken all the narratives of the *Bhagavata* as factual, doubts were cast on Krishna's historicity by the early

Orientalists of the 19th century, and Krishna was treated as a mythical figure even by the historically-minded Hindus. But scholarly opinion has now changed, as there is as much data about Krishna's historicity as of any other world teacher. He must have flourished not later than 900 B.C. according to Pargiter in his book on *Ancient Indian Historical Traditions*. Chandogya Upanishad makes mention of Devaki-Putra Krishna as the disciple of Ghorangiras, and the teachings of these are in several respects in accordance with those of the Gita. Panini, the founder of Sanskrit grammar, who, according to R. G. Bhandarkar, 'lived in the beginning of the 7th century before the Christian era, if not earlier still,' speaks of 'Vasudevakas', or 'the sect who followed Vasudeva', indicating that before his time Krishna or Vasudeva, the Vrishni hero and philosopher, had already been recognised as a divine personage and that His followers had spread far and wide, even up to Gandhara or Afghanistan where Panini lived. Information about the wide-spread prevalence of the Krishna cult is got from the reference to it by the Greek ambassador Megasthenes (4th century B, C.); from the Ghosundi stone inscriptions (200-150 B. C.) informing of a Bhagavata setting up the compound wall of a temple of Vasudeva; from Basnagar inscriptions (100 B. C.) mentioning of a Greek named Heladorus as a Paramabhagavata; and from Nanaaghar inscription (100 B. C.) which describes Vāsudeva as a Deity.

Krishna was on his mother's side Devaki-putra (son of Devaki) and on his father's side Vāsudeva-Krishna (son of Vasudeva). He is therefore known both as Krishna and Vāsudeva. The Vrishni clan, to which he belonged, was a very important and wide-spread Vedic clan, and Krishna, its leader, by the power and holiness of his personality and the great part He played in the cultural and political life of His times as we find from the *Mahabharata*, became canonised among his clan and among many other people. He was looked upon as the Incarnation of Vishnu, the Godhead in the Vaishnava theology. In the Chandogya Upanishad we find Ghorangiras instructing Krishna in meditation centring on the Solar Deity. Vishnu is identical with the Solar Deity of the Vedas, and it is He who is invoked in the great Gayatri Mantra of the Vedas. In course of time Vishnu became the most dominant among the Vedic Deities, and came to be accepted as the Supreme Being, of whom the other Vedic Deities like Indra and Varuna became minor expressions. Krishna, being an exponent of a theology extolling Vishnu, came to be recognised as an Incarnation of Vishnu Himself. It is not unusual in the history of cults for the founder or prophet of a cult to be recognised as the manifestation of the Cult-Deity Himself.

The main facts of Krishna's life can be gathered from the *Bhagavata* and the *Mahabharata*. He was born in captivity in the prison of king Kamsa of Mathura, as the son of Vasudeva, a leader of the Vrishnis, whom Kamsa was trying to suppress. He was transferred immediately after birth from the dominion of Kamsa to the cowherd settlement (Gokula) of a chieftain of herdsmen called Nanda. It was in the Gokula of Nanda and at Vrindavana that he grew up into youth. Some of the most important spiritual manifestations of Krishna the Incarnate took place in those places. From Vrindavana he migrated to Mathura, the capital of Kamsa, and killed Kamsa, the oppressive king. From this time onwards he gradually became the leader of his Vrishni clan, though he did not assume their kingship. He suppressed many tyrant kings of his times, the chief of these being Jarasandha of Magadha, Yavana, Bana, Salva, Sisu-pala etc., and made the Vrishnis one of the most powerful people of the times. He founded a new capital at Dwaraka[1] on the western seashore and played a very important part in shaping the cultural and political life of the India of his times. He took a leading, though inactive, part in the great conflict between the two lines of the Kurus, the sons of Dhritarashtra and those of Pandu, culminating in the great war described in the *Maha-bharata*. While his life was full of activity, he was also a philo-sopher and teacher of a gospel which came to be known as the Bhagavata Dharma, and is chiefly expounded in the *Bhagavad Gita* and the *Bhagavata Purana*.

The Bhagavata Dharma is noted for the fact that it is meant for every man. The Vedic teachings catered mainly to the elite.

1 Recent archeological excavations on the shores of the pilgrimate called Dwaraka in Gujarat have revealed the raruparts and other structures of a fortified city under water in the sea there. This is a positive archeological evidence for the historicity of Krishna.

The Vedic religion had, on the one hand, got elaborated into a vast system of complicated sacrificial rituals, to which only the Brahmanas and the Kshatriyas were eligible. On the other hand, it had developed the philosophy of the Upanishads which required high intellectual training and moral efficiency for their comprehension. It was to the credit of Sri Krishna that, when the common man in India was without a simple and vital religion, he provided him with a devotional gospel in which action, emotion and intellect played equal parts, and a universal Iswara who could be communed with through love and service and who responded to the prayers and the deepest yearnings of man.

The Mystical Krishna in the Context of the Puranas

While the skeleton of the historical Krishna is clearly visible through the narratives of the *Bhagavata* and the *Mahabharata*, the finished personality that we get as the central figure in the *Bhagavata* is not a mere man or a hero or a philosopher or even a saint, but the very God whose contact transforms sinners into saints, ignorant men into sages, sense-bound beings into spiritual ecstatics and even animals into devotees of God. He is of the essence of Satchidananda personified into a human form, so that weak man, who cannot rise through meditation and Samadhi into communion with the Divine forming his own spiritual substratum, may get an opportunity to contact the very same Divinity through the senses. All His human actions during the span of His earthly life are meant not only to bless His contemporaries and establish righteousness on earth, but to provide, for the pious contemplation of posterity, the spiritually potent account of His earthly deeds, by meditating on which they could establish with Him the same devotional relationships, which His great devotees had with Him in His life-time. He is depicted as an expression of the redeeming love of God (Anugraha-sakti of Iswara) which manifests in different ages and in different lands, bringing spiritual enlightenment and bliss into the otherwise dreary life of humanity.

The highly idealised life of the Krishna of the *Bhagavata* based on the assumption of His divinity, may often puzzle a modern mind that swears by historicity. But the authors of the

2

Puranas looked at it from an entirely different point of view. History has to be differentiated from mere events. Events become history only to the extent they affect the physical environment of man through natural cataclysms, or impress the mind of man in a way that they are remembered as a tradition. As mere events history is as fleeting and insubstantial as a line on water, but as a remembered tradition stimulating man's thought and action, it becomes a lasting and substantial force. In the hands of Pauranika thinkers the external ends of history often got lost in the stimulation they gave in the realm of eternal values, and they reappeared in idealised forms bearing the reactions of the impact they made on the highly sensitive and saintly philosopher-poets who composed the Puranas.

Attempts have been made in the past by Orientalists with a Christian theological bias to ignore this supra-historical validity of the Puranas and the Itihasas of the Hindus and dub them as cock-and-bull stories at the worst or as fanciful imaginations at the best. And as a conclusion following from this, as it were, is drawn the picture of Christianity as built on the bed-rock of Christ's historicity in contrast to Hinduism built on the quicksands of Pauranika mythology. This view is the result of a total misunderstanding of the springs of validity and power in Christianity and Pauranika Hinduism alike, in both of which they happen to be the same. History as such has no special spiritual value, as events are only at the moment and are not in the next. Events become history, as stated before, to the extent they are remembered and become a tradition, and historical facts become spiritual reality to the extent they stimulate a Myth and become a Psychic Verity. For example, in itself the much vaunted historicity of Christ gives no spiritual significance to that religion, but its Christ Myth does. That a carpenter's wife gave birth to a son out of wedlock, that he became a teacher of some ethical and devotional doctrines, that his own clansmen became jealous of him because of his claim to their leadership, and that they had him executed—may all be facts of history but they have no significance to posterity. But when it is accepted that he was the expression of the Second Person of the Trinity, that he was im-

maculately conceived, that he was the Redeemer of men, that his
suffering on the cross was in atonement of man's sins, that he
rose from the dead, and that all who take refuge in him would be
saved—then Christ transcends history and becomes a Myth and a
Psychic Verity of world-wide significance. No man in his senses
will offer to prove the above cited statements as historical, but
because they have been accepted by the psychic being of the community, they have a value far transcending events of so-called
history. The same is the case with Krishna and Rama. Their
validity lies in the fusion their traditions have achieved with the
supra-historical foundations of life.

The Right Approach to the Puranas

In fact the Puranas are not at all to be read as history and
geography, nor are they to be regarded as fictions. Pandits who
often interpret all the accounts of the Puranas as facts of our
three dimensional space and time do as much harm to the minds
of people as many moderns who brush them aside as cock-and-
bull stories. They belong to an order different from both history
and fiction, though they may have superficial affinities with both.
Even as the rivers and mountain ranges of a country are the expressions of the natural forces working from within and without
this planet of ours, the Puranas are the up-throw of a people's
mind struggling to express their quest for a meaning for life and
their findings in this respect. They represent the more enduring
and enriched reactions of the psyche of a race to the fleeting events
of space and time. It is in their cumulative effect and not in the
validity of their individual statements or in a critique of their
methodology that we should seek the values they embody. They
attempt to make the dry bones of philosophy, history and traditions into an integrated literature of high psychic potentiality,
capable of stimulating in man a keen sense of an omniscient,
omnipotent and all-loving spiritual Reality, who can be communed
with, prayed to and visualised in various forms of spiritual glory.
God in formful aspects and Divine personages have become
concrete to the Hindu mind through the Puranas. In so far as
they are facts of memory in the minds of men, they fulfil the role

of history, but in so far as the stimulations they give belong to spiritual dimensions, the Puranas are linked with Eternal Verities that transcend history.

The *Brihadaranyaka Upanishad* (2.2.1) says that Brahman has two aspects, Formful (Murta) and Formless (Amurta). The Puranas, including the *Bhagavata*, accept both these aspects, but concentrate particularly on the Formful Aspect, which is the more significant for the devotional mind. What is called the Formless is the Non-dual Absolute and the Formful is the Sakti or the manifesting Power of the Formless, without which the Formless will be indistinguishable from a Nihil (Sunya). In the same way if the Formful alone is accepted without the Formless or the Infinite and Absolute Being as its complement, the former will be only a limited entity indistinguishable from an exalted man. So the Puranas in general, and the *Bhagavata* in particular, accept the Supreme Being as both Murta and Amurta, with a greater stress on the Murta aspect and call Him the Bhagavan. The Bhagavan is Parama-Purusha, the Supreme Person, but not an individual. He has an Arche-typal Form, but it is a potential Multiform that can take any form in which He is invoked. An anthropomorphic veneer is put on Him, as man could think of Him only in terms of the highest that he could conceive of, and that is himself in an idealised state of existence. So the Puranas try to depict, and impress on man, the Divine majesty of the Bhagavan through symbolic and, at the same time, highly realistic descriptions of this Arche typal Form, – His divine attributes, His abode, paraphernalia, decorations, weapons, attendants, creative and redemptive activities, incarnations, associations with sages and devotees—in fact with such a variety of details and highly poetic touches, and with such a realism as we cannot imagine with regard to any noted individual in our earthly plane of existence. In these highly artistic descriptions, care is taken at every step to impress on man the supra-human and transcendent nature of the object dealt with, and that accounts for many of their unearthly and unusal features. When the details of these descriptions are taken in isolation and scrutinised, they look queer and bizarre; but the cumulative or synergistic effect they produce, when taken as a whole, with a receptivity born of Sraddha, is to make a tremendous impact of Divine consciousness on the mind. No literature in the world has succeeded in making God a reality to man by such vivid and realistic descriptions as the Puranas have done.

VII

The Bhagavan in The Bhagavata : His Abode and His Form

The *Bhagavata* styles itself as such because it is entirely concerned with the depiction of the majesty and greatness of the Bhagavat. The Bhagavat (familiarly written as 'Bhagavan') is the term specially used to indicate that God is the Supreme Person but not an individual, that He is the Absolute Being but is yet responsive to worship and prayers, that He could be communed with as one's Master, Father, Mother, Friend or any other relationship one prefers. In the Upanishads and the Buddhist texts the term Bhagavan is used as a term of address to any exalted and venerable human teacher. But in the Puranas it has come to be applied to God or His Incarnations. The *Vishnu Purana* describes the Bhagavan as one having Bhaga or majesty. The Bhaga or majesty is described as six-fold: "Ominipotence (Aisvarya), Virtue (Dharma), Glory (Yasas), Beauty (Sri), Omniscience (Jnana), Non-affectedness (Vairagya)—the full manifestation of all these six excellences is called Bhaga" And He who is distinguished by these is the Bhagavan. For the Vaishnava Puranas—and the *Bhagavata* is one such—Mahavishnu, including all his Emanations and Incarnations, is the Bhagavan. Though He is the Absolute (Amurta) also, He has an Arche-typal Form, the source of all forms. It is sometimes represented in a realistic form as the Purusha, the Universal Person, who includes all the fourteen manifested spheres in a fragment of Himself and also transcends them into infinity in His subtle unmanifest aspect. In His transcendent aspect He is described as an Ideal Form amidst the sublime splendour of His heavenly abode known as Vaikuntha Dhama (the state beyond all sorrow, darkness, sin and ugliness). The Vaikuntha and all its denizens are formed not of matter (Prakriti), but Suddha-sattva, which is an etherial stuff of luminous consciousness and bliss. The description given of this supra-sensual abode of Bliss is, however, in terms of the most highly artistic and sublime conceptions known to us in this world. Warbling birds, vernal flowers with humming bees, fruit-bearing trees, enchanting scenery, joyous inhabitants of both sexes with explosive beauty, golden planes gliding about—such are some of the features that enter into these descriptions. But there is no touch of sensuality or voluptuousness in these, as all details are subordinated to the devotional sentiment. For example, the chirpings of birds stop when the beetles begin their humming, resembling the utterance of Omkara. The sweet-smelling garden flowers give way to the holy fragrance of Tulsi leaves. The men and women in the golden Vimanas, though possessed of rare physical charm, are unmindful of it in their absorption in singing the name of Hari. Dominated by devotion, beauty only subserves the purpose of the former in the setting provided by the luminous abode of Vishnu. Vishnu seated in Vaikuntha is described with a wealth of symbolic imageries which fall under four heads: physical features (Anga), weapons (Ayudha), decoration (Akalpa) and accessories (Upanga). In order to emphasise that the formful aspect of God is not a mere anthropomorphic imagination but a spiritual concept, He is described as simultaneously manifesting Himself in four conditions—as moving, as seated, as reclining and as dwelling in the heart of man. Seated on His eagle vehicle Garuda, symbolising the three Vedas, He moves about the worlds. At the beginning of the creative cycle He is conceived as floating on cosmic waters, reclining on the bed constituted of the thousand-hooded serpent Adisesha who stands for infinite Time or the unmodified Prakriti. In Vaikuntha He is described as seated under a huge white canopy and fanned with white Chouries by attending divinities standing on both sides A host of Divine attendants, who are His powers personified, are arrayed about His seat in a hierarchical order, all humming the praise of Hari with devotional fervour. On one side are arrayed His various attributes personified—His eight Mahimas or majesties, His eight Maha-vibhutis or spiritual glories, His three Vibhutis or material powers, His three Saktis or powers of manifestation and creative activity. On the other side are His Parshadas or constant attendants, next the Brahmarishis and Devarishis

or sages of great spiritual power and attainment, the Ashtadik-
palas or the gods protecting the eight directions, and Bhagavatottamas or the highest human devotees. His weapons like Sudarsana
or celestial discus are described as devotees attendant on Him. In
this vast assemblage of devotees and attendants brimming with
holiness and devotion, Mahavishnu is conceived as seated on the
resplendent serpent bed constituted of the thousand-hooded
Ananta (Infinity). The form of Vishnu is thus described from
foot to head in the *Bhagavata* in a meditation on Him : "I meditate on the lotus feet of the Lord, bearing on their soles the auspicious marks of the thunderbolt, hook and lotus, and His big, red
and rounded toe nails whose brilliance dispels the gloom of ignorance from the minds of persons meditating on them. Those feet are
so holy that even Siva felt purified by them. And the thunderbolt
marks on them are so powerful that one meditating on them will
have his mind steady in meditation. I meditate on the legs of the
Lord, whose brilliance gets mixed with that of the hands of
Lakshmi, the Universal Mother, as She shampoos them with great
tenderness. I meditate on His thighs which rest on the shoulders
of Garuda as He rides on him, and which are as powerful as they are comely with their blue complexion. I meditate on
His waist covered with a dangling brilliant yellow silk tied with a
waist band of luminous metal. I contemplate on His abdomen
with all the worlds potential in it, and His navel from which
comes the Lotus of World–formation having the creator Brahma
seated in it. I contemplate on His chest, luminous with Lakshmi's
eternal presence and with the brilliance of the mark Srivatsa and
of the rare jewel Kausthubha dangling round His neck. I contemplate on the arms of the Lord, with their upper ornaments
burnished by friction with the mountain Mandara, with the eight
guardian deities of the quarters seeking strength from them, with
the many-faced discus called Sudarsana of irresistible powers
held in one of them, and with the swan-like conch Panchajanya
resting in the lotus-like palm of another. Further, I meditate on
His club called Kaumodaki which delivers the death-blow to the
forces of evil and ignorance, and on the floral wreath on His neck
with numerous honey-seekers gathered round it. I now contem-

plate on the lotus-like face of the Supreme Being who has assumed this form for blessing the devotees. He has a most comely nose, and His cheeks reflect the lustre of His slightly tremulous earrings. His lustrous face resembles a huge lotus flower in a pool, having His two moving eyes for fishes and flowing curls of hair for water weeds. Long should one contemplate on His gracious looks full of mercy for the sufferings of the suppliants, as also on His bewitching smile potent enough to dry the pools of tears caused by the sufferings of creatures, on His eye-brows scattering holiness that calms the passions agitating the minds of His votaries, and on His pearl-like teeth that have taken a slightly reddish hue on account of the reflection cast on them by His brilliantly red lips. On this form of Vishnu residing is one's own heart, let one meditate with the mind melting in love and feeling attraction for nothing else." (Bh. 3. 28. 21–33)

Interpretation of the Symbolic Form

While the *Bhagavata* would have a devotee meditate on the form of the Lord it describes, it is none the less too metaphysical to leave it there. To impress on the votary that the Deity it depicts is not a mere anthropomorphic cult-deity but the all-inclusive Absolute Being as He presents Himself to the illumined minds of the sages, the *Bhagavata* also gives a symbolic interpretation of the form and paraphernalia of Mahavishnu in the 11th chapter of its 12th Canto. His form, the essence of Sat-Chid-Ananda, is the support of the fourteen spheres of the manifested universe, whose parts constitute, as it were, the limbs of His being. The ornament Kausthubha worn on His neck is the Jiva-consciousness dependent upon Him for its existence. The mark Srivatsa on His chest is the spreading brilliance of the same. The floral wreath (Vanamala) on His neck is His own Maya Sakti having the three Gunas and their evolutes as its flowers. The brilliant yellow garment He wears is the Chchandas (Vedic Metres), and the thread across His chest (Brahmasutra) is the sacred Om with its three syllables. His ear rings are the Jnana Yoga and Ashtanga Yoga, the spiritual disciplines leading to Him. The diadem He wears is the Brahmaloka, the highest sphere attainable by spiritual striving. The serpent of infinitude called Adisesha, on whom He rests, is Prakriti (Matter, Objectivity) in its unformed condition. The Sattva Guna, which stands for morality, knowledge, beauty etc., is the lotus on which He is seated. The mace (Gada) Kaumodaki in His hand is Prana, the cosmic energy, which is the source of all strength, stamina and impressiveness. His sword Nandaka is the bluish element Sky. His shield is the dark element Tamas (darkness, inertia). His bow Saranga is the category of Time. His quiver of arrows is the potential Karmas. His discus (Chakra) Sudarsana is the element Fire. His conch Panchajanya is the element Water. The lotus He playfully holds in hand is His sixfold Bhaga (Divine Majesties). His finger postures (Mudras) indicate the bestowal of boons and salvation to votaries. The two ceremonial fans (Chamaras) held on His sides are righteousness and glory. With Yajna (Vedic sacrificial rite) for His form, He rides on His vehicle, the eagle Garuda, who is none but the three Vedas, and sits under a ceremonial umbrella which stands for His Divine Abode Vaikuntha Dhama, the state of bliss and freedom from fear. His eight door-keepers are His eightfold Divine Powers (the Ashtaisvaryas), and the chief of His attendants, Vishvaksena, is the embodiment of Vaishnava Tantras (ritualistic codes) like the *Pancharatra*. Sri Devi, His consort, is His Sakti (Divine Power) ever inseparable from Him like heat and light from fire. The disc of the sun, the sacrificial altar and the holy images constitute the symbols for His worship, and fitness to worship Him consists in initiation and other purificatory rites. He manifests Himself for worship and meditation as the four Emanations (Vyuhas)—Vasudeva, Sankarshana, Pradyumna and Aniruddha, and correspondingly in consciousness as Turiya (Samadhi), Prajna (deep sleep), Taijasa (dream state) and Visva (waking state). Thus Hari in His fourfold aspect with His physical features (Anga), accessories (Upanga), decorations (Akalpa) and weapons (Ayudha) is to be worshipped and meditated upon. He it is that manifests Himself as the whole world of Becoming, and sustains and withdraws it into Himself by virtue of His Divine Power (Maya), Himself remaining unchanged and unaffected by these processes.

It will be seen from the above summary of the Vishnu conception in the *Bhagavata* that it is not inculating any crude anthro-
pomorphism of a narrow cult.   Left to himself man cannot have
any concrete sense of Divine majesty and attributes.   The mind
has to be stimulated into a sense of these, and the highly sublime
and evocative descriptions of Divine Personality contained in the
Puranas achieve this for the votaries of particular cults. Questions
of three dimensional factuality, dates and location are irrelevant
matters, provided the thought-forms have sufficiently soaked into
the psychic substratum of the people concerned and remain potent
enough to stimulate the response of the whole being of man.   The
Cult-Deity becomes then a channel of contemplation and communion for generations of pious devotees and high-souled saints, and
the Supreme Personal-Impersonal Being responds to them through
these thought forms.   These forms, much more enduring and dynamic than anything that the so-called history can offer, thereby
become Psychic Realities and channels of communion through
which the Supreme Being could be approached and realised.   The
cult of Vishnu is one of those channels culled out by the human
mind and infilled by the Divine Spirit for man's attainment of the
spiritual goal. And the *Bhagavata Purana*, one of the great texts of
this cult, would be fulfilling its purpose if it could produce through
its descriptions, narratives, hymns and philosophical disquisitions, a whole-hearted acceptance of the Vishnu concept and evoke
devotional responses of the highest order from the mind of man.
Who can dispute the fact that the *Bhagavata* has amply succeeded
in this?

VIII

Theology of the Bhagavata: the four Pada Theory

As regards the theology of the Bhagavata, the generally
accepted idea of it has been that the Supreme Being in His personal
aspect is the Mahavishnu as described above, together with His
Sakti, Emanations (Vyuhas), and Avataras (Incarnations). But in
the recent research work[1] of Prof. Siddheswar Bhattacharya

---

1. It is not entirely new, as it is mainly a justification and restatement
of the position adopted by the Bengal or Chaitanya School of Vaishnavism, of
course with some important differences.

entitled *The Philosophy of the Bhagavata* already referred to earlier, an attempt has been made to spell out a new theology of a more elaborate and complicated nature. The following is the substance of the conclusions he arrives at, after a thorough-going research of the text of the *Bhagavata* :

From the Rig Vedic hymns down to the Upanishads, the Reality of Supreme Being is conceived as having three and sometimes four Padas (aspects or parts). The Sun or Savita, who is the basic concept behind Vedic Vishnu, is conceived as covering the heavens and the earth with three strides and transcending these by His fourth stride. The Purusha Sukta, which presents Vishnu as Cosmic Man, speaks of Him as manifesting as the world with one Pada and transcending it by the remaining three Padas. It is further said : "That transcendent state (Pada) of Vishnu is seen by the Suris (mystic devotees) like an eye spread in the sky " The *B*-*ahmanas*, which specially deal with sacrifices, conceived of sacrifice as having three Padas, of which one is manifest as the Vedic ritual called sacrifice. In the Upanishadic literature where the theory of Brahman is propounded, we find the Chandogya Upanishad, speaking of Brahman as having four Padas— *Tat etad chatushpād Brahma* Ch. U. 3. 18. 2).In the *Mandukyopanishad* also we get the philosophy of four states of consciousness spoken of as the four Padas of Brahman. All this resulted ultimately in the synthesis effected in the concept of Chatushpad Brahman (Brahman with four parts) propounded in the *Tripād-vibhūti-mahānārā-yanopanishad*, which, according to Dr. Battacharya, seems to have inspired the theology of the *Bhagavata*.

Krishna Conception versus Vishnu Conception

According to Dr. Bhattacharya, the *Bhagavata*, following the analysis of *Tripād - vibhuti-mahānārāyanopanishad*, conceives of Reality as having four Padas or aspects or degrees of manifestation. By this it is not meant that the Infinite Being has four divisions in Him, but only that He could be studied in depth only if we approach Reality in these four aspects, each aspect being included in the other. Just as when gold is formed into ornaments, vessels etc., the substance gold remains the same, so the Supreme

Reality is not broken by its manifestation as four degrees of manifestation. Reality in its fourth degree is the Non-dual Absolute. As
the Absolute is beyond the grasp of the human mind, the *Bhagavata* leaves it with the assertion that the 'Absolute is what it is '.
It functions as the Supra-transcendental to remind that the other
degrees of Reality posited afterwards are not Cult-Deities of a
purely personal nature, but the unlimited Absolute Itself manifested as apprehendable by human conceptions in a hierarchical
order. The Absolute or the fourth grade of Reality is indicated as
Sat-Chit-Ananda.

Its full manifestation as the Supreme Person or the third
degree of Reality is Sri Krishna, with His Dhama (abode) in
Goloka (the land of light). Such an idea is foreign to the *Bhagavata*, but is found only in later Puranas like the *Brahma-Vaivarta*
and others. This is however a theological doctrine of the Chitanya
School of Vaishnavism, and Dr. Bhattacharya endorses it and justifies it, though the name of this particular school is not mentioned.
On a solitary passage occuring along with the catalogue of Incarnations – ' Krishna is Bhagavan Himself ' (*Krishnastu bhagavan
svayam*)—it is assumed without any justification that the *Bhagavata* puts Krishna as the third degree of Reality in the hierarchical order, and we are told that the absence of any mention of
Goloka as His Abode in the *Bhagavata*, is made up by the description of Gokula where Krishna spent his infancy and boyhood.
Krishna thus displaces Mahavishnu. Critical remarks on this
have already been made elsewhere. In order to accommodate
Krishna as the Supreme Person, Mahavishnu of the Bhagavata is
given a lower status in the hierarchy as the second degree of Reality, by changing His name into Adi-Vishnu, and that of His
abode Vaikuntha into Adi-Vaikuntha, both of these changes being
without any sanction in the *Bhagavata* text.

Adi-Vishnu, it is said, is also known as Adi-Narayana and as
Pramatman. He is primarily the embodiment of Sat (existence)
and Chit (intelligence), with Ananda (bliss) only as a subordinate
element. Next there is the first grade of Reality known as Brahman, who is only Sat—the all-comprehensive, undifferentiated
and self-luminous being who provides the background for the

world of Becoming with all its heterogenous and contradictory factors, and also forms the seminal condition into which everything dissolves at the end of cycles. Brahman is thus to be distinguished from the Non-dual Being, the fourth grade of Reality, spoken of earlier. Brahman is also called Purusha, the immanent self.

All these grades of Reality have their own Saktis or Potencies conceived as female. Sri Krishna, the third grade of Reality, has Yoga-Maya as His Sakti. She is the expression of the inherent bliss of the Bhagavan and manifests herself as the Gopikas when Sri Krishna appears in the Gokula. Adi-Vishnu, the second grade of Reality, has Mahamaya, also known as Vishnu-Maya, as His Sakti or Potency. She is also known as Sri and Ramā ocupying the Vaikuntha Dhama of Adi-Vishnu. Brahman, the first grade of Reality, also called Purusha, has, as His Sakti, Atma-Maya, who bifurcates into Chit-Sakti and Maya, in the creative process.

World Manifestation and Salvation

Creation (Srishti) is in cyclic order, having a vast period of manifestation followed by an equally long period of unmanifested state (Pralaya)[1]. A new eycle is set in motion by the creative will (Ikshana Kriya) of Adi-Vishnu, the second grade of Reality. With this divine will to be many, Adi-Vishnu, the second grade of Reality, becomes Brahman, the first grade of Reality. Thereupon Atma-Maya, the dynamic energy of Brahman or the first grade of Reality, manifests itself in its twofold contradictory

---

1. There is first the individual's daily Pralaya or dissolution when he sleeps, and his Srishti or creation when he wakes. This is subjective and is called (daily) Nitya-pralaya. In contrast there is cosmic Srishti and Pralaya according to the waking and sleep of Brahma. Then there is total Pralaya when the lifetime of a Brahma ends. So dissolution and manifestation depend on Brahma's time. The same is calculated as follows by the Pauranikas: 320000 human years=1 Chatur Yuga (period of time comprising the four ages of Krita, Treta, Dwapara & Kali). 1000 Ch. Yugas=1 Kalpa or 1 day time of Brahma when the universe is manifested. It is followed by an equally long period of time (Kalpa) when Brahma sleeps and the universe is in dissolution. So 2 Kalpas are termed Dviparardha=one day and one night of Brahma (when one periodic projection and one dissolution are completed and the next projection begins). 360 such Brahma's days=1 year of Brahma. 100 such years=

conditions as Maya and Chit Sakti, the first standing for
materiality and the second for spirituality. Brahman, the first
grade of Reality, becomes Purusha (God) when these contradictory Saktis operate. Of these two Saktis, Maya evolves into Kāla
(time), Karma (the residual impressions of the acts of Jivas) and
Svabhava (Nature) on the one hand, and into Vidya (spiritual knowledge), Avidya (ignorance causing bondage) and Prakriti (root-
matter consisting of the three Gunas, Sattva, Rajas and Tamas)
on the other. By the impetus given by Kāla, Karma, and Svabhava
to Prakriti or Matter, material evolution of the twenty-four categories takes place. These categories are four psychological categories consisting of Chitta, Ahamkara, Buddhi, and Manas; the
ten physiological categories consisting of the five sense organs and
the five motor organs; and the ten physical categories of five
Tanmatras (subtle elements) and the five gross elements springing
from them. The minds and bodies of Jivas of all grades of evolution and the fourteen gross and subtle regions for them to dwell
in are evolved out of these categories by the will of God inter-
penetrating them. With the five gross elements, Brahma the
Demiurge, charged with the strength of the Purusha, forms at the
beginning of a Kalpa, the Brahmanda (Cosmic Egg) and gradually
manifests it into the fourteen Lokas or planes of existence—seven
inferior worlds called Atala, Vitala, Sutala, Talatala, Mahatala,
Rasatala and Patala, and the seven regions of higher evolution
called Bhuloka, Bhuvarloka, Svarloka, Maharloka, Janaloka,
Tapoloka and Satyaloka. In these various planes of existence

---

the full life time of a Brahma, when one Brahma is absorbed into Mahavishnu
and another Brahma assumes creatorship. There is then total Pralaya or dissolution. That is, in the Pralayas at the end of each Kalapa or day of Brahma
all the worlds up to Satyaloka only dissolve. But in this Pralaya at the end of
Brahma's life time, which is called Prakrita Pralaya, Satyaloka of Brahma,
together with Brahma and all manifested Prakriti, attains dissolution in the
Supreme Being, who never sleeps but only winks. In winking, when He opens
the eyes, the whole of creation represented by Brahma's life time (which on
computation of the data given above will come to 311.04 trillion human years)
takes place, and when he closes His eyes, it relapses into its primordial condition, that is, into Himself. The Supreme being Himself is above time and is
eternal.

Jivas are embodied in bodies formed for them by Brahma according to their deserts arising from Karma. By the power of Avidya (ignorance), one of the off-shoots of Maya, Jivas feel identified with bodies and forget their nature, until through purification by good deeds and devotion in the course of repeated embodiments, Vidya (illumination) is generated by the grace of Chit-Sakti (spiritual aspect of Atma-Maya) and the Jiva is set on the path of liberation from the imprisonment of Prakriti. If an aspirant is a seeker after Moksha and freedom from embodiment, the Jiva attains to non-dual consciousness and is merged in the Absolute (Sayujya). If he is for Divine love and service, the Jiva becomes a Bhagavatottama, an eternal companion of the Divine, delighting in service of Him and participating in His redemptive activity.

Brahman, Paramatman and
Bhagavan the Denotation of the Terms

The learned research work of Dr. Bhattacharya is very comprehensive and expounds many themes other than what is given above. What is summarised here is mainly his findings on the Mahavishnu conception, and the following critical remarks are confined to this topic alone. Students of the *Bhagavata* would have been happy if such a fourfold structure of Reality as adduced by Dr. Bhattacharya was clearly discernible in the *Bhagavata* text, just like the Vyuha theory, the incarnation doctrine, the scheme of cyclic evolution and other doctrines expounded by him on the basis of the *Bhagavata* text, on which no student of the *Bhagavata* will have any difference from his views. The solitary verse in the *Bhagavata* (1.1.11) on which he bases his special theological doctrine is as follows : ' That which truth-knowers speak of as the Non-dual Consciousness, is called (*Sabdyate*) as Brahman, Paramatman and Bhagavan.'' Following the interpretation of the Chaitanya School of Vaishnavism, Dr. Bhattacharya takes the word '*Sabdyate*' (meaning only 'is called') to signify the three grades of Reality in the hierarchical order of Bhagavan, Paramatma and Brahman. There is nothing in the quoted line or its context to indicate any such hierarchical order of Reality and in the whole Bhagavata text of eighteen thousand verses, nowhere is such a gradation to be found.   The verse concerned only states the liberal and syncretic view of the *Bhagavata* that what the Upanishadic philosophers call Brahman, the Yogis speak of as Paramatman and Bhaktas as Bhagavan, indicate the same One without a second and are only *synonyms* for the one Reality. This is only a reiteration of the traditional Vedic doctrine declared in the well-known Vedic passage. "The Truth is one; the sages speak of it in many ways." The only other passage he quotes from the *Bhagavata* in support of his gradation theory relates to the description of the spiritual progress of Kardama Prajapati (Bh. 3. 24. 43-47).   The words Brahman, Bhagavan and Pratyagatman are all used there only in apposition or as synonyms as in the earlier passage, and not in the sense of gradation of Reality. All that it can show is that according to the *Bhagavata*, perfect spiritual realisation consists in experiencing the Non-Dual Reality as Impersonal-Personal Being.

Tripad-vibhuti-mahanarayanopanishad and the Bhagavata

That the *Bhagavata* is deeply rooted in Vedic tradition has to be conceded, but whether the doctrine of the four Padas (aspects of Reality), so often found in the Vedas and the Upanishads, is reflected in it is very doubtful.   It is nowhere clearly stated in the text, although a vague reference to it can be found in the four Vyuha theory.   Dr. Bhattacharya attributes this doctrine to the *Bhagavata* on the assumption that it draws inspiration for its theology from the *Tripād-vibūti-mahānārāyanopanishad*.   This is a Vaishnava Upanishad, non-dualistic in trend.   It speaks definitely about the four Padas (quarters or aspects) of Reality— Avidya Pada (Ignorance Aspect), Vidya Pada (Knowledge Aspect), Ananda Pada (Bliss Aspect), and Turiya Pada (Transcendental Aspect). Avidya Pada alone is completely distinguished as being a gross manifestation modified by ignorance (Avidya), while the other three are treated together as a unity of the subtle (Sukshma), the potential (Bija) and the transcendental (Turiya) aspects of Reality, free from the sway of ignorance. Unlike in the case of Avidya Pada, there is in the unity of the other three the pure Radiance of sentiency and unalloyed bliss.   In that Radiance is manifest the eternal Vaikuntha, with which Mahavishnu, the Personal aspect of Reality, is identified. This Mahavishnu Himself is also called Adi-Narayana. Both the Impersonal Non-duality and the Personal Mahavishnu are accepted as involved in Reality or Brahman, because the Upanishad contends that the so-called Absolute and Impersonal Being (Turiya) can only be understood as insentient Akasa if the Personal Bliss-Sentient Aspect is not conceded. Thus the analysis of this particular Upanishad gives not a hierarchy but an Impersonal-Personal Deity denoted by mutually equatable synonyms like Mahavishnu, Adi-Narayana, Paramatman and Brahman, who .manifests also the world of materiality and ignorance and indwells it as Purusha. The Bhagavata position also seems to be the same.

Though the research done by Dr. Bhattacharya is thorough-going and illuminating in many respects, it is thus difficult to accept the doctrine of gradation of Reality in spite of the fact that the new arrangement would have given greater regularity to the *Bhagavata* theology. Vaikuntha is everywhere in the *Bhagavata* associated with Mahavishnu, the Supreme Being, according to this text, and there is no higher state than His Paramapada. There is nothing to show that the *Bhagavata* displaces Mahavishnu by Krishna, reducing Him into Adi-Vishnu, an inferior emanation of Krishna. There is no Adi-Vishnu distinguished from Mahavishnu of Vaikuntha in the *Bhagavata* text. The *Bhagavata* all through treats Krishna as an Incarnation of Mahavishnu only, no doubt, the most complete. The solitary controversial line "Krishna is Bhagavan Himself" has already been discussed. In consistency with several other passages on the subject, it can be taken only to mean that Krishna is the most perfect of all Incarnations. There is not the slightest reference in the *Bhagavata* to a Goloka and to an Adi-Vaikuntha foisted on it as Abode of Krishna and of Adi-Vishnu respectively. The conception of Sakti as threefold—Yoga-Maya, Maha-Maya and Atma Maya—to suit the first three grades of Reality cannot also find clear support in the *Bhagavata* text. These words are there, no doubt, in the text, but there is justification only to regard all these expressions as synonyms of the power of Vishnu and not as a hierarchy of pow-

ers pertaining to the hierarchical grades of Reality—the Bhagavan, Adi-Vishnu and Brahman. The interpretation of Brahman
as the last grade of Reality in the research work of Dr. Bhattacharya can only create confusion, as this word is always used for
the Supreme Being of the Upanishads in all Indian religious and
philosophical literature. This is admitted by Dr. Bhattacharya
himself, and he criticises the Bengal School of Vaishnavism for
considering the Brahman of the Upanishads as the external splendour (Tanu-bha) of Krishna. The better course is not to use
this word at all in this confusing sense in the absence of any clear
sanction for it from the *Bhagavata* text.

All that can be said with certainty about the theology of the
Bhagavata is that it proclaims the glory of Mahavishnu, the Non-
dual Being, who is both the Impersonal Absolute and the
transcendent Divine Person with Vaikuntha as His Dhama
(Abode). Though transcendental, He also manifests Himself as the
Viraja Purusha, whose body is constituted of the Brahmanda
(cosmic whole) with its fourteen Lokas (worlds) and the Jivas
inhabiting it, and who, as indwelling spirit, pervades it. The
Mahavishnu conception also includes His transcendental emanations known as the fourfold Vyuhas, His threefold Gunavataras
and His twenty-three Descents (Incarnations) known as His
Leelavataras. Of these Leelavataras, Krishna is the most complete Descent of Mahavishnu, and the *Bhagavata* devotes itself to
the depiction of the glory of Krishna's life, actions and teachings.

VII
Manifestations of Mahavishnu : Vyuhas

The doctrine of Avatara or Divine Descent is of supreme
importance in the devotional doctrine of the *Bhagavata*.
Though this word is usually associated with what is considered as
God's appearance in the society of men, it is taken for treatment in
a wider sense to include all the different types of Divine Epiphany
mentioned in the *Bhagavata*. The terms indicating these different
types are as follows : Vyuha, Gunavatara, Leelavatara, Purnavatara, Amsavatara, Kalavatara, Amsa-Kalavatara and Avesavatara.
To take the Vyuhas first, they constitute a fourfold transcendental

Emanation of Mahavishnu, hypostatic or co-substantial with Him. They are distinct from the Avataras proper in so far as they do not form an Epiphany occasioned by cosmic situations, but constitute an intrinsic expression included in the structure of Mahavishnu and inseparable from Him. The names of the four Vyuhas of Mahavishnu are Vasudeva, Samkarshana, Pradyumna and Aniruddha. The Vaishnava codes of worship represent them as Murtis or forms with distinctive Anga (physical features , Upanga (paraphernalia), Ayudha (weapons), Akalpa (decorations) etc., and present them as objects of meditation and worship, which constitute the adoration, not of different Gods but of the one Mahavishnu, the Supreme Being, Himself. Though the Vyuhas are thus spiritual entities, the *Bhagavata*, perhaps to imply their unity, brings their names together as a family group in the life of Krishna. Vasudeva is the name of Sri Krishna Himself ; His brother Balarama is equated with Samkarshana ; Krishna's son is known as Pradyumna, and his grandson as Aniruddha. A cosmic and psychological status is also given to the Vyuhas by relating them as uninvolved witnesses of the evolutionary categories and states of consciousness. Thus Vasudeva is related to Chitta (mind stuff) Samkarshana to Ahamkara (egoity), Pradyumna to Buddhi (intellect), and Aniruddha to Manas (mind). They are also conceived as presiding over Turiya (super-consciousness), Sushupti (deep sleep), Svapna (dream state) and Jagrat (waking state) respectively.

Gunavataras

As distinguished from the Vyuhas of Mahavishnu, are His Gunavataras - Brahma, Vishnu and Mahadeva—generally known as the Trinity of Hinduism, though their conception is entirely different from that of the Christian Trinity. These constitute the one Mahavishnu in association with the three Gunas of Prakriti, for which reason they are called Gunavataras—Descents in association with Gunas. Mahavishnu is the one Supreme Being. When in His creative role He associates Himself with an impure Guna like Rajas (desire-prompted energy), He is called Brahma; when for purposes of dissolution or destruction He puts on the other impure Guna, Tamas (dullness, inertia), He is called Maheswara or Rudra; and when in His preservation-cum-redemptive role He assumes the Sattva Guna (light, purity, intelligence), He (Mahavishnu) is Vishnu, forming the object of worship for all who seek devotion, enlightenment and salvation. Invested with the two impure Gunas, His Bhaga (sixfold Divine majesty) is obscured, whereas Sattva being pure and fully revealing, His manifestation through it possesses all the majesties of the Bhagavan, and He alone is therefore the object of worship and prayer for all who seek devotion, spiritual enlightenment and liberation.

Leelavataras

Besides, out of abounding love for the Jivas and in order to bring them the light of spiritual illumination and freedom from the misery of transmigratory cycles (Samsara), as also for the achievement of some special cosmic purposes, Mahavishnu incarnates in the universe of sentient beings as one of them. Such Incarnations are called in general Leelavataras (Sportive Divine Descents), and these are the most significant from the point of view of man in need of spiritual enlightenment. The *Bhagavata* makes mention of twenty-three such, including the original Purushavatara, which stands as a class by itself. Some of the Leelavataras are in the ranks of Devas, some among Rishis, some among men, and some among sub-human species of beings. The twenty-three Incarnations listed in the *Bhagavata* are as follows :

1· Viraja Purusha : He is the first cosmic manifestation of the transcendental Mahavishnu and the original Incarnation out of whom all other Incarnations come. The Vedas speak of the transcendental Mahavishnu manifesting by a fourth of His being as the Viraja Purusha. The *Bhagavata* represents Him, "as lying in Cosmic Waters in Yoga-nidra (sleep of spiritual absorption)." That form, free from Rajas and other impurities of Prakriti, and endowed with all powers, is seen by the spiritual insight of sages, as shining with countless legs, arms, faces, ears, eyes and heads and decorations. He is the source of all future Incarnations. Out of his navel comes out the lotus bud of the worlds in their subtle form, and from it emerges Brahma, the Demiurge, with the creative urge. On the petals of that lotus are plotted by him, all the fourteen spheres constituting, as it were, the gross body of that original Incarnation. This Viraja Purusha, the Original Incarnation, remains always, unlike the other Leelavataras which come for particular purposes at particular times. 2. In Kumara Sarga He manifested Himself as Sanat Kumara evincing the power and greatness of Brahmacharya. 3. He assumed the shape of Yajna-varaha (Boar as embodiment of sacrifice) to re-establish the worlds in their equilibrium. 4. In Rishi Sarga, He appeared as Narada to preach the Sāttvata doctrine of devotion and non-attached work. 5. He embodied himself as Rishis Nara and Narayana who engaged themselves in severe austere practices. 6. He became the perfect sage Kapila. and restated the forgotten philosophical doctrine known as Samkhya. 7. He next appeared as sage Datta-treya and imparted the knowledge of the Atman to the sages. 8. As Yajna, the son of Prajapati Ruchi, He presided over the Age of Svayambhuva Manvantara (the period of a certain Manu's rule). 9. He was born as Paramahamsa Rishabha when He exemplified the highest spiritual ideas through his life. 10. He became the Empe-ror Prithu who exploited the resources of the earth for the benefit of all beings. 11. In the deluge that took place in the Chakshusha Manvantara He assumed the shape of a Fish and saved Vaivas-wata Manu in a boat, the shape of which the earth assumed. 12. He appeared as the Cosmic Tortoise to support the Mandara mountain used as a churning rod for churning the milk ocean. 13. He took the form of Dhanvantari for presenting Amrita (the elixir of life) after the churning of the milk ocean. 14. He became Mohini (charming maiden) to infatuate the Asuras who took away the Amrita by force. 15. He became the Man-lion for the dest-ruction of Hiranya Kasipu, the demoniacal and anti-God tyrant. 16. He embodied Himself as the Vamana or the Dwarf to restore the worlds to Indra from Bali. 17. As Parasurama He destroyed all the tyrannical Kshatriya kings. 11. Coming as Vyasa, the son of Satyavati, He re-edited the Vedas for their easy comprehension. 19. As Rama, He destroyed Ravana and other Asuras. 20-21. He became afterwards Balarama and Sri Krishna to lighten the bur-dens of the earth. 22. In the Kali age He is born as Buddha to confuse the demoniacally minded. 32. In future, towards the end of the Kali age, He is to appear as Kalki.

After citing these twenty-three Incarnations, including the original one, the Purusha, the *Bhagavata* says that there is no limit to their number. "The Incarnations of Hari are as numerous as water channels coming from a lake." This over-liberal view, while it has helped the Hindu mind to avoid putting exclusive claims in regard to any particular Incarnation, has, however, contributed also to water down the significance of the Incarnation idea. When they are so numerous, on what criterion can an Incarnation be distinguished? It is sometimes said an Incarnation inaugurates a new age and marks an elevation of consciousness in humanity. But this can be recognised only after his time. It is also said an Incarnation lessens the tensions of society by destroying the forces of Adharma represented by evil doers. In our historical times this is very difficult to recognise, as destructive wars are fought only by political and military figures having no spiritual touch in their lives. It is, however, noteworthy that in the list of Incarnations given in the *Bhagavata*, at least some like Parasumara come on a purely destructive mission. But all the significant Incarnations are centres of holiness, transforming even sinners and confirmed rebels against God, and they bring the light of knowledge and devotion into the lives of countless men for generations that follow. After discussing the various purposes of the advent of Incarnations, the *Bhagavata* finally concludes that their most important object is to provide ways of spiritual enlightenment and salvation for men at large. The immediate purposes described in their lives are secondary. The Lord incarnates not as a solitary personality but as the central figure among a group of His eternal companions and highly advanced souls whose Karma brings them into the orbit of His Divine mission. All of them become means for the accomplishment of His mission, but besides this, through their relationship with Him and in accomplishment of His work, they exemplify various devotional ideals and set patterns of devotional life for others to imitate. The earthly lives of the Incarnation and His inner circle of devotees thus provide a rich record of activities full of spiritual significance. It may be that only the contemporaries of the Incarnations are immediately benefited by direct physical contact with them, but their teachings and the rich record of their doings, glorified in Puranas and Itihasas, leave devotional material for generations to contemplate upon and to develop the sentiment of devotion. The life of Krishna, Rama and other Incarnations are examples of this. Besides their spiritual teachings, their actions and relationships with devotees have inspired the production of Puranas, Itihasas, temples, images, musical compositions etc., which have gone to light the flame of devotion in countless minds. In the text of this Anthology it will be found how the life of Krishna, as recorded by the *Bhagavata*, becomes a means for Sravana (hearing), Kirtana (praising) and Smarana (remembrance) the three of the most important devotional disciplines. So also the Incarnation, being hypostatic with Vishnu, can become an Ishta Devata (Chosen Deity) for worship and meditation. Though the physical bodies of historical Incarnations may disappear, they continue as spiritual embodiments in oneness with the Supreme Being and become channels for worship and communion with the Divine. The various attitudes of Dasya (servitude), Sakhya (friendship), Vatsalya (parental love) and Madhura (conjugal love), as practised by His devotees towards Krishna during His earthly sojourn, have become ways of Sadhana (spiritual practice) through imitation for countless generations of devotees that followed. Thus the purpose of every Incarnation is to bring God into the life of mankind without any limitation of time or place.

Other Classifications of Avataras

The *Bhagavata* has attempted, though not in a very precise and systematic manner, a classification of these Avataras into different categories on the basis of the manifestation of Divinity in them. Five expressions are used for this classification—Purna, Amsa, Kala, Amsa-Kala, and Avesa. Purnavatara means, complete or perfect Incarnation, and the one and only Purnavatara known to the *Bhagavata* is Sri Krishna, the Divine Personage, whose glory the *Bhagavata* has undertaken to expound. He is called Purna in the sense that the Bhaga or the sixfold majesty of omnipotence, goodness, glory, beauty, omniscience, and renunciation associated with the Bhagavan or Mahavishnu, was fully manifest in Him. It should be once again reiterated here that

the *Bhagavata* does not at all mean thereby to displace Mahavishnu, the Supreme Being, by Krishna who is everywhere treated
as an Incarnation of Mahavishnu only. While in verse 1-1-11 of
the *Bhagavata,* He is spoken of as Bhagavan Svayam (Bhagavan
Himself) because of the full manifestation of Bhaga in Him, He is
also spoken of as a Kala (a portion or particle) in Bh. 2-7-26
and as Amsa-bhaga (a part of an aspect) in Bh. 10-2-26. These
are very inconvenient expressions for interpreters of the Krishna
cult, and in spite of all their skill in deriving whatever meaning
they like from Sanskrit expressions, no impartial reader can find
reason to accept Krishna as other than an Incarnation, may be
an Incarnation with much fuller manifestation of all Divine
majesties than others. But since all Leelavataras are hypostatic
with Maha-Vishnu, they are all Bhagavan in the same sense that
Krishna is, and are worthy of worship.

In contrast to the Purnavatara, are the Amsas and Kalas, both
of which mean more or less the same thing—a part and a portion.
In Dr. Siddheswar Bhattacharya's work, he has tried to distinguish these by calling an Amsa as 'part' and Kala as 'particle',
meaning thereby "that the term Amsa might be applied to a
reality homogeneous in character and substance with its prototype and that the term Kala would be applicable to a different
kind of reality heterogeneous in character and substance from its
proto-type." Most of the commentators have taken it more or
less in the same sense. By Amsavataras they mean Divine manifestation revealing only some of the Divine majesties (Bhaga)
needed for the occasion, though, being one in consciousness with
God, they possess all powers. A Kala is described as a Vibhuti,
or a manifestation of divine power in separation (Bhinnamsa).
Kalas of Vishnu are individualised expressions of His power as
souls of exceptional potency. Some Kalas are taken as His eternal
companions and attendants like Sesha, coeval with Him, and some
like Manus and exceptional souls of high evolution, are described as
Adhikarikas to whom cosmic functions are allotted by Him. They
may also be liberated souls (Muktapurushas) who have realised
their oneness with Him but yet retain their individuality and are
ever at His service. Such divinised individualities are His Vibhu

tis (Powers) or Kalas. The Bhagavan can be conceived as manifesting His Amsa (aspect), or His Bhaga, (majesties) through the medium of these Kalas. If such a conception is accepted, the term Amsa-Kala used by the *Bhagavata* becomes specially appropriate to indicate this combination. God may be conceived as formful, but He is not an individual. So when He is said to manifest, it is proper to conceive Him as doing this manifesting as an individuality through His Kalas. This idea of combination is conveyed by the expression Avesāvatara, or Descent by infilling. It means the Divine Spirit infills a Kala or perfected individual and becomes incarnate thereby as a personality. According to some commentators of the *Bhagavata* like Jiva Goswami, a very limited manifestation of Divine power through a Kala is called a Vibhuti, but when the infilling is of a very great magnitude, the mighty expression of Divinity that results is called an Avesaavatara. It will thus be seen that the Amsa and Kala conceptions of Incarnation become unified in the idea of Avesāvatara.

A grouping of the twenty-three Avataras as found in an unspecified old work on the basis of the manifestation of Bhaga or divine majesties in them, is given in the commentary of Viswanath Chakravartin on the *Bhagavata*. It is as follows: Nrisimha, Parasurama, Kalki and Purusha are manifestations of God's Bhaga called Aiswarya (omnipotence); Narada, Vyasa, Varaha and Buddha, of Dharma (goodness); Rama, Dhanwantari, Yajna and Prithu, of Yasas (glory); Balarama, Mohini and Vamana, of Sri (beauty); Dattatreya, Matsya, Kumara and Kapila, of Jnana (omniscience); Narayana, Nara, Kurma and Rishabha, of Vairagaya (renunciation). Krishna, the ocean of all sweetness, is, on the other hand, the manifestation of all the six above mentioned divine majesties. He underlies all the Avataras.

Avatara as an infilling (Avesa) of
Anugraha-sakti or Redeeming Power

The above grouping introduces some system into the rather amorphous list of Incarnations given in the *Bhagavata*. A better systematisation is to be found in the unification of the conceptions of Amsa and Kala, often indiscriminately used in the

Bhagavata, by the theory of Avatara as an Amsa-Kala or an Avesa (infilling of a Kala by Divinity) as stated earlier. Leaving aside the non-human Descents, the Incarnation concept can be understood as an expression of the Anugraha-Sakti (redeeming aspect or Amsa) of Mahavishnu through a Kala (a perfected individuality ever associated with the Lord's work of redemption). An Incarnation becomes significant to man only when He is an expression of the Divine through humanity and one could see in Him both God and man. In some conspicuous examples like Krishna Incarnation, Divinity predominates and humanity is a thin veil only, for which reason He is called Purnavatara and Bhagavan Svayam (Bhagavan Himself). The implication of this predominance of Divinity in Krishna is that man can follow only His instructions and not his actions which are of superhuman dimensions. The sportive activities of His life were meant for blessing His devotees, and so they provide matter for devout contemplation and not for imitation What is suited for imitation is the attitude and actions of His devotees in relation to Him. But there are other Incarnations like Rama in whom humanity and divinity are equally matched and who provide examples for imitation. It is, however, confusing to note that Varaha (Boar), Matsya (Fish), Nrisimha (Man-lion) etc. are included in the list of Amsa-Kala or Leelavataras (Sportive Descents) along with Rama, Krishna, Buddha, Kapila, Rishabha, Dhanwantari, Datta-treya etc. who can be easily understood as Amsa-Kalas. They are obviously historical personages, though our limited knowledge of the dimensions of history may raise problems for such accommodation. As regards non-human Incarnations, they may be taken as psychic manifestations in the consciousness of devotees or as relating to other dimensions than ours.

Some clever attempts have been made to explain the usually enumerated ten Avataras from an anthropological point of view. These ten Avataras are Matsya (Fish), Kurma (Tortoise), Varaha (Boar), Nrihari Man-Lion), Vamana (Dwarf), Parasu-Rama (Rama with Axe), Rama (Prince of Ayodhya), Krishna with Bala-rama (the full Incarnation of the *Bhagavata*), the Buddha (the historical Siddhartha) and Kalki (the future destructive Descent).

The non-human Avataras are described by some as the totems of different clans, and as these clans came to be accommodated in the Vishnu cult, the totem animals etc. were sanctified and the legends associated with them were incorporated as materials of the Puranas. Others find in the arrangement of the list, the recapitulation of the evolutionary ascent of life from water-bound creatures, through amphibians and land-bound creatures, to primitive man clearing forests with the axe, and thence to civilised man. These theories are interesting but far-fetched. What is more, they shed no light on the devotional developments centring on these Incarnations

With the Amsa-Kala doctrine of Incarnation unified under the idea of Avesavatara, the *Bhagavata* conception of Mahavishnu is complete. He is the ultimate source of creation, revelation and redemption. Through Brahma, who comes out of his Navel-Lotus, He creates, and through Him, He also reveals the Veda, the Word of power and wisdom, and His redeeming aspect (Anugraha Shakti) comes as the Leelavatara from age to age for resuscitating the eternal spiritual law and providing the Jivas with various means of salvation through the contemplation of His activities and teachings. The Leelavatara, as an Amsa-Kala or Avesa, may be described as the Transcendental manifesting through a perfect Person who is one with Iswara in consciousness but keeps up a distinctive individuality for the purpose of world redemption. And if we conceive that perfect Person to be the same eternally, then He becomes the very embodiment of God's redeeming power and the distinction between the two becomes inconsequential. Unless some such doctrine is accepted, it is impossible to understand the statements of some of the great personalities accepted as Incarnations like Sri Krishna and Sri Ramakrishna. "Many have been the births undergone by Me as also by you. I remember them all, but you do not," says Sri Krishna. "The same One who appeared as Rama and as Krishna has now appeared as Ramakrishna but not in the Vedantic sense," says Sri Ramakrishna. These statemens can be understood only as meaning that the same Divine Personality, one with Iswara in consciousness but keeping up a distinct entity, appears from

age to age as the Divine Incarnation, the embodiment of the re
deeming power of God (Anugraha Sakti). A Leelavatara is therefore both God and Man. It is God approaching man through
humanity, so that even ordinary people who cannot practise
philosophic reflection and concentration can have communion
with Him through the study and contemplation of the sportive
activities of the Lord Incarnate and the devotional attitudes of
His associates.

Finally, in addition to the Leelavataras, the spiritual traditions of India and the world at large record the lives of many
great personages known as prophets, Adhikarika-purushas, Alwars, Acharyas etc. All these may be understood as coming
within the concept of Kalas interpreted as Vibhutis or manifestations of limited powers of the Lord through highly evolved personalities. When the *Bhagavata* says that the Incarnations of Hari
are as numerous as streamlets from a lake, it has to be understood
to mean such Kalas or Vibhutis. They are thus to be distinguished from the rather rare Leelavataras in whom Divine majesty,
especially the power of redemption, that is, of bestowing salvation
on Jivas at will, is conspicuously manifest.

VIII
The Metaphysics of the Bhagavata

It has already been pointed out that the *Bhagavata*, though
a Bhakti scripture, accepts Non-duality as the ultimate nature of
things. This Non-dual existence is described as Sat-chit-ananda.
There is a general impression that a non-dualist metaphysics
(Advaita) gives no scope for devotion as the ultimate end of
spiritual living. This is due to the exclusive identification of
Advaita with the school called Kevaladvaita, which maintains
that every manifestation of the Non-dual Being, including
Iswara, is a superimposition and therefore only an appearance.
But this is too exclusive an idea. All Vedanta or Upanishadic
philosophy is Advaita in the sense of accepting the unity of
existence as the ultimate nature of Reality. The differences of the
schools of Vedanta come in the interpretation of the relation
between this Unity or Brahman and multiplicity. In Kevaladvaita,

Brahman, the Impersonal-Absolute, alone is real and everything else, including Iswara, is an appearance only. In the Suddhadvaita of Vallabhacharya and in the Achintya-bhedabheda of the Chaitanya School of Vaishnavism, Brahman is both supra-personal and personal, and He becomes, through His Sakti, the universe and the Jivas in reality, without being affected in the least thereby. In the Vishishtadvaita of Ramanuja, Brahman is the all-inclusive Whole to whom the universe and the Jivas are organically related, as the body and limbs are in an organism. In Madhwa's Brahmadvaita, Brahman is the one Indpendent Being and the multiplicity, though separate from Him, has only an existence dependent on Him like that of reflection on its prototype.

It may be possible to find passages to support all these views in the text of the *Bhagavata*. It is even so with the Upanishads, the source book of Vedanta. Attempts have been made in the past to interpret all such scriptural passages with apparently diverse meanings as supporting one or the other of these philosophic trends exclusively, under the presumption that all scriptural passages can have only one meaning or purport as in the case of words arranged as a sentence. We find this is not so even in the writings of great literary geniuses like Shakespeare and Kalidasa, wherein we get passages having more than one meaning. In Sanskrit there are Kavyas (poetical works) which seem to present one story when read from one end, and a different one when read from the other end. Why should not this kind of versatility be conceded in the case of revelations like the Upanishads that are meant for the spiritual needs of men of diverse tastes and at different stages of evolution? It is quite possible for a scriptural text to have different philosphies in it. These may look contradictory when viewed from a purely intellectual stand-point, but when philosophy is viewed only as a scaffolding to build up the edifice of spiritual experience—as conceptual aids for different spiritual types to evolve to their fullest stature— then these contradictions cease to be of any consequence. It is far better to conceive of God as a poet than as as a logician.

At least as far as the *Bhagavata* is concerned, no metaphysics seems to be obnoxious to it, if it does not question the

ultimacy of the Bhagavan and the supermacy of Bhakti. Its leaning
seems to be towards some form of realistic monism which recognises the Reality as Personal-Impersonal, manifesting in a real
sense as the Bhagavan, the infinite Divine Person, and as the Jivas
and the Jagat (living beings and the changeful world system), without undergoing any diminution or change of entity in the process.

The first verse of the *Bhagavata*, a verse in praise of the Supreme Being gives us a clue to the metaphysics of this scriptural
text. The verse is as follows: "From whom the origin etc. of the
universe took place; who exists in and through the universe as its
material cause and also without it when the universe is naught;
whose awareness of Himself as the whole and whose mastery over
everything are ever unaffected; who at the beginning of creation
imparted to Brahma the knowledge of the Veda which transcends
the understanding even of the great sages; whose transformation
into the universe, unlike in the case of primordial elements like
water, fire etc., never affects His own entity; in whom the threefold creation exists as a reality; in whose light of intelligence there
is no place for anything false; —to that Supreme Truth my salutations."

With all the flexibility of construing that the Sanskrit language affords, this verse can be interpreted—in fact has actually
been intrepreted — to yield meanings agreeable to all the different
schools of Vedanta. The reason for this is not difficult to see.
All schools of Vedanta teach that the end of spiritual life consists
either in Jnana (unitary knowledge with effacement of the
difference between the personal self and Universal Self), or in
Bhakti (unitary consciousness retaining the *distinction* between
personal self and the Universal Self meditated upon with loving
devotion). The *Bhagavata* concedes both these ideals, with a preference for Bhakti under a kind of doctrine that can be described
as theistic Absolutism. Its teachings may differ from schools of
classical Advaitism which relegate Iswara (God) also to the
realm of pseudo-realities like the individual self and the external
world. But the *Bhagavata* would never allow the elimination
of the God of love at any stage. It is ultimately only by God's

grace that the individual realises his unity with the Absolute, although his spiritual strivings may make him deserving of that grace. The Absolute is God, and the realisation of unity with the Absolute does not therefore eliminate God as an appearance. For it is God that reveals Himself as the Absolute to the Jiva that seeks unity with Him. In the attainment of that unity it is not the 'I' that engulfs God, but God that engulfs the limited 'I', just as it is not the Ganges that merges in the wave but the wave that merges in the Ganges. It is the 'I' or the ego that is sublated, and the sublation leaves 'Him' as the one without a second. When unitary consciousness is viewed in this way, it does not conflict with Bhakti, nor does it reduce Bhakti to a lesser value. But the *Bhagavata* has got its own preference, and that is in favour of devotion, which helps the devotee keep up his distinction from the Lord, so that he may be 'tasting the sugar and not become the sugar.' In support of it, the *Bhagavata* mentions the cases of several great spiritual men like Suka, Narada, the Kumaras, the Nava Yogis, Prithu, Prahlada and others who preferred doing loving service to the Lord, to becoming one with Him. And the *Bhagavata*, in extolling Bhakti, puts in the mouth of Sri Krishna Himself, that He bestows Mukti (liberation or oneness with Him) freely, but seldom Bhakti. Bhakti is thus the Super-Value, and metaphysical insight (Jnana) and liberation (Mukti) form only its concomitants. It will be seen from this that the *Bhagavata* has no objection to any system of metaphysics which will give scope for the fullest expression of Bhakti, without denying the prospect of being one with the Lord to those who are for such a consummation. Probably it is appropriate to call it a philosophy of Theistic Absolutism.

IX

Bhakti in the Bhagavata: its Definition

The concern with the sentiment of devotion to the Supreme Being is as old as the Vedas themselves in the Indian tradition. The *Rig Veda Samhita* is full of it, although it is true that at a later time even the purely devotional hymns were adapted for ritualistic use and propitiatory rites. In the *Upanishads* the

predominant direction of the quest is to find out the unity of
existence, to know that by knowing which everything is known
and man is helped to transcend all fear. But the path of devotion is very clearly observable even in the oldest Upanishads
like the *Brihadaranyaka* and the *Chandogya.* The doctrine of
grace finds expression in the *Katha* and the *Kausitaki Upanishads,*
while the *Svetasvatara* teaches a full-fledged devotional attitude
and discipline, along with the conception of a Deity who can be
communed with and prayed to and who responds to such prayers
of the votary. The *Svetasvatara* goes to the extent of telling :
" It is only in an aspirant having supreme devotion to God and
also to the Guru that the truths of the *Upanishads* will fructify
as realisation." What the Puranas in general, and the *Bhagavata*
in particular, do is to supplement this Vedic development with
highly personalistic conceptions of the Deity suited for purely
devotional purposes without losing link with the Upanishads, and
to elaborate the devotional Sadhanas into a highly specialised
system.

The word Bhakti is derived from the root ' Bhaj ' which has
several meanings, among which one,—'to serve', 'to honour', 'to
love', 'to adore',—has given the expression its current meaning of
'devotion to God'. But the earliest use of the word as found in
Yaska's *Nirukta* is in the sense of 'ornamental' (Bahu-Bhakti-
vādini) and of 'relationship' (agni-bhaktini). But by long usage in
devotional literature, it is now commonly understood as love of
God and the way of life conducive to it. Narada and Sandilya,
the most authoritative theoreticians on Bhakti, have described it
as follows : According to Narada it is the whole-hearted and
supreme love of God. Obtaining it, a man feels he has gained the
highest attainment in life ; he rises above fear of death ; and he
finds himself in unalloyed bliss always. He becomes indifferent
to everything except God, and he depends on nothing except Him.
Bhakti is characterised by absorption in His worship and in
remembering His excellences. Its most conspicuous sign is
complete self-dedication to Him and the feeling of intense anguish
whenever the mind slips away from Him. Sandilya describes it
as 'Parānuraktirīsvare'—which means 'the highest form of

ensuing and *ever continuing* attachment to God. The particle 'anu' can be interpreted as 'following' or 'ensuing' some previous attainment or condition. This condition consists in a general understanding of God's greatness and attributes, especially his lovability or dependability, without which no love and attachment can arise. Narada is probably more pronounced in this respect. He thinks that Mahatmyabodha (consciousness of God's unique greatness and His attributes) is always present in devotion, as without it, devotion will be indistinguishable from human love. The other meaning of 'Anu' is 'unabating or unslackening' attachment to God. It is probably better to understand the definition as having both these implications instead of one only, because, some general understanding about an object must necessarily precede the birth of love and attachment for it and their continuance. It is also true that worldly attachment may be eroded, slackened or even totally obscured by adverse circumstances, but not genuine and deep-rooted love of God. It retains its intensity and freshness at all times, even when adversity visits a man in spite of his devotion to God.

The *Bhagavata*, however, gives its own definition of Bhakti as follows : "When all the energies of the mind, including those of the organs of knowledge and of action, become concentrated as a unified mental mode directed to the Supreme Being, spontaneous like an instinct and devoid of any extraneous motives, the resulting state of mind is called Bhakti. It is superior even to Mukti. Like fire it burns up the soul's sheath of Ignorance" (Bha. 3.25.32-33).

There are several other descriptions of Bhakti in the *Bhagavata* more or less on the lines of Narada and Sandilya, but it looks that in describing Bhakti as 'absorption of all the energies of one's intellect, mind and senses in the Bhagavan' the *Bhagavata* seeks to enlarge the frontiers of Bhakti beyond what the theoreticians like Narada and Sandilya have in view. While love and attachment can arise only towards a being apprehended as a person, attractive and favourably disposed, absorption through concentration can arise even in respect of an impersonal

4

entity and also through the stirring of fundamental instincts like curiosity, fear and hatred. Three consequences follow from this:

X

Types of Bhakti: Vidvesha–Bhakti

1. The first is the *Bhagavata* idea of Vidvesha-Bhakti or communion through confrontation. Such a conception is not found in the Sutras of early Bhakti theoreticians, nor is it looked upon with favour even by later writers on Bhakti like Madhusudana and Rupa Goswami. Unlike the *Bhagavata*, they consider that only absorption resulting from a sense of Anukulya (favourableness) in the object of love, can be the genesis of devotion. It is not possible to have 'favourableness' in respect of a dreaded enemy with whom one is in confrontation. Besides, whatever the *Bhagavata* may say, it has no application in the life of man ordinarily. In the *Bhagavata* narrative this attitude of confrontation is represented in the case of some Titanic souls like Hiranyakasipu, Ravana, etc. and that under unusual circumstances. They were once servants of God, but due to their haughtiness they were cursed by some great sages to lose their heavenly status and become embodied in worlds of sin and strife. They were, however, to regain their status after spending three successive lives in hatred of, and in confrontation with, God. In each of these births they were to be killed in battle by the Lord incarnate, and that would purify them and restore them to their original condition. As the result of the sages' curse, intensely instinctive antagonism to God and an obsessive dread of Him possessed their soul. Impelled by this antagonism they thought of Him with all the intensity of their mind, as only an inveterate enemy can do with regard to his dreaded antagonist. According to the *Bhagavata* such a state of mind can have a transforming effect on the mind. "The worm imprisoned in a cavity and guarded by the beetle," says the *Bhagavata*, "lives in constant dread of it, and through such identification through fear, gets transformed into the form of the beetle. Even by constantly thinking of Krishna as their dreaded enemy, they became washed of all their sins and attained to Him" (Bh. 7. 1.

23-28). In fact it is even stated that the purification which they could have got only in the course of seven embodiments if they followed the path of love, they obtained through three births of confrontation. It is also to be noted that the Lord approached these 'devotees in confrontation' in a manner appropriate to their attitude. Challenged in battle, He 'blessed' these devotees by responding to their attacks with mighty weapons, and destroyed them and their following. Slaughter at His hands was the blessing they got for their peculiar brand of devotion. It effected their purification and raised them to their original condition.

The logic behind this is evident. Mortal dread and antagonism can produce as much absorption of the mind in an object, as love and attachment can. Now if the object is God, concentration on Him, even though it is motivated by antagonism, must purify the soul, just as a potent medicine consumed, must necessarily effect a cure, whatever be the attitude of the patient towards it.

It is obvious that this has no application in the life of man ordinarily. It is doubtful if even the fear of God, which some cults inculcate, can come under this confrontation doctrine. There are some devotional cults which depict God as a mighty Power who inflicts devastating punishments through storms, earth-quakes and floods on men who break covenants made with Him, or as a dreaded terror-inspiring Energy which holds the votaries' attention by the display of awful forms and shudder-generating might. Surely if God as a creator-preserver is sweet, loving and lovable, His might as the destroyer must manifest in awe-inspiring forms. In modern times Professor Otto has worked out the theory that the origin of religion is in the sense of 'awe' generated by the experience of the mysterious and the tremendous. A cult based purely on such an experience is considered primitive, and the passage from fear of God to love of Him is supposed to be the course of evolution in religion. Yet in most cults of the world the sense of awe continues to be an abiding factor in the devotional sentiment. Though the *Bhagavata* theory of confrontation cannot be equated with this—for confrontation in the real sense is possi-

ble only for Titanic souls   yet an element of it enters into all
forms of religious sentiment based on awe.

In non-Hindu religious thought we find a sense of confrontation in the attitude of Satan towards God in Christianity, but its
spiritual implication is entirely different from that of the *Bhagavata.*

It should be noted that spiritual indifference, shallow atheism,
and superficial agnosticism—the pitiable attitudes of many worldlings and the so-called intellectuals in spiritual matters—has nothing to do with the Vidvesha-Bhakti concept of the *Bhagavata.*
For indifference and superficiality have nothing in common with
concentration and absorption in God, which are presupposed in
the conception of Vidvesha-Bhakti. Further elaboration of this will
be found in the Notes on verses 6. 12 & 13 of the *Bhakti Ratnavali.*

Jnana-Bhakti of the Bhagavatottama

2.   Another implication of the *Bhagavata* definition of Bhakti
is that Jnana or Knowledge has got a much more important place
in it than in the conceptions of Narada and Sandilya. Curiosity,
the genesis of the quest for knowledge, is as much an urge of the
soul as any other passion, though it is cold and calculating in its
operation. The Gita therefore recognises a Jijnasu, an enquirer,
also in its classification of Bhaktas (devotees). If the enquiry
takes a purely inward turn as an investigation of the nature of the
'I-sense' and its source, it becomes Jnana Yoga in the strict sense
of the term. It becomes a type of psychology. But if the enquiry
takes an outward form also and ends in the acceptance of a Supreme Being, Sat-Chid-ananda, who is the originator and master
of all creation and the prototype of all individual souls, the enrap
tured contemplation of whose majesty and attributes as formless
non-particularised Being leads uitimately to a total surrender and
absorption in Him—then that discipline may be called one of intellectual love, to use an apt expression of Spinoza, the great
Western philosopher, or as Jnana-Bhakti (devotion dominated by
knowledge) ending in Sayujya or oneness with the Divine. The
contrast between these two may be stated thus :   In pure Jnana

discipline the mind and the ego sink in the 'I'; whereas in the Jnana-Bhakti discipline they sink in the 'He'. The final meaning of both may be the same, but in their setting, the former is idealistic and solipsistic, whereas the latter is realistic and object-centred.

Later theoreticians on Bhakti have described this form of devotion as Santa-Bhakti or devotion of the peaceful mood—peaceful because it is without any personal element. The *Bhagavata* abounds in the lives of several sages like Rishabha, the Kumaras, Muchukunda, Bharata, Prithu, Narada, Suka and others who attained to union with God through combination of Knowledge and Bhakti. Knowledge of divine majesty produces the sense of adoration, which leads to complete self-surrender and unity with Him. This in turn leads to a fuller understanding of the extent and depth of Divine Life (Tattvajnana) – to an acceptance of God as both Impersonal and Personal, as both Nirguna and Saguna. In Sri Ramakrishna's words, such deeper understanding is called Vijnana, and a Jiva with Vijnana retains an enlightened ego which manifests unitary consciousness and the sense of loving relationship with the Divine at the same time. As the *Bhagavata* accepts the Supreme Being as both Saguna (with attributes) and Nirguna (without attributes), this harmonious combination of Jnana and Bhakti, knowledge of unitary consciousness and of devotional attitude, is possible in its synthetic spiritual outlook.

But the *Bhagavata* is against pure intellectualism as a means for attaining the spiritual goal. It ridicules such attempts as trying to get rice by pounding chaff, and agrees fully with the' *Svetasvatara Upanishad* that the truths regarding the Supreme Spirit will shine only in one who has supreme devotion to Iswara. It is of the firm conviction that devotion generates both knowledge of God and renunciation of self-centred values. It is aptly put that just as eating a morsel of food will simultaneously produce enjoyable taste, satisfy the hunger and increase strength, so too devotion and surrender to God generate simultaneously love and knowledge of Him together with the spirit of renunciation of worldly enjoyments. A deep apprehension of Divine

excellences thus leads to Santa Bhakti which ends in complete
surrender ; surrender generates Tattvajnana (unitary conscious¯
ness); and Tattvajnana elevates devotion to universal love. So
speaking incisively of this devotion based on Tattvajnana and
comparing it with narrow forms of devotion, the *Bhagava¹a* says:
"The Bhagavatottama (the highest type of devotee) is one who
sees the glory of the Bhagavan reflected in all beings, high and
low, and also perceives all beings as dwelling in Him. The
second-rate devotee is one who makes a distinction between God,
His devotees, common people and evil-minded ones, and maintains towards them attitudes of reverential love, friendship, pity
and avoidance respectively. And one who worships images of
God with great devotion but has no regard for His devotees and
no consideration for others, is the most inferior type of a devotee" (Bha. 11.2.45-47).

Mudha-Bhakti : its Uniqueness

3. A third, and perhaps the most unique result of the
Bhagavata definition of Bhakti as mental absorption in Iswara, is
the doctrine of Mudha Bhakti, or devotion without the aid of
knowledge. In place of being based on considerations of God's
majesty and excellences or on any idea of dispassion for the
world, this kind of love has its source and sustenance in the sense
that God is 'mine'. Madhusudana, the great Advaita philosopher
and latter-day theoretician on Bhakti, has remarked in a verse:
" 'I am His', 'He is mine', 'I am He',—devotion takes these three
forms according to the maturity of one's spiritual striving." It
looks that in the view of the *Bhagavata* 'I am His' and 'He is
mine' need not necessarily follow in this order, but can, on the
other hand, proceed independently and reach the unitary cons
ciousness represented by 'I am He'. 'I am His' represents the
Jnana-Bhakti described earlier. 'He is mine' stands for blind
devotion based on the sense that God is one's 'own'. It results in
the development of loving personal relationship with Him in any of
the familiar forms of human love, as master and servant, parent and
son, friend and friend, husband and wife, and the lover and the
beloved. The object of the devotee's attention is not attributeless

(Nirvisesha) Brahman or even attributeful and formless (Savisesha Nirvakara) Brahman, but God with a divine form or His Incarnations. The identification of that form with the Supreme Being and the cultivation of the sense that He is one's 'own' master, mother, father, friend, husband or lover is the essence of this discipline. God can have any form but the Divine Incarnation is the most suitable for this type of loving personal relationship with Him, as the Incarnate is more human and lovable in a personal sense than a Deity. And of all divine forms, Krishna is the most versatile Divine manifestation, as every form of loving relationship could be established with Him. This probably is another reason why the *Bhagavata* regards Krishna as the most perfect Incarnation.

The uniqueness of the *Bhagavata* consists in its specialisation in depicting this form of divine love through the life of Sri Krishna and His relation with various devotees. The inhabitants of Vraja knew from His extraordinary achievements that Krishna was divine, but the feeling that He is our 'child', 'our friend', 'our lover' etc. dominated over the sense of His greatness, and removed all inhibitions that the thought of majesty might have created against the intimacy of personal relationship. Theoreticians of the Bhakti doctrine, especially Narada, have discussed this question as to how this form of love can be distinguished from worldly love. It is pointed out that all worldly love is motivated by thought of selfish gains and pleasure for oneself, whereas in spiritualised forms of love the gain and the pleasure of the person concerned is found to consist in the gain and the pleasure of the object of love. Further, Narada maintains that the consciousness of Krishna's greatness as the Divine Incarnate (Mahatmya-bodha) is present in the minds of the Gopikas. This has to a large extent to be conceded from an examination of the *Bhagavata* text. In some places some of the Gopikas speak of Krishna as being "not the son of Devaki but the witness of the innermost 'conscious essence' in all beings" (10. 31. 4). Yasoda saw His cosmic form when He opened His mouth. Many examples of his superhuman powers also were witnessed by them. The consciousness of His greatness arising from memories of such experiences, came to some of the Gopikas sporadically, but it was made inoperative by the overpowering sense of nearness and tender relationship they entertained towards Him. Had it not been for this, their devotion would have been indistinguishable from Santa-bhakti. The great God of the universe appeared to them to be 'our child', 'our friend', 'our lover', and they developed towards Him feelings and behaviour corresponding to these relationships. So it has to be accepted that the stress here is on 'mineness' (Mamata) and not at all on greatness (Mahatmya), although the latter sense was also present in the background. In the light of the *Bhagavata* teaching, what transmutes this love into a Divine sentiment is not any subjective excellence in the person concerned, but the objective fact that this love is fixed on Krishna, the Divine Incarnate, the alchemist of human souls. Krishna reacts to this love in a manner appropriate to its form — as a child if He is looked upon as a chiid, as a friend if He is looked upon as a friend, as a lover if He is looked upon as a lover. As a medicine taken knowingly or unknowingly cures a disease, concentration on Krishna, whatever form it might take and however ignorantly it is practised, has got its purifying effect on the person concerned. The touch of Krishna purifies the soul and converts even the most sensuous passion into sublime selfless love and takes one to the highest spiritual goal. So the *Bhagavata* lays down the dictum : "By feeling alone the Gopis and even unintelligent creatures like cows, deer, elephant, serpent, etc., attained to spiritual consummation in Me. They never learnt the Vedas, they never served any teacher, they practised no austerity; but by association with holiness they attained to Me" (Bha, 11. 12.7 & 8)

"Lust, anger, fear, affection, friendship, sense of oneness — whichever sentiment man entertains towards Hari, he will attain to Him through that" (10.29.15). "The Gopis through lust, Kamsa through fear, Sisupala through enmity, the Vrishnis through clannishness, the Pandavas through affection and sages through devotion attained to Him" (7.1.30). Again the *Bhagavata*, contradicting Narada's dictum, as it were, puts it in the mouth of Krishna Himself "Hundreds of women attained to Me, the Supreme Brahman, though not knowing my real nature but loving me as a paramour in whom they took delight" (11.12.13). The

descriptions of these relationships in the *Bhagavata*, though
centring upon Krishna, will therefore resemble very much the
depiction of human love, the most noteworthy of these being the
highly erotic poetry employed in the description of the relation
between Krishna and the Gopikas of Vrindavan as between a
paramour and his beloved.

XI
Gopi-Krishna Episode: its Interpretations

Critics have not been wanting who have cavilled at the moral
stature of Krishna for His questionable relationship with the
Gopikas and the propriety of a devotional text like the *Bhagavata*
including in itself such highly erotic episodes and their graphic
descriptions. So various attempts have been made to get over
these difficulties by several theories, some of the most important
of which are as follows: 1) The whole episode of Krishna and the
Gopikas is symbolical and not factual. The Gopikas stand for the
soul (Jivatman) and Krishna for the Supreme Soul (Paramatman),
and the intense aspiration of the former for the latter is depicted
through sex love. The Jiva in this philosophy is taken as the
Prakriti of the Lord and therefore depicted as female. In this
theory historicity of the events described is denied and only a
symbolic meaning is attached to them. 2) The *Bhagavata* states
that Krishna was only a boy of ten or eleven at that time. So the
highly erotic descriptions of the relationship between him and the
Gopikas, who are depicted as ladies of mature years, are only poetic
exaggerations of some innocent pastoral sports of Krishna with
boys and girls of the cowherd community among whom he spent
his boyhood days. The eroticism superimposed on these should
be taken only as an aberration of decadent sectaries. Here
historicity is accepted in a modified form and the existence of any
ethical problem is denied. 3) According to the third theory,
while historicity is accepted, it is maintained that the Gopikas
were devoid of bodily consciousness and they met Krishna at a
spiritual level. Therefore there is nothing carnal about it, as the
descriptions are of purely mystical significance. In support of this,
is pointed out the *Bhagavata* verse 10.33.38, which states that

while the Gopikas were away engaged in Rasa Lila, their people
found them at home also. This mystic element is also hinted at
in the very beginning of the description of Rasa Lila in the statement that Krishna took part in it assuming his Yoga Maya
or Mystic Power (Bha. 10.29-1).

Bhagavata Interpreation of the Love of the Gopikas

Now what does the *Bhagavata* itself say on the point? While
it is true that the *Bhagavata* text holds forth hints justifying all
the three explanations given above, the overwhelming evidence
of language and description of the text declares unequivocally
that the Gopika episode was a physical fact and that all aspects
of love were involved in the relationship. Raja Parikshit, to
whom the *Bhagavata* was narrated, takes it in that sense and
questions Sri Suka whether there was any ethical justification at
all for it. Suka's famous reply, as given in the *Bhagavata*, is as
follows: "Divine personages are found to override the rules of
Dharma (ethics) and do actions of a shocking nature. But just
as no impurity affects fire which consumes everything, nothing
causes blemish to such persons of immense potency. But lesser
men should not imitate them in these respects even in mind.
If they do so foolishly, they will perish, as one will do if one
drinks poison following the example of Rudra. The instructions
of godly persons are valid; so are *some* of their actions too.
A wise man will follow only such of their actions as are consistent
with their words. It is admitted that for enlightened men without ego sense, there is no selfish gain to be attained by their
actions and no evil to be warded off by abstinence from them.
What good or evil can then affect the supreme Lord Krishna who
is the Master of all beings—gods, men, animals and the rest? By
devotion to His holy feet the great sages derive that Yogic power
by which they become free from the bondage of all actions. How
can there be any bondage or sin for the Universal Being who has
assumed a body out of His own will, and by devotion to whom
even these great sages derive their spiritual excellence? He who
permeates all beings, including the Gopikas and their husbands,
and directs the minds and sense of every one – even He out of

sportive intention has assumed a body as Krishna. For bestowing His blessings on all beings he has assumed a body, and He sports with that body in ways that will interest and attract men to Him. By Krishna's mystic power the inhabitants of Vraja found their women in their homes all the time, and had no occasion to be displeased with Krishna" (Bha. 10.33. 30-40).

From this it is clear that just as Krishna faced Kamsa and Sisupala (examples of communion through confrontation) with weapons in hand and raised them to the height of spiritual glory by delivering deadly blows on them, He received the Gopikas who came to Him with passionate love stimulated by His exquisite physical charm and the ravishing strains of His flute (Venugana), as an earthly lover receives his beloved, although mentally He was unperturbed and ever-poised in His spiritual Essence. But what starts as a physical passion in the Gopikas gets transformed into a pure spiritual experience in the course of their association with Krishna. By the touch of Krishna, who in the words of the Gita is 'Brahman Supreme, the most exalted state of Existence and the seat of all purity and holiness', the Kamukis (lustful females) and the Abhisarikas (the passionate women going in search of the lover) became converted into Premikas (persons endowed with rapturous loving devotion), transcending body consciousness like the Paramahamsas. If we remember this aspect of the Gopi-Krishna episode, we shall find that Krishna needs no defence and we need not be apologetic about Him by taking refuge in allegorical interpretations. The allegory and symbolism are there, and are very important too, but we should not use them to overlook or cover up the *Bhagavata* doctrine that when the mind is firmly fixed on Him, whatever might be the motivating feeling or circumstance, He responds to the Jiva in a manner appropriate to the Jiva's attitude and transforms him by His touch. As the verse 10. 87.23 of the *Bhagavata* states. " The Yogis concentrating their mind on Him as the indwelling self, the philosophers who try to see Him as prevading everything, the Asuras who live in mortal dread of, and in confrontation with, Him, and the passionate women who seek physical union with Him in violation of all social and ethical sanctions—

they are all alike to Him." The fact that the minds of all these are directed to Him with intensity is sufficient reason for their transformation when they receive His response in the manner appropriate to their respective attitudes. In a study of Krishna's life we should not forget that the *Bhagavata* looks upon Him not as an ordinary man but as Bhagavan Svayam, the Supreme Being Himself manifest as man, to reveal how He becomes the many but continues to be the One uncorrupted and Perfect Being inspite of His transformation into the many through His Sakti. To attribute corruption to Krishna for any of His actions is therefore as correct or as absurd as attributing corruption to God for manifesting this enigmatic world. All His actions were without any self-centred purpose, and were only the expression of the Lord's redeeming love for the Jivas. Being the One existence that has become the many, He is supra-moral and human standards have no relevance in respect of him.

Why the Medium of Erotic Poetry is used

Regarding the other allied question about the propriety of these erotic descriptions in a devotional scripture, the *Bhagavata* has got its own answer. The Lord incarnated as Krishna not merely for scholars, philosophers, ascetics, puritans and moralists, but for the good of all who could develop faith in Him, irrespective of their spiritual, cultural and moral attainments. A philosopher will be interested only in abstract thought and not in heroic exploits and adventurous stories ; on the other hand a boy or a person without education will only be bored by philosophy, but thrilled by a narration of the Lord's majesties and his sublime attributes. A diplomat or a politician will not, however, be moved by these ; he will probably be interested in accounts of state-craft and human relationship. An artiste or a connoisseur of beauty will have a dread of philosophy and ethics but will be attracted by highly artistic depictions of romantic love and beauty in all its phases. The life and teachings of Krishna, the Purnavatara, is meant to attract men of all these types. So in a life abounding in dealings with persons of varied temperements—philosophers, devotees, ascetics, common folk, cowherds, love-lorn women, cruel monsters, oppressive kings, righteous rulers, diplomats, etc.—Krishna has left for mankind a rich and varied record of events which have been taken up and glorified by the Puranas for edifying and attracting even the so-called sense-bound humanity to the devotional cult founded by Him. In later times a great devotee poet of India, Jaya Deva, has, probably for this very reason, taken up the love relationship of Krishna with the Gopikas as the theme for his famous. *Gita-Govinda*, a poetical work of rare literary and musical excellence, noted alike for its devotional significance as for its high eroticism, observing all the rules of Sanskrit poetics. No one can gainsay the fact that this work has exercised a great influence on the devotional and artistic life of India and drawn to Krishna large numbers of people who would not have otherwise been attracted to Him at all. So in justification of its description of these amorous accounts, the *Bhagavata* itself says: "Having assumed a human body for the blessing of mankind, He adopts such sportive activities as will interest and attract men of various types to Him...He who, with faith in Krishna in his heart, hears, reads and narrates these amorous dalliances of His with the Gopis, that intelligent man will obtain deep devotion to the Lord, and will easily *overcome* lust, the real 'heart-disease' of mankind" (Bha. 10. 33. 37 & 40 .

The idea is that the mind of an aspirant with faith in Krishna will gradually be filled with the symbolic and spiritual significance of these descriptions, that it is the passion of the purified soul of man for God that is represented in the Gopika's longing for Krishha, and that if we imitate that passion within ourselves, we shall attain to the Divine. To several of his puritanical disciples who expressed disapproval of the Gopikas' love for Krishna on moral grounds, Sri Ramakrishna, who never questioned the factuality of the Gopi-Krishna episode, nevertheless replied that if they did not like the Gopikas, they might forget them, but they must consider themselves blessed if they could manifest towards God a hundredth of that intensity of feeling that the Gopikas had towards Krishna, the Lord of all that exists. The contention of the *Bhagavata*, however, is that the Gopikas have dug this unique channel of devotion to God by their example, and that none can reach Him in that form of intimacy and intensity unless they sail their boat along the channel they have dug.

A careful reader of the *Bhagavata* will note that the text is careful to trace the growth of the love of the Gopikas for Krishna from a passionate personal love to love of Him as the Universal Being. Unlike devotees in general, they did not, it is true, pass through the earlier phases of devotional discipline. Being fortunate enough to be the contemporaries of Sri Krishna, the Lord Incarnate, their purification was effected by direct contact with Him. Sexual attachment is ordinarily a cause of spiritual downfall, but in the Gopikas, such attachment, being directed to Sri Krishna, the Lord incarnate, had the opposite effect of purifying and uplifting them. Reciprocating their love, Krishna blessed them with His divine company, but they were soon separated from Him when he left Gokula for Mathura, from where He sent them the message, "Separation only strengthens love. Soon will you attain to the joy of Brahman which will make you experience separation and union as equally bisssful" (*Narayaneeyam*). When they met him again at Samanta Panchaka some years after, they were found to have developed that depth of love through the tormenting yet delightful pangs of separation. On that occasion Krishna gave them full enlightenment that enabled them to realize His presence in everything and everywhere. He conveyed to them the following as His last message : "Devotion to Me is the only means for attaining to Bliss undecaying. It is fortunate that you have developed attachment to Me, which is the means for attaining to Me. Just as all material objects have their beginning and their end in the five elements, and are also covered and infilled by these elements, in the same way understand Me to be the basis of, and the substance pervading all the worlds, living and non-living. Living beings only experience objects, but the latter do not rest in them but in the elements constituting them. It is, however, in and through Me, the supreme and imperishable Being, that both these—the experiencing Jivas and the experienced objects constituted of elements—have their entity and subsistence" (Bha. 10. 82. 45-47).

GENERAL INTRODUCTION 63

It will also be seen from this that this kind of Bhakti is not that Mudha, ignorant of Divine excellence; it brings full enlightenment too. Enlightenment only leads to the enrichment and not the elimination of devotion.

XII
Bhakti as the fifth Purushartha

Devotion of this type also can end in the sense of unity, in the understanding 'I am He'. In the description of the Gopi-Krishna episode, it is stated that at a stage of their love for Him, they felt themselves to be He. Regarding the state of their mind, it is further stated by Krishna Himself: "By the strength of their attachment to Me, they became oblivious of their individuality and the whole objective world, just as the mind of a contemplative in Samadhi and a river merged in the ocean overcome all distinction created by name and form" (Bha. 11-12-12). But this union contemplated has necessarily to be distinguished from Sayujya, which is the goal of Bhakti based on Jnana. In Sayujya the individuality merges in the Bhagavan, who is also the Absolute of philosophy, and the Jiva ceases to be an individual by becoming one with the Absolute, as a river ceases to be a river and becomes one with the sea when it has joined the sea. This is Mukti or release. But in devotion based on personal relationship of the type represented by the inhabitants of Vraja and of those who follow their path, the goal of spiritual striving does not consist in Mukti of the above type. In the ripeness of their devotion, devotees get the knowledge of the unity of all existence in Him, but unity in consciousness does not, for the devotee, entail an ontological cessation through dissolution in Him. The sense of personal relationship and the urge for serving the Lord result in the retention of individuality, and the devotee becomes an eternal servant of the Lord. So long as he has his human body, he lives as a Bhagavatottama, one who sees the Lord in all beings and all beings as resting in the Lord, and he serves the Lord in all and in every possible way. After he gives up the human body, as also the subtle mental sheaths of Prakriti which have been vehicles of all his transmigrations, he assumes a non-

material form of Suddha sattva (non-material pure stuff), serves
the Lord in regions of Light and Blessedness called Vaikuntha, and
also comes as a participant in the Lord's redemptive work as
the Incarnate. Through the concept of such Bhagavatottamas and
their preference for the bliss of Divine service to liberation (Mukti)
and to absorption in the Godhead, it is said that the *Bhagavata* has
raised Bhakti to the position of the fifth Purushartha (ultimate
value) over the usually recognized four Purusharthas—Dharma
(virtue), Artha (power), Kama (pleasure), and Moksha
(liberation).

Contrast between Bhakti and Priti

Leaving aside communion through confrontation, it will
thus be seen that Bhakti in the *Bhagavata* takes these two forms—
one, as Santa-Bhakti based on the feeling ' I am His ', and consequently dominated by knowledge and consciousness of Divine
majesty and ending in absorption in Him, and the other, as
Prema Bhakti based on the sense ' He is mine ', manifesting itself
through idealised channels of personal affection as a passion for
communion and service of the Divine as servant, child, friend,
husband or lover. To distinguish these two types of devotion in
the *Bh.gavata*, Dr. Bhattacharya has suggested in his learned work
on this text that the word Bhakti (adoration) leading to merger
in the Divine may be taken to denote the devotion based on
knowledge, and that the personality-based devotion may be
distinguished from it as Priti (self-abnegating love and joyful
service of the Divine Person) — a term that has become specially
significant by its use in the Chaitanya School of Vaishnavism.
Among the later theoreticians on Bhakti, the celebrated Advaita
thinker, Madhusudana Saraswati has championed Santa-Bhava
based upon knowledge of God and His attributes as the purest
form of Bhakti. By an apprehension of the infinite excellences of
the Lord, the infinite bliss that is His, manifests as supreme joy
in the heart of the aspirant. In the heart that is molten, as it
were, by this joy, the impress of the Lord, like that of a seal on
wax, always remains as pure attachment to Him without the bias
of any personal limitation. Thus, according to Madhusudana,
Santa-Bhakti alone is the purest and perfect form of devotion.

The more this Rati (attraction and attachment for God) takes personal forms as that of servant and master, son and father, husband and wife etc., the more it becomes limited in nature and also mixed with unspiritual elements In spite of this outlook, he is not, however, behind any devotional thinker in his acknowledgement of the uniqueness of the Gopikas.

The purely personal type of devotion based on Priti (joy of personal love and service) is upheld by the Chaitanya School of Vaishnavism, of which Jiva Goswami is the most noted exponent. He maintains that the Supreme Being has two aspects—one as the all-pervading Impersonal Brahman, and the other as the Bhagavan possessing countless blessed attributes, with whom personal relationship on the basis that 'He is mine' (Mamata) can be maintained. The former of these aspects is secondary and peripheral in the Supreme Being while the latter represents His fundamental and basic nature. Those who entertain the knowledge-dominated Santa-Bhava can get only the peripheral understanding of Him. For, in their attitude, the sense of 'mineness' (Mamata' cannot be entertained with regard to Him, and without that sense and the intimacy resulting from it, the depths of His being as Rasa, or pure Bliss, cannot be adequately apprehended. In place of this attainment, these votaries become one with His Impersonal aspect. The perfect expression of Priti is possible only where 'mineness' comes into play, and therefore what the advocates of Santa Bhakti consider as a defect, becomes the distinguishing excellence by means of which the depths of the Bhagavan as Bliss is explored. A follower of this ideal of Priti rejects Sayujya (merger in the Lord) as a stumbling block in spiritual evolution, and considers intimate personal love and eternal service of the Bhagavan as the highest goal (Purushartha) of an aspirant.

This view no doubt, gets ample support in many passages of the *Bhagavata*. For example, it is put in the mouth of Sri Krishna Himself in the following *Bhagavata* passage: "The holy men who have deep-rooted love for Me and see Me in everything, win Me over as a faithful wife does a dutiful husband. Having attained to life's fulfilment by My service, they do not care for the four forms of Mukti (liberation) to which they are eligible by virtue of their service of Me. How little would they care for the perishable attainments of this world !" (9.4.36-37).

In pursuance of such teachings found in the *Bhagavata*, the followers of the Chaitanya school of Vaishnavism maintain that one who aspires to be a true Vaishnava should eschew all the four usually accepted Purusharthas of Dharma, Artha, Kama and Moksha, and have Bhakti of the nature of Priti, the fifth Purushartha according to them, as their goal. Bhakti in this sense is eternal service of the Lord with unflagging love for Him as ' one's own '.

Priti the Result of Poshana or Pushti (the Divine Choice)

This unique form of devotion denoted by the expression Priti cannot be had by a Jiva in its natural state. By practice he can have Santa Bhakti, tinged with the relationship of Dasya (servitude). It is only in one whom God chooses that the sentiments based on Priti can arise. Krishna, says the Chaitanya school of Vaishnavism, is Sat-chit-ananda, and He has got three Saktis or Potencies of manifestation. These are called Swarupa Sakti, Jiva or Tatastha Sakti and Maya Sakti. The last of them is His power of manifesting as insentient matter, and the second, as limited centres of sentiency or Jivas. The first, namely, Swarupa Sakti, is His innate and most essential nature. Swarupa Sakti is analysed into Sandhini, Samvit, and Hladini. By Sandhini, corresponding to Sat (existence), He sustains His own existence as also of all His manifestations. By Samvit, corresponding to Chit (consciousness), He makes Himself self-conscious and makes others also conscious. And by Hladini, corresponding to Ananda (Bliss), He enjoys His own Bliss and makes others enjoy it. He is described as Rasa (another Upanishadic term for Bliss) as also Rasika or enjoyer of His own Rasa. As the Rasika, He not only enjoys His own innate Bliss, but also that Bliss as reflected from the Jivas. On the Jiva whom He chooses, His Hladini Sakti, the potency of His Bliss-nature, is cast, and the same as reflected from the Jiva is devotion of the highest order (Priti). As a result of this bestowal of grace, the Jiva is, as it were, nourished and enriched with motiveless devotion, which is thus an expression of the Lord's Hladini Sakti and not of any innate endowment of the Jiva. Expressing itself as motiveless love and service of the Lord, this reflected Hladini evokes a unique type of Bliss in the Lord Himself as also in the devotee when the latter expresses himself in loving service, the sole object of which is the pleasure of the Lord and not of himself.

This is a further development of the *Bhagavata* conception of Priti at the hands of the theoreticians of the Chaitanya school of Vaishnavism. Though the *Bhagavata* definitely speaks of Bhakti as the highest gift of God, bestowed on aspirants even more rarely than Mukti itself (Bh. 5.6.18), it will not be correct to say that the concept of Hladini Sakti and its part in the genesis of Bhakti are to be found in it with any clarity. They are the doctrinal elaborations by the Chaitanya school of Vaishnavism. But without some such elaboration, it is impossible to understand how the Jiva can entertain the idea of 'mineness' with regard to the Supreme Being and how the *Bhagavata* doctrine that Bhakti is superior to Mukti can be sustained. With the power of understanding that the Jiva is endowed with, purified and augmented by devotional disciplines, he can develop the attitude of self-surrender and feel 'I am Thine', and be lost in the sense of Divine majesty and excellences. This is Santa Bhava tinged with a sense of servitude (Dasya), and the goal of it is Sayujya or merging in the Divine. But Priti Bhakti, based on the sense of 'mineness' towards God, manifests only when graced by His Hladini Sakti.

For, to experience such closeness to the Bhagavan, who creates, sustains and dissolves the universe, who is omniscient and endowed with countless majesties, as to feel that He is one's own child or friend or sweetheart, and experience a sense of 'mineness' with regard to Him—does not seem to be natural to a limited being like the Jiva. A totally new consciousness of closeness to the Divine, consistent with the awareness of His unique majesty, has to be born in the human spirit. This is accomplished only by the bestowal of grace. This is called Poshana, enrichment by the divine nutrient, which consists in Hladini, the Divine Sakti of Bliss, reflecting in the Jiva and rendering it capable of grasping the Divine as one's 'own' without any inhibition from the awarenss of His majesty. The Lord permits the devotee to be greater and Himself looks smaller, subjecting Himself to the Devotee's attitude. So the Lord says, "I am subordinate to my devotee, and am therefore in a sense without freedom. Being extremely fond of devotees of exalted mind, my heart is under their control" (Bh.9-4-63). There are innumerable events in the life of Sri Krishna as depicted in the *Bhagavata* to illustrate this. Such Jivas as receive this grace, become Nitya-Siddhas, ever retaining their individuality and engaged in the bliss of Divine service. This is the highest goal that the doctrine of Bhakti holds forth. Hence Priti-Bhakti becomes the fifth Purushartha.

Significance of Parakiya-bhava

While all forms of love where there is the sense of 'mineness' with regard to God like that of a servant to a master, of a child to a parent, of a parent to a child and of a friend to a friend are considered as forms of Priti, the most unique expression of devotion of this type consists in Kanta-bhava (wifely relationship), and especially in Parakiya-bhava (relationship of illicit love) as manifested in the wives of Sri Krishna at Dwaraka and in the Gopikas in Vrindavan respectively. Of these, the second is considered the acme of Priti, because it is in it that, like a girl who goes away with her paramour staking everything, her past and her future, in full trust of, and absorption in, her object of love, the devotee abandons himself unreservedly to God in utmost confidence and without any calculation or expectation of return. It is considered superior even to wifely attitude, because a wife's dedication does not involve that total revolution, abandonment and non-expectation characterising the love for a paramour. It is for this reason that the *Bhagavata* places the Gopikas of Vrindavan above the wedded wives of Sri Krishna in the scale of devotees endowed with Priti.

Stages in the Development of Priti

Savants of the Chaitanya School of Vaishnavism have analysed the development of this unique form of Priti, which is called Madhura-bhava (relationship of sweetness), into the following eight progressive stages: (1) Prema: This is characterised by attachment that never wanes under any condition. (2) Sneha: It is the stage when the heart melts in love. (3) Mana: It is the augmentation of love through assumed or real obstructions. (4) Pranaya: It is unreserved confidence, friendship and comradeship (5) Raga: It is the state in which the pangs of separation augment love and happiness. (6) Anuraga: It is characterised by experience of unceasing novelty in love. (7 & 8) Bhava and Maha Bhava: These are states of absorption in Krishna-consciousness characterised by some twenty-four physical and mental modes of expression. The latter is manifest only in Divine Incarnations, and not in ordinary Jivas struggling for the attainment of a little of God-love.

Vrindavana as a Transcendental Fact

It is, however, to be noted that according to these new theological innovations introduced by the Chaitanya School of Vaishnavism, the Vrindavana episode of the Gopikas' love for Krishna is not a mere historical fact, but the expression, in history, of a transcendental fact, and as such the unethical implication of illicit love cannot be imputed to it. The idea is that Sri Krishna is the Absolute Person, the Eternal Truth, in the transcendental realm of Goloka, and all manifested beings are expressions of His Sakti (Potency). He is not a mere phenomenal expression of the Absolute of the Kevaladvaitins but is Himself the Absolute (Advaya-Tattva), and what the Advaitins call Impersonal Brahman is only the peripheral brilliance of His being. The Gopikas are eternally present with Him in Goloka as His Parikaras and Parshadas (associates and attendants). They are the embodiments of His essential potency (Hladini Sakti), and are as such free from all touch of gross matter and have no physical body and the physical passions associated with it. Their forms are immaterial (Suddha-sattva). As His Saktis, they are the eternal properties of Krishna and are ever engaged in his service, which is their only delight and the sole meaning of their existence. Though they are described as many, they are all the expressions or emanations of the principal Gopika by name Radha, who is Herself the Hladini Sakti conceived as the serving Counter-whole of Krishna. It is this one Sakti that manifests as the countless Gopikas. To delight Krishna without any self-centred consideration is their sole function, and this service of Krishna takes the form of the eternal dance called Rāsa. This transcendental and eternal Divine sport is what is described in the 10th Canto of the *Bhagavata* dealing with the Gokula and Vrindavana episodes of Krishna's life. It is to be taken neither as only historical nor as merely symbolical. It is the transcedental Truth, revealed in history no doubt, but not deriving its truth or validity from its historicity. The Transcendental is the sanction of history, and not history the sanction of the former. Nor is the Gopi-Krishna episode in any way to be interpreted as the highest expression or expansion of human love, in spite of the language used in its description for want of a better medium. For the Transcendental is not moulded on the worldly forms, but the worldly forms are distortions of the Transcendental. Krishna's dalliance with the Gopikas, the emanation of His Hladini Sakti, has no element of sex-love in it. It is the expression of the self-delight of the Pure Spirit in His own blissful Self, and it is eternally going on as Rasa Dance in Goloka. When the Lord manifested in Vrindavana as the Purnavatara, (perfect Incarnation), He revealed this eternal dance along with all His Parikaras (the eternal associates) involved in it. The soul, being a Sakti of the Lord and therefore considered as feminine, can derive spiritual inspiration through identification with the whole-hearted longing of the Gopikas for Krishna, but this in itself does not convert the transcendental Gopi-Krishna relation into a symbol, nor invest it with any taint of human sexuality, nor subject it to the ethical ideas of human sex relationship. Thus it is fundamentally transcendental and spiritual; historicity is considered only to be a subordinate aspect, and sexual symbolism and ethical implications are denied.

But while such a theory of transcendental identity for the Gopikas may remove some moral objections, this is done at the expense of the *Bhagavata* doctrine that by the mere association with Krishna,

even depraved people are raised to the highest level of purity
and holiness. The greatness of Krishna, the *raison d'etre* of calling
Him the Purnavatara, is the full manifestation of the redeeming
power in Him. Besides, this idea of a transcendental identity
for the Gopikas would also make the doctrine of divine Grace or
Choice (Pushti) redundant; for the Gopikas would then become
holy divinities by nature. So whatever the theological notions
of later Vaishnavism might be about the Gopikas, the *Bhagavata*
text itself maintains that they belonged to a promiscuous society,
that they were at the start attracted by Krishna's physical
charms, and that it was Krishna's association that raised them to
the summit of purity and holiness. So says Uddhava, a great
disciple and follower of Krishna, in utter astonishment on seeing
the unexpected devotional exaltation of the Gopikas: "How low
are these women, belonging, as they do, to a forest tribe given to
adulterous sex-relationship! And how exalted is this deep-rooted
devotion to Krishna, the Supreme Being, found in them! As a
potent medicine swallowed 'with or without knowledge of its
efficacy' invariably cures a patient, so the Lord brings about the
spiritual regeneration of a person whose mind settles well on Him,
however ignorant he might be" Bha. 10-47-57. It is evident
from this that the main stress of the *Bhagavata* is on the transforming power of love and holiness manifest in Krishna, the
Purnavatara, but it does not exclude the relevancy of any theological or symbolical explanation. It is also to be noted that accord
ing to the Chaitanya School of Vaishnavism the attitude of the
Gopikas towards Krishna should not be directly practised by any
aspirant. What he could do is only to participate in the feeling
of the Gopikas through impersonation in consciousness with them.
So it is called Raganuga Bhakti—or devotion consisting in the
imitation of love manifested in Vrindavana. Imitation can ultimately lead to Prema—deep and abiding love for Krishna. This
path is also called Pushti-Marga or the Path of Divine Nourishment, as the development of Priti of this type is the result of the
rich nourishment that the Jiva receives from the Grace of the
Lord.

XIII

Devotional Discipline in the Bhagavata: the Place of the Four Yogas in it

What has been discussed till now is the experience of devotion (Bhakti) when it has become deep-rooted in the human mind. It is only when devotion is deep-rooted, whether it be of the Santa type or of the Priti type, that the mind will flow naturally and irresistibly towards God as the Ganges flows to the ocean, as described by the *Bhagavata*. It is the final fruit of devotional discipline and is therefore called Para-Bhakti or Sadhya-Bhakti. It is the end product of a long evolution of the Jiva extending over several lives, the result of the sedulous practice of preliminary devotional disciplines generally described by the terms Sadhana-Bhakti (disciplinary devotion) or Vaidhi-Bhakti (devotional practices according to scriptural injunctions).

According to the *Bhagavata* all genuine spiritual disciplines are parts of Bhakti Yoga (discipline of Bhakti), because the Lord has declared that He can be grasped only through Bhakti, that morality, pursuit of truth, charity etc., though good in themselves, cannot purify the soul if devoid of Bhakti, and that the gold of the human spirit shines, rid of all its dross, only when put into the fire of Bhakti. Still it recognises the distinctiveness of three Yogas—Jnana, Karma and Bhakti. Sometimes it speaks of Yogas being only two, of Jnana and Bhakti, that of Karma being only preparatory to them. To Sannyasins of very high renunciation, jnana Yoga is prescribed; to those who are moved by desires, Karma Yoga is applicable; and to those who, through listening 'by chance' to the recitals of the excellences of the Lord, feel strongly drawn to Him but are only partially fit for renunciation, Bhakti Yoga is recommended (Bh. 11. 20. 7 & 8). By this the *Bhagavata* is not down grading Bhakti, which it considers to be the highest Purushartha attainable by a Jiva and also as unavoidable for success even for a seeker after Mukti through Jnana Yoga. For, it is stated (Bha. 10. 14. 4) that pure intellectual effort to attain to an abstract truth without the elevating influence of faith and devotion is like milling chaff, resulting in vain labour and exhaustion alone. True Jnana Yoga is only Bhakti with a higher degree of intellectual, and less of sentimental, element in it, — a form of 'intellectual love of God' and absorption in Him· The Jnani looks upon the Lord as his own Higher Self and seeks communion with Him through the ' I ' sense. The spirit of detachment and renunciation required for this discipline must be of a very high order even at the very start. But, as pointed out above, the discipline of Bhakti can be started even by one of less endowment in this respect. Besides, while a Jnani aspirant has got to rely on his own strength, the Bhakta has always got the backing of the Bhagavan whom he approaches in a personal relationship and who responds to him accordingly. So Sri Krishna says : "A genuine devotee of mine, who, even if he happens to be temporarily subjugated by sense objects, is never lost. He is backed by the power of his devotion to Me" (Bha.11. 14.8.). According to the *Bhagavata,* devotional discipline generates both renunciation of worldly objects and knowledge of God in a natural and simultaneous process of spiritual evolution, despite initial deficiencies.

As far as Raja Yoga and Karma Yoga are concerned, they only subserve the purpose of the discipline of Bhakti Yoga. Raja Yoga consists in the systematic practice of inward concentration which is immensely helpful in deepening the devotional sentiments and thereby in the continued fixation of the mind on God. Regarding Karma, the *Bhagavata* holds it to be an important aid to Bhakti discipline in the early stages. The Vedas prescribe various Karmas or ritualistic actions either as daily duties or as means for the fulfilment of desires here and in other worlds. Besides, there is another kind of Karma, consisting in the discharge of the various duties of man as a member of society. Both these kinds of actions or Karmas are technically called Dharma. The *Bhagavata* considers that if any of these activities are to deserve the sacred name of Dharma, they must be conducive to the generation of devotion in man. If they are not so motivated, they are vain and meaningless efforts. So the *Bhagavata* looks upon the offer of rich rewards of heavenly enjoyments for proper performance of Karma by the ritualistic sections of the Veda, as mere eulogy and an indirect way to attract sense-bound and child-like man to a life of faith and discipline, just as children are persuaded to take medicines by promises of sweets and savouries. Their ultimate purpose is to teach man to do Vedic Karmas and his worldly duties with a sense of detachment and in dedication to God. When so performed, Karma, otherwise known technically as Dharma, becomes Karma Yoga or communion through dedicated action, and it becomes an integral part of devotional discipline.

The Stages of Sraddha, Rati and Bhakti: Bhagavata Dharma

In the generation and growth of devotion, the *Bhagavata* mentions three main stages as follows "By living in intimate contact with holy men and hearing their discourses on the Lord's excellences, man develops progressively faith (Sraddha), attachment (Rati), and loving devotion (Bhakti) to Him" (Bh. III.25.25). Loving devotion is what was described earlier as Sadhya-Bhakti (mature and well-established devotion). The other two are stages of development, and the devotional disciplines necessarily belong to them. Development of a living faith in God and in the supreme importance of devotional life is the first and foremost discipline. Quite a vast number of people profess to have faith in God, but it is mainly a formal or conventional acceptance, which fails to move them powerfully from within to aspire and work for knowledge and love of God. God and spiritual life become real matters for which man feels it worth while to stake his all, only when he moves closely with others whose life and conduct have the stamp of powerful God-love and spiritual experience. It is only from one light that another lamp can be lighted. So the *Bhagavata* holds that association with holy men and listening to their talk on the Lord and His excellences form the one single factor that lights the flame of genuine faith (Sraddha) in the hearts of men. Faith or Sraddha, the first stage of true devotion, is a state of mind in which the spiritual value is accepted as more fundamental than any other, and man shows readiness to sacrifice and strive for it. The very important part that holy company plays in generating faith is amply elaborated in the second section of this Anthology.

For men of faith who want to develop attachment (Rati) and loving devotion (Bhakti) for God the second and third stages of devotion—the *Bhagavata* prescribes a course of discipline called Bhagavata Dharma, which it claims is applicable to all men of right intentions. It is claimed to be much more easy and practicable than the disciplines prescribed in the Vedas and Yoga-sastras. "For aspirants who are not learned in the Vedas and other scriptures, the Lord has given the Bhagavata Dharma (the path of devotion) as an easy way for attaining to Him," says the *Bhagavata*. " A person following this path never sustains any spiritual fall. Even if he runs along this path with eyes closed, his feet do not slip and he does not topple down. Whatever a devotee does with body, mind, senses, intellect or spirit—not necessarily scripture-ordained duties, but all activities natural to him - , let him consecrate it all to Narayana by making them an offering unto Him" (Bh. 11.2.34-36).

XIV

Ninefold Specific Bhakti Discipline

Supplementing the above statement, the more direct devotional disciplines are thus enumerated elsewhere: " Hearing narratives of the glorious actions and the excellences of Vishnu; chanting His name and reciting hymns in praise of Him; remembering Him continuously : serving him ; worshipping Him ; paying obeisance to Him ; practising servitude to Him ; befriending Him ; and making total self-surrender to Him—these are the nine aspects of devotion to Vishnu to be practised by men who have received proper instruction from a teacher" (Bh. VII. 5. 23 -24).

The quintessence of devotional disciplines is given in the above-cited verses. The nine disciplines mentioned are specific devotional practices, and the one cited earlier, namely, discharge of duties as worship of God, is a general discipline, the importance of which in devotional life at all stages has to be specially stressed. It has necessarily to be practised along with the nine disciplines, because without the refinement got through it, the latter will not be effective. The practice of devotional disciplines will bear fruit to the extent that man's mind is pure and he is absolutely sincere in his practice. It is comparatively easy for a man to make a show of devotion by chanting, attending discourses and devotional recitals, worshipping, serving holy images etc., but if he is full of what the *Bhagavad Gita* calls Asuri Sampat, demoniacal nature, gloating in self-aggrandisement through greed, lust and violence, his devotional practice will be completely useless. So combating this demoniacal nature in an aspirant is the foundation on which the edifice of devotional life is to be built up, and this is done by whole-hearted dedication of one's actions and their fruits to the Lord. If all actions are to be dedicated to Him, one in whom Sraddha (true faith) has been generated will be very particular to eliminate unethical action: for nothing corrupt and tainted should be offered to the Lord. For man dominated by body sense, physical values are the most real of all categories. Mere ritualistic worship or mental adoration cannot give him the sense of realism which dedication of all actions can give. Dana (material gift), Daya (loving disposition) and Dama (self-control) are declared in the Upanishads as the keynote of the ethical discipline for Asuras, men and gods respectively. In every person there are all these three. So to combat Asuric nature, a quantum of physical worship is required, and this consists in dedicated action, service of fellowmen, charities, observance of vows, austerities etc. It is only through long practice of dedicated action that devotional sentiment will take root. There is no time limit fixed for this discipline. So long as man has not developed dispassion for the objects of senses and begun to feel delight in Divine contemplation, at least works of the nature of duty and service of fellowbeings must be performed. In fact, according to the *Gita*, work of this purifying type should be kept up all through life.

Simultaneously, man should follow the nine specific devotional disciplines beginning with 'hearing', enumerated earlier. Selected verses on each of these disciplines are included in the text of *Bhaktiratnavali* from Section 4 onwards. These, together with the sectional Introductions and Notes, state most of what has to be said on these disciplines. Among the few additional points to be elucidated, is the significance of the grouping into which these nine devotional disciplines fall. As pointed out by Dr. Siddeshwar Bhattacharya in his learned book on the *Philosophy of the Bhagavata* (Vol. II), the two disciplines, Sravana (hearing) and Smarana (remembering), correspond to the Vedantic disciplines of Sravana (hearing the Upanishads) and Nididhyasana (deep meditation). The two are linked by Kirtana (praising by songs, hymns etc.,) which corresponds to Vedic Swadhyaya (scriptural study and chanting of the Vedas). Thus through these three disciplines the *Bhagavata* links itself with Vedic tradition. Padasevanam (service), Vandanam (obeisance) and Archanam (worship) are essentially Tantric disciplines introduced by the Pancharatra for the worship of God in holy images and service in temples. Dasya (servitude), Sakhya (comradeship) and Atmanivedana (self-dedication) are pure devotional attitudes that form the core of the Bhakti discipline. While one or more of these attitudes in their rudimentary state may find expression in the earlier devotional disciplines, their firm establishment in the mind represents the state of Rati or continued attachment to the Lord, marked by the automatic involvement of the mind in uninterrupted thought of the Lord even without the help of any of the more external practices. Rati, when mature, becomes the deep loving devotion of the Santa type, if one is dominated by knowledge and apprehension of the Lord's majesty; or of the Priti type, if the Lord is grasped as one's 'own' through a sense of personal relationship. A person who has firm Faith should also take initiation from a Guru, which will facilitate regular spiritual practice.

Another question that arises in regard to the nine Bhakti disciplines is whether they are expressions of devotion or whether

they are only disciplines to be practised one after another or all at
a time. The consensus of opinion among authorities is that they
are as much disciplines of devotion as expressions of devotional
experience. They are the charateristic forms in which even the
greatest devotees give expression to their longing for God and love
of Him. For them, they become the spontaneous expressions
coming from within. But for persons who are only at the preparatory stage (Vaidhi or Gauni Bhakti), they are the means by
which they could keep remembrance of the Lord, purify their
understanding and nourish the tender sapling of devotion planted
in them at the awakening of Sraddha through some holy contact.

Nor is any grading contemplated in the enumeration of these
disciplines. In other words, by sticking exclusively even to one or
a combination of a few of them, one can rise to the higher levels of
devotion. For example, the *Narada Bhakti Sutras* cite the opinion
of different Bhakti teachers on this point as follows: The
disciples of Parasara hold that delight in worship and allied
disciplines constitute devotional practice. The teacher Garga
thinks that it consists in being devoted to the recital and the hearing
of narratives about the Lord and His excellences. Narada considers
that the sign of devotion is dedication of everything to Him and
the experience of intense anguish when one fails to remember
Him.

It will be seen from the above remarks that one or a combination of a few of these disciplines are accepted by the teachers of
Bhakti as self-sufficient for the cultivation of God-love. While
this cannot be denied, a combination of most or all of the disciplines will be the best. The object of all the preparatory disciplines is to keep up the constant remembrance of God, and by
engaging oneself in hearing and singing, alternated with Puja
and service, one will be helped to have that constant remembrance (Smarana), which is the essence of the early disciplines
until Rati (natural and continuous attachment to God) is generated. Smarana then becomes natural without any external aid.

XV

The Glory of the Divine Name

Among these devotional disciplines there is one closely connected with Smarana (remembrance), which the *Bhagavata* emphasises specially through the lives of several devotees. It consists in the utterance of the Divine Name (Nama), the unique power of which finds a place among the most important teachings of the *Bhagavata*. It is dealt with at length in the 5th Section of *Bhaktiratnavali*, in which quotations from the Ajamila episode are given. The uniqueness of the Name is that its utterance is the most powerful expiatory discipline for men suffering from sin-consciousness, and also the most effective practice for gaining concentration, remembrance and devotion to God. Sri Ramakrishna also advocates this as the Sadhana (spiritual discipline) *par excellence* for man. It is sometimes said that the Hindus have no church to administer the last sacrament to a dying man. The *Bhagavata* comes to fill up the gap with its doctrine that the mere utterance of the Lord's Name 'Narayana' by a dying man, as in the case of a sinner like Ajamila, is sufficient to take him towards higher evolution. It says: "Those who resort at the time of death, in a mood of helpless supplication, to the Names of the Lord, quickly overcome the sins of many births and attain to the True Being.. ...The Name of the Lord, uttered with or without knowledge of its power and holiness, destroys the sins of man, as fire consumes fuel. A potent drug, even when used casually without any awareness of its powers, manifests its inherent curative power. Even so is the utterance of the Lord's Name" (Bh. 5. 12,23 & 24).

Further, it states that the continuous repetition of the Lord's Names and excellences is the best and the most potent of spiritual disciplines in the age of Kali. "In this age of Kali," says the *Bhagavata*, "they indeed are the fortunate and the blessed who themselves remember the Names of Hari and help others to remember the same. Though the age of Kali is dominated by evil, it holds forth one great advantage. What an aspirant attains in Krita Yuga through meditation, in Treta Yuga through sacrifices, in Dvapara through service of holy images, the same is attained in

Kali Yuga through hymning the praise of Hari" (Bh XII. 3. 51-52).

It may be said that the whole teaching and philosophy of the *Bhagavata* is compressed in the doctrine of the infinite power of the Divine Name, which is veritably an Avatara (Descent) of God for every one with faith to commune with—whether he is a saint or a sinner, a learned man or one in ignorance. The Lord has made Himself easy of access to every one through His Name.

BIBLIOGRAPHY

1. The text of the *Bhagavata*

2. Commentaries on the *Bhagavata* : By Sridhara Swami, Viswanatha Chakravarti, and Vaisravanam Raman Nampudiripad.

3. *Cultural Heritage of India* : The Ramakrishna Mission Institute of Culture, Calcutta.

4. *The Philosophy of the Bhagavata* Vol. I and II : By Dr. Siddheswar Bhattacharya (Shantiniketan).

5. *Vaiṣṇavopaniṣads*, Adyar Library, 1945

BHAKTI RATNĀVALI

(THE NECKLACE OF DEVOTIONAL GEMS)

PROLOGUE

THE *Bhakti Ratnavali* is an Anthology of verses selected by a medieval ascetic named Vishnu Puri from the Srimad *Bhagavata*, which is the *magnum opus* on Bhakti (devotion to God), and is accepted as authoritative by all schools of Vaishnavism. The *Bhagavata* is held in high esteem by non-Vaishnava devotees also, especially because of the harmony it effects between devotion and knowledge (Bhakti and Jnana). It consists of about 18,000 verses, including several passages of prose-poetry, divided into twelve Cantos. Devotion to the Supreme Being as Vishnu, especially His incarnation as Sri Krishna, is its theme. This theme is expounded through elaborate narrations dealing with cosmic cycles, dynastic histories, lives of sages, saints and saintly kings, and lives of Divine Incarnations, and by means of long conversations between teachers and disciples, by philosophical and ethical disquisitions, and by hymns in praise of God and Divine Incarnations. In fact every topic through which devotion to God can be inculcated is brought in.

Vishnu Puri, the Anthologist, has selected from all this vast and amorphous literature, four hundred and five verses, which according to the metaphor he has himself used, have been 'strung' by him into a 'necklace of devotional gems', consisting of thirteen Virachanas or strands. In these verses we get a clear outline of the doctrine of Bhakti, both in its theory and practice, as conceived by the great devotional text, the *Bhagavata*. Though he has selected the verses from different parts of the work, the Anthologist has arran-

ged them with an eye to the continuity of the theme, and has further established this continuity by connecting each verse with the
succeeding one by his brief introductory notes, which have also
been translated with some minor alterations or elaborations. Thus,
the work, far from being a stray selection, has a unity of its own.
In three or four verses of his own composition, incorporated into
the Anthology, Vishnu Puri compares his efforts to those of a
diver gathering gems from the bottom of the sea, the sea here being Srimad *Bhagavata*. Further he speaks of himself as stringing
these gems of devotion gathered from the *Bhagavata* into a necklace of thirteen strands, which, as tradition says, he offered at the
feet of Jagannatha (Lord of the Universe at Puri) through another
contemporary Master of the devotional school, Sri Chaitanya.

About Vishnu Puri, we have no authoritative information except that he was an ascetic hailing from Tairabhukta (Tirhut in
Mithila), and that he made the Anthology probably at Banares
(Varanasi). These details are gathered from his own statements
contained in the work. Scholars are very uncertain about the time
when he lived. According to tradition, he seems to have been a
contemporary of Sri Chaitanya (1485 to 1533 A.D.), to whom he
was personally known. This is disputed by others who consider
him to have lived two centuries before Sri Chaitanya. There is
also a view that he lived as late as 1633, but on various considerations this is dismissed, this date being likely to be on which the
copyist of the particular manuscript completed his work.

All lovers of Srimad *Bhagavata*, which is the most outstand-
ing work in Hindu devotional literature, will feel thankful to
Vishnu Puri for this Anthology, which is undoubtedly the result of
deep thought, very careful study, and much painstaking effort at
selection. As stated by him in verses six to eight of the Text, he
"dived deep into the ocean of the *Bhagavata*, and discovering, by
the Lord's Grace, these invaluable gems of devotion in it, hastened
to lift them up with great effort and make them into this necklace
of an Anthology fit to 'adorn' the necks of (i.e. to be studied and,
recited by) votaries who have no time or facility to go into the
immense text of the original *Bhagavata*.

An edition of the work was published in the 'Sacred Books of the Hindus' series in 1912 from Allahabad, and later another edition from Calcutta.   It is doubtful whether these are now available in print, and a fresh edition with a new English translation and annotation will not therefore be out of place. It is hoped that with the help of the English translation those who have a working knowledge of Sanskrit will be able to enter into the not too easy literary structure of the original verses and catch a glimpse of the soul-stirring beauty and grandeur of Srimad *Bhagavata*.

STRAND 1

GENERAL REFLECTIONS ON BHAKTI

Sectional Introduction : The first section, the longest of all the 13 sections of the Anthology, consists of 116 verses out of its total of 405 + 11* verses. These verses deal with Bhakti in a general way. Some of the teachings included in it are as follows: Vasudeva is the Supreme Being. Man's highest duty in life is to practise devotion to Him. All other duties in life should subserve this supreme duty, and a man who neglects it and lives merely for physical and social values would be spending his life in vain. All are eligible to practise devotion to Vasudeva, the only qualification for it being unfailing faith in Him. Birth, culture, refinements etc., are of no consideration in the path of Bhakti. Bhakti, in its mature form, is the tendency of the mind to go naturally and irresistibly to the Lord in place of worldly objects. This state is reached only after long practice of Bhagavata Dharma consisting in the dedication of all one's actions to Him, and of the ninefold discipline of Bhakti. Ultimately it is a matter of Divine Grace also. Every one is eligible for this Grace, provided he yearns for it intensely. For, the Lord is the same to all, and he who takes refuge in Him, gets Him, while he who keeps aloof, excludes himself from Grace. A true devotee has always got the unfailing support of the Lord, and even if he has some defects and deficiencies, they are soon made up, if he is sincere in his devotion. The practice of Bhakti simultaneously develops in one, all other spiritual excellences like renunciation, purity, knowledge and realisation. Even non-Bhakti disciplines have to be mixed with some element of devotion, if they are to be successful. Bhakti is not only the easiest and the least risky path to Divine realisation, but also the most direct. It is both the means and the end, and great devotees seek Bhakti in preference to Mukti itself. It is thus a super-value excelling even liberation. But liberation, however, follows it automatically.

---

*These eleven verses have been added by us to those selected by the Anthologist. Besides, seven verses included at the beginning and the end of the selection are of the Anthologist's own composition.

In accordance with the Hindu tradition, Vishnupuri, the Antho-
logist, begins with a salutation to Sri Krishna for the successful
accomplishment of his work, quoting a verse from the end of the
10th Canto of the **Bhagavata:**

जयति जननिवासो देवकीजन्मवादो
यदुवरपर्षत्स्वैर्दोभिरस्यन्नधर्मम् ।
स्थिरचरवृजिनघ्नः सुस्मितश्रीमुखेन
व्रजपुरवनितानां वर्धयन् कामदेवम् ॥

(1) **Obeisance to Lord Sri Krishna, the Indweller in all
beings as also their Abode. Though reputed as born of Devaki, He
is really the Eternal and Ancient One. Surrounded by attendants
of the Yadu clan, He destroyed the forces of unrighteousness by
the prowess of His arms. He redeems all beings, animate and
inanimate, from their sins. By His benign and smiling countenance,
He inspired Divine love into the hearts of the womenfolk of
Vraja and Mathurapuri.** (Bh. 10.90.48)

Note : This is the first of the three verses with which the
10th Canto of the *Bhagavata,* narrating the life of Sri Krishna,
ends. It is therefore a brief statement of the life and work of Sri
Krishna, who is the Purnavatara (full Incarnation) according to
the *Bhagavata.* The avowed purpose of the *Bhagavata,* as shown
in the Introduction, is to preserve and present the life and message of this Divine Incarnation. This verse briefly summarises the
three features of his life and message: first, though possessing a
human body as the son of Devaki, all Divine attributes were
present in Him and as such all His actions are to be looked upon
as those of God and not as of a man;   second, He was the embodiment of dynamic powers which He used for the destruction of
the evil-minded and the establishment of virtue; third. He was also
the embodiment of redeeming love and sanctifying holiness by
which *a)* he gave salvation even to all who hated Him and opposed
Him in battle; *b)* liberated men and gods who had been reduced
to the state of plants and animals as a result of the curses of sages
for their misdeeds, and *c)* raised into paragons of holiness, purity

and Divine love, women who approached him out of carnal affection under the influence of His overpowering physical beauty.
His sanctifying power is praised in the succeeding verses.

The potency of the Lord's name is stated in the words of Suka:

यत्कीर्तनं यत्स्मरणं यदीक्षणं यद्वन्दनं यच्छ्रवणं यदर्हणम् ।
लोकस्य सद्यो विधुनोति किल्बिषं तस्मै सुभद्रश्रवसे नमो नमः ॥

(2) By whose praise, by whose remembrance, by whose sight,
by whose salutation, by whose hearing, by whose worship men get
rid of their sinful tendencies immediately—to that Lord, the reputed centre of abounding grace and benevolence, our repeated
prostrations.   (2.4.15)

Repeated salutations are offered in the words of Sri Suka:

भूयो नमः सद्वृजिनच्छिदेऽसतां असंभवायाखिलसत्त्वमूर्तये ।
पुंसां पुनः पारमहंस्य आश्रमे व्यवस्थितानामनुमृग्यदाशुषे ॥

(3) Salutations again to Him who destroys the sins of devotees,
who effaces unrighteousness, who is manifested as all beings, and
who bestows Self-knowledge to the Truth-seekers following the
path of discrimination—the way of the Paramahamsas.   (2.4.13)

*The Chosen Ideal is praised as the all-comprehending Univer-
sal Being in the words of Sri Suka:*

श्रियः पतिर्यज्ञपतिः प्रजापति-र्धियांपतिर्लोकपतिर्धरापतिः ।
पतिर्गतिश्चान्धकवृष्णिसात्वतां प्रसीदतां मे भगवान्सतां गतिः ॥

(4) The Lord of Sri (or Mahalakshmi), the master of all
Yajnas (sacrifices), the progenitor of all living beings, the controller
of Buddhi (intellect) and all mental faculties, the master of the
worlds, the protector of the earth, the guide and refuge of all
devotees, the final end sought by all virtuous men—may He, the
Perfect Being, be propitious unto me.   (2.4.20)

*Suta, the narrator of the scriptural Text, in praise of Sri
Suka, the revealer of the Bhagavata:*

यः स्वानुभावमखिलश्रुतिसारमेकं अध्यात्मदीपमतितितीर्षतां तमोन्धम्
संसारिणां करुणयाह पुराणगुह्यं तं व्याससूनुमुपयामि गुरुं मुनीनाम् ॥

(5) I seek shelter at the feet of Sri Suka, the son of Vyasa
and the spiritual teacher of all contemplatives (Munis), who, out
of compassion for those entangled in the world, revealed this most
esoteric of all Puranas, which has got its own uniqueness (doctrinal and poetical), which contains the essence of all Vedas and
Vedantas, which is of unrivalled excellence, and which is verily a
spiritual lamp unto those who want to cross the blinding darkness
of ignorance.   (1.2.3)

Vishnu Puri's task in his own words:

दूरान्निशम्य महिमानमुपेत्य पार्श्वं अन्तःप्रविश्य शुभभागवतामृताब्धेः
पश्यामि कृष्णकरुणाज्ञननिर्मलेन हृल्लोचनेन भगवज्जनं हि रत्नम् ॥
तदिदमतिमहार्घं भक्तिरत्नं मुरारे-रहमधिकसयत्नः प्रीतये वैष्णवानाम् ।
हृदिगतजगदीशादेश-मासाद्यमाद्य-निधिवरमिव तस्माद्धारिधेरुद्धरामि ॥

(6) Hearing from afar about its greatness, I approached and
plunged deep into this blessed nectarine ocean of the *Bhagavata*
and with my mind's eye clarified by the collyrium of Krishna's
grace, I perceived the gems of Divine Love deposited in it. [*Vishnu
Puri's composition*]

(7) With very great effort I am lifting up, like a precious
treasure, this great gem of Divine Love out of the ocean of the
Bhagavata for the enjoyment of the Lord's devotees (Vaishnavas).
In this I am following the command of the Supreme Being lodged
in my heart. [*Vishnu Puri's composition*]

*The excellences of the Anthology are stated in Vishnu Puri's
own words:*

कंठे कृता कुलमशेषमलंकरोति वेश्मस्थिता निखिलमेव तमोऽपहन्ति ।
तामुज्ज्वलां गुणवतीं जगदीशभक्ति-रत्नावलीं सुकृतिनः परिशीलयन्तु ॥

(8) Worn round the neck (means also 'recited'), it is an
adornment to the wearer. Placed in the house (means also 'esta-

blished in the heart") it removes darkness (ignorance). May all
good people wear always on their bosom (means also 'apply themselves intensely to the study of') this brilliant and precious necklace made of the gems of Divine Love (also means 'this book called
Bhakti-ratnavali'). [Vishnupuri's composition]

When there is the Bhagavata, why this Anthology?

निखिलभागवतश्रवणालसा बहुकथाभिरथानवकाशिनः ।
अयमयं ननु ताननु सार्थको भवतु विष्णुपुरीग्रथनग्रहः ॥

(9) There are many, who though not apathetic, cannot study
or hear the full original *Bhagavata* owing to their preoccupation
with the various affairs of life. Let this effort of Vishnu Puri (a
Sannyasin of Tairabukta or Tirhut) to bring together the gems of
verses from various sections of the *Bhagavata* and string them
together into a consistent whole, become useful to such devotees.
[Vishnu Puri's composition]

*The first five verses, quoted early from the Bhagavata, are by
way of salutation to the Lord. The next four are the compiler's
Introduction in his own words. Now the Text proper begins with
the Suta's verses stating that religion and spirituality are based
on devotion to God:*

स वै पुंसां परो धर्मो यतो भक्तिरधोक्षजे ।
अहैतुक्यप्रतिहता ययात्मा सुप्रसीदति ॥

(10) The supreme duty of man consists in following such
activities as will generate in him pure devotion to God (Adhokshaja
or Vishnu), free from all extraneous motives, and unshakable by
antagonistic circumstances. By such devotion a person's mind
attains to supreme peace.   (1.2.6)

Note: At the start Vishnu is praised as the Supreme Deity
deserving the adoration of all devotees. The *Bhagavata*, being a
Vaishnava text, has necessarily got to exalt Vishnu as the Deity.
But this is not done in a narrow sectarian way. There is in the
Text no antagonism to other conceptions of the Deity. Besides,
the appellations for the Deity such as Vasudeva, Vishnu, Narayana

etc. have highly philosophical and universally acceptable meanings. Vasudeva means, 'He in whom all beings dwell'; Vishnu is 'He who prevades everything'; Narayana is 'The resting place for all Jivas'; and Adhokshaja means 'One who is beyond the ken of the senses'.

The generation of devotion is put forward as the meaning and purpose of life. Pursuit of all other values has to subserve this purpose. The Dharmas (duties) of man are many—those imposed by scriptures, by society, by family, by the State etc. According to the *Bhagavata*, practice of devotion to God is supreme over them all, as that alone makes life ultimately meaningful. But this does not mean that the so-called secular duties should be completely separated from our devotional life and water-tight compartments made of them as the spiritual and the secular. If all our duties are done as an offering to the Lord, they become a part of devotional life, and thereby life becomes dominated by the pursuit of devotion, as instructed in these verses. It is the main teaching of the *Bhagavad Gita*, too. Such a life of integration of spiritual and secular pursuits is called Bhagavata Dharma. It is discussed in detail in the Introduction and in the Bhakti Ratnavali text too. If a man does not consciously strive to develop devotion through all his activities in life, he has lived his life in vain. This is the sum and substance of all the teachings of the *Bhagavata*.

According to the accepted Vedic teaching, the discharge of duties (Svadharma) in the right spirit is said to make a man fit for Jnana (knowledge). How can Dharma then be the cause of Bhakti? The answer is given through the following words of the Suta that it is Bhakti that produces Jnana, and Svadharma is only indirectly generative of Jnana, devotion (Bhakti) being that intervening factor.

वासुदेवे भगवति भक्तियोगः प्रयोजितः ।
जनयत्याशु वैराग्यं ज्ञानं यत्तदहैतुकम् ॥

(11) The practice of communion with Lord Vasudeva through loving devotion (Bhakti Yoga) quickly generates dispassion

for worldly objects as also the intuition of the Supreme Being,
without the aid of the ratiocinative processes of logic.   (1.2.7)

*Why Vasudeva (Mahavishnu or the Supreme all-pervading
Spirit) alone should be the object of worship, is stated in the words
of Sri Suta:*

सत्त्वं रजस्तम इति प्रकृतेर्गुणास्तैः
युक्तः परः पुरुष एक इहास्य धत्ते ।
स्थित्यादये हरिविरिञ्चिहरेति. संज्ञाः
श्रेयांसि तत्र खलु सत्त्वतनो्नृणां स्युः॥
अतो वै कवयो नित्यं भक्ति परमया मुदा ।
वासुदेवे भगवति कुर्वन्त्यात्मप्रसादनीम् ॥
मुमुक्षवो घे.ररूपान् हित्वा भूतपतीनथ ।
नारायणकलाः शान्ता भजन्ति ह्यनसूयवः ॥

(12)   The one Supreme Being, uniting Himself for the purpose
of cosmic manifestation with the threefold aspects of Prakriti
(Nature), known as Sattva, Rajas and Tamas, assumes the names
of Hari (Vishnu), Virinchi (Brahma) and Hara (Siva).   Of these,
the Lord's manifestation in the Sattva aspect of Prakriti is
especially conducive to the highest good (liberation), as it is
Sattva that generates spiritual illumination (Jnana).   (1.2.23)

(13)   For this reason sages practise loving devotion towards
the Supreme Being as Vasudeva, with their hearts full of joy.
Devotion gives supreme peace to the mind.   (1.2.22)

(14)   Persons seeking liberation through Bhakti (loving devotion) worship the beatific manifestations of Narayana in preference to terror-inspiring forms of the Deity.   But they do not
cavil at any form of worship.   (1.2.26)

Note : The reference here is to the very well-known doctrine of
Trimurti—the Supreme Being in the three aspects of Brahma,
Vishnu and Maheswara (Siva) associated with creation, preservation and dissolution of the universe. Though the Supreme Being
is the one all-inclusive Non-dual Entity, He has His inherent

Sakti or Power of manifestation. Saktimat and Sakti, the Possessor of Power and the Power are not two but one and the same entity like fire and its heat. This Sakti is here called Prakriti, a term originally used by the Samkhyas but afterwards adopted by the other schools also with the enlarged meaning that it is not an independent matrix of insentient matter, but the Power of the Supreme Being (the Sat-chid-ananda). It is His Sakti that manifests as the universe. The transformations are in the Sakti and therefore they do not affect Him. Thus by Sakti coming between God and the world of Becoming, we are helped to understand how God manifests as the world without Himself being affected. So the Text speaks of the One Supreme Being manifesting the worlds as the Trinity by uniting with Prakriti having its threefold constituents of Sattva, Rajas and Tamas.

According to the Samkhya philosophy, Prakriti is a complex of the above mentioned constituents which are technically called Gunas (qualities . Even when Prakriti was accepted as the Sakti of God, its conception in this respect did not change. Sattva stands for purity, light, intelligence, harmony, tranquillity etc; Rajas for passion, energy, strife etc; and Tamas for dullness, ignorance, darkness, inertia etc. All things, mental and physical, are the evolutes of Prakriti, and are as such, permutations and combinations of the basic three Gunas. In the process of world manifestation, the Supreme Being, Vishnu, is described as associated with each of these Gunas of Prakriti—with Rajas for creation (Srishti), with Sattva for preservation and redemption (Sthiti), and with Tamas for dissolution (Pralaya). It should be clearly understood that they are not three Gods, but the one and only Supreme Being (Vishnu), of whom the other two are manifestations in Rajas and Tamas. So they should really be called Vishnu-Brahma and Vishnu-Siva. Vishnu Himself manifests also in Sattva, but Sattva, being pure, His manifestation through it is not in the least distorted by the medium of manifestation, unlike in the case of the Brahma and the Siva manifestations through Rajas and Tamas. In Him therefore there is the full expression of the Bhagas, the six glories, which qualify Him to the term Bhagavan (See Introduction). He is the one Supreme Being to be adored and prayed to, and through His worship, both Brahma and Siva, besides other subsidiary Divine manifestations, are all worshipped. The manifestation of the Supreme Being as Trimurti is called Gunavatara—descent through the Gunas of Prakriti (See 'Avataras' in the Introduction).

It should be noted that the *Bhagavata* exalts Vishnu as the Supreme Being, because it is a Vaishnava Purana. Saiva Puranas and Sakta Puranas will do the same with Siva and Sakti.

All kinds of devotees, whether Sakama or Akama, are exhorted to be devoted to the Lord in the following words of Suka:

अकामः सर्वकामो वा मोक्षकाम उदारधीः ।
तीव्रेण भक्तियोगेन भजेत पुरुषं परं ॥

(15) Let a man be desireless, or let him be with many desires (owing to his situation in life). If he is an intelligent and sincere aspirant after liberation, let him worship the Supreme Being with intense devotion.   (2.3.10)

That all paths of spiritual upliftment are dedicated to Vasudeva, is stated in the two following verses of Suta:

वासुदेवपरा वेदा वासुदेवपरा मखाः ।
वासुदेवपरा योगा वासुदेवपरा क्रियाः ॥
वासुदेवपरं ज्ञानं वासुदेवपरं तपः ।
वासुदेवपरो धर्मो वासुदेवपरा गतिः ॥

(16-17) The Vedas have Vasudeva as their subject matter; the sacrificial rites are dedicated to Vasudeva; all Yogas have Vasudeva as their end; all religious ceremonies have Vasudeva in view; the spiritual science of Self-knowledge is devoted to Vasudeva; all austerities are meant to propitiate Vasudeva; Dharma consists in the dedicated service of Vasudeva; Vasudeva is, indeed, the supreme goal of man!   (1.2.28—29)

Narada on why devotion is superior to other disciplines:

यमादिभिर्योगपथैः कामलोभहतो मुहुः ।
मुकुन्दसेवया यद्वत्तथास्माद्धा न शाम्यति ॥

(18) The mind of man under the sway of passions and greed will not attain to real and lasting peace through the restraint of the senses and the other practices of Rajayoga, as it will through the service of the Lord with loving devotion.   (1.6.36)

The self-sufficiency of Bhakti Yoga in the words of Suta:

भक्तियोगेन मनसि सम्यक् प्रणिहितेऽमले ।
अपश्यत्पुरुषं पूर्णं मायां च तदुपाश्रयाम् ॥

(19) (Vyasa) attained to the perception of the Supreme Purusha, and of Prakriti as dependent on Him, with his mind made steady and pure by the practice of communion through loving devotion.   (1.7.4)

Kapila on the nature of the highest form of devotion:

देवानां गुणलिङ्गाना-मानुश्राविककर्मणाम् ।
सत्त्व एवैकमनसो वृत्तिः स्वाभाविकी तु या ॥
अनिमित्ता भागवती भक्तिः सिद्धेर्गरीयसी ।
जरयत्याशु या कोशं निगीर्णमनलो यथा ॥

(20-21) When the powers of the organs of knowledge, as also of those of action, manifest as a unified mental mode directed towards the Supreme Being, spontaneous like an instinct and devoid of any extraneous incentive—that (state of mind) is called Bhakti (devotion) to the Lord. It is superior even to liberation (Siddhi.) It quickly burns up the soul's sheaths of ignorance (Linga Sarira) as the fire consumes all objects.   (3.25.32—33)

Superiority of Bhakti to Mukti in Kapila's words:

नैकात्मतां मे स्पृहयन्ति केचित् मत्पादसेवाभिरता मदीहाः ।
येऽन्योन्यतो भागवताः प्रसज्य सभाजयन्ते मम पौरुषाणि ॥

(22) There are some rare aspirants who do not desire to become one with My being (or attain to non-dual consciousness), because they are eager to do personal service unto Me. Such devotees assemble together and render homage to Me by singing about My glories.   (3.25.34)

Kapila on what happens to the above-mentioned type of devotees:

पश्यन्ति ते मे रुचिराण्यंब सन्तः प्रसन्नवक्त्रारुणलोचनानि ।
रूपाणि दिव्यानि वरप्रदानि साकं वाचं स्पृहणीयां वदन्ति ॥
तैर्दर्शनीयावयवैरुदार-विलासहासेक्षित-वामसूक्तैः ।
हृतात्मनो हृतप्राणांश्च भक्ति-रनिच्छतो मे गतिमण्वीं प्रयुंक्ते ॥

(23) O Mother ! These great devotees, who reject even the state of oneness with Me, perceive and talk with My lovely Divine forms having beautiful faces, rosy eyes, and sweet voice, and showering blessings on votaries.   (3.25.35.)

(24) Being drawn heart and soul by the attraction of My beautiful forms, My sportive ways, smiles, glances and speech so ennobling to the mind, they attain, though not desiring, to My subtle nature (Sayujya or intimate union) by virtue of their loving devotion (Bhakti).   (3.25.63)

अथो विभूतिं मममायाविसृष्टा-मैश्वर्यमष्टांगमनुप्रवृत्तम् ।
श्रियं भागवतीं वाऽस्पृहयन्ति भद्रां परस्य मे तेऽश्नुवते तु लोके ॥
न कर्हिंचिन्मत्पराः शान्तरूपे नङ्क्ष्यन्ति नोऽनिमिषो लेढि हेतिः ।
येषामहं प्रिय आत्मा सुतश्च सखा गुरुः सुहृदो दैवमिष्टम् ॥

(25) They do not hanker for any of the splendours that are manifested by My Maya (Power) in the seven worlds. They do not care for the eightfold powers that automatically come to them with their spiritual development. Even the glory of Vaikuntha (the heavenly abode of Vishnu, the Supreme Being as manifested Person) is not sought by them. Yet in my supreme Abode they attain to bliss unmixed with sorrow. (Though they do not care for anything except serving the Lord, He confers on them all fulfilments.)

(26) Those who resort to Me as the Supreme never meet with a fall (destruction) from that Abode of peace. The wheel of Time which I wield continuously, brings all beings except them

under its sway. For, to them I am the beloved, the self, son, friend, teacher, well-wisher and Chosen Deity. (3.25.37-38)

Note : In this and the succeeding verses, it is hinted that devotees of the highest type have no special aspiration for what is called Moksha or cessation from the cycle of birth and death. Their bliss consists in loving and serving the Lord. Yet union with Him, here called 'subtle state' comes automatically to them. But the Bhakti tradition maintains that some of His greatest devotees retain their individuality and remain as His eternal servants and associates. They are the Nitya-Siddhas who appear as the associates of the Lord in His Incarnations to serve as exemplars of various patterns of devotion and loving service.

That those who have real renunciation and devotion automatically get liberation also, is confirmed by Kapila in the following three verses:

इमं लोकं तथैवामुमात्मानमुभयायिनम् ।
आत्मानमनु ये चेह ये रायः पशवो गृहाः ॥
विसृज्य सर्वानन्यांश्च मामेवं विश्वतोमुखम् ।
भजन्त्यनन्यया भक्त्या तान्मृत्योरतिपारये ॥
नान्यत्र मद्भगवतः प्रधानपुरुषेश्वरात् ।
आत्मनः सर्वभूतानां भयं तीव्रं निवर्तते ॥
तस्मान्मां सर्वभावेन भजस्व परमेच्छिनम् ।
तद्गुणाश्रयया भक्त्या भजनीयपदांबुजम् ॥

(27-30) This world and the worlds attainable hereafter; the transmigrating subtle body that goes from one world to another; wealth, houses and other properties pertaining to one's present physical body—renouncing these and all other similar encumbrances, man should, with unswerving devotion, worship Me, the all-pervading. By granting him such devotion, I liberate him from the cycle of birth and death. In none but Me, the Supreme Person, the Master of matter and souls, the all-pervading Spirit, can one find shelter from the great terror (the cycle of birth and death).   Therefore apply yourself heart and soul to the service of the Supreme Being, the Adorable One, with devotion inspired by an apprehension of His excellences.   (3.25.38–41)

After concluding Kapila's instructions, two verses from Suniti's advice to Dhruva are taken to show why Maha Vishnu (the Supreme Being in whom everything dwells) alone should be worshipped :

तमेव वत्साश्रय भृत्यवत्सलं मुमुक्षुभिर्मृग्यपदाब्जपद्धतिम् ।
अनन्यभावे निजधर्मभाविते मनस्यवस्थाप्य भजस्व पूरुषम् ॥

नान्यं ततः पद्मपलाशलोचनात् दुःखच्छिदं ते मृगयामि कंचन ।
यो मृग्यते हस्तगृहीतपद्मया श्रियेतरैरङ्ग विमृग्यमानया ॥

(31)   Depend only on Him who is .fond of His ·servants and whose adoration is the path to be chosen by men in quest of liberation.   Install the Supreme Being in your heart purified by your good deeds, and adore Him with unswerving devotion and dedication.

(32)   There is none other than the lotus-eyed Lord Vishnu to whom you can look for the relief of your sorrows.   His greatness is such that Sri Devi, (the Divine Consort of Vishnu, otherwise known as Lakshmi), whom all the worlds seek (because of Her being the Goddess of Wealth), is ever in quest of Him with lotus flowers in hand for His adoration.   (4.8.22-33)

Why Sri Devi seeks Him alone, is now stated in two verses of Prithu :

अथो भजे त्वाखिलपूरुषोत्तमम् गुणालयं पद्मकरेव लालसः ।
आप्यावयोरेकपतिस्पृधोः कलिः नस्यात्कृतत्वच्चरणैकतानयोः ॥

जगज्जनन्यां जगदीश वैशसं स्यादेव यत्कर्मणि नः समीहितम् ।
करोति फल्ग्वप्युरुदीनवत्सलः स एव धिष्ण्येऽमिरतस्य किं तया ॥

(33–34)   If, like Sri Devi (the Divine Consort), I also serve Thee, the Supreme Being, the repository of all excellences,—is it not likely that rivalry and consequent ill-feeling will arise between us two for the reason that both of us are seeking one and the same Being as our Lord and Master with our affections centred on Him ? Even if I incur the displeasure of Sri Devi, the Mother of the worlds, I am bent on rendering service unto Thee. Thou, who art the friend of the lowly, dost certainly consider as great even a trifling service of a devotee. And to Thee, who art always established in Thy infinite glory, what special attraction does Sri Devi hold forth? (4.20.27-28)

Note : Prithu, a great king and devotee, compares himself, with a poetic touch, as one courting the love of the Lord in competition with Sri, the consort of Vishnu. So he apprehends that Sri will be jealous of him, but consoles himself with the thought that the Lord, who is above every want, cares more for the lowly devotee than for all the attractiveness of Sri.

Rudra to Prachetas on the identity of Vishnu and Siva :

यः परं रंहसः साक्षान्त्रिगुणाज्जीवसंज्ञितात् ।
भगवन्तं वासुदेवं प्रपन्नः स प्रियो हि मे ॥
अथ भागवता यूयं प्रियाः स्थ भगवान् यथा ।
न मे भागवतानां च प्रेयानन्योऽस्ति कर्हिचित् ॥

(35-36) Those who have surrendered themselves to Bhagavan Vasudeva, who transcends Nature (Prakriti) constituted of the three subtle Gunas (qualities) as also the Jivas (souls),— they are indeed dear to Me. O Bhagavatas! (Devotees of Vishnu!) As Lord Vishnu is dear to Me, so are you all dear. And for true Bhagavatas also, there is none dearer than Me. (4.24.28&30)

Note : These verses, put in the mouth of Rudra (Siva), have been selected by the Anthologist to establish that there is no need for sectarian hostility between the followers of these two aspects of Godhead, because both are the same.

Narada on the supremacy of devotion to Hari :

तत्कर्म हरितोषं यत्सा विद्या तन्मतिर्यया ।
हरिर्देहभृतामात्मा स्वयं प्रकृतिरीश्वरः ॥

7

(37) Whatever leads to propitiation of Sri Hari, that is real
Karma (and not rituals and worldly activities done for one's own
worldly advancement). That indeed is learning which generates
faith in, and experience of, Sri Hari. And Sri Hari is the soul
of all embodied beings, the lord of all, and the self-sufficient First
Cause.   (4.20.49)

*Prahlada contends that devotion is the hallmark of a great
man :*

यस्यास्ति भक्तिर्भगवत्यकिंचना सर्वैर्गुणैस्तत्र समासते सुराः ।
हरावभक्तस्य कुतो महद्गुणा मनोरथेनासति धावतो बहिः ॥३८॥
हरिर्हि'साक्षाद्भगवान् शरीरिणा-मात्मा झषाणामिव तोयमीप्सितम् ।
हित्वा महांस्तं यदि सज्जते गृहे तदा महत्त्वं वयसा दंपतीनाम् ॥

(38-39) He who has motiveless devotion to Sri Hari, in him
all virtues and all divinities abide. If one has no such devotion,
how can noble qualities (like renunciation, discrimination,
universal love etc.) arise in one, as a mind without devotion to
God always goes outward to petty objects and imaginary sense
enjoyments ? Just as water is to fish, so is Sri Hari to the life
of a devotee. People who ignore His majesty and get attached to
mere domestic felicities,—how can they pretend to be, or be
accepted as, great men ? To do so is as ridiculous as the world's
convention of recognising the superiority of married couples
merely by considering their age.   (5.18.12-13)

Note: For example, a husband is considered superior to the
wife because the former is usually elder to the latter. So also in
Dampati-pooja (worship of a married couple) older couples are
preferred to the younger for worship.

*That Sri Hari alone is worthy of worship is stated in the words
of Rama :*

स वै पतिः स्यादकुतोभयः स्वयं समंततः पाति भयातुरं जनम् ।
स एक एवैतरथा मिथो भयं नैवात्मलाभादधि मन्यते परम् ॥

(40) Sri Hari is the Lord of all. By His very nature, He is free from the fear of any one else. He gives protection to persons oppressed by fear, in every way. He being the One without a second, there is none to cause Him fear. Nor is there anything external to Him to give satisfaction considered greater than His own biissful self-awareness.   (5.18.20)

Hanumat on the qualification of all to worship Hari :

सुरोऽसुरो वाप्यथ वानरो नरः सर्वात्मना यः सुकृतज्ञमीश्वरम् ।
भजेत रामं मनुजाकृतिं हरिं य उत्तराननयत्कोशलान् दिवम् ॥ ४१ ॥
न जन्म नूनं महतो न सौभगं न वाङ् न बुद्धिर्नाकृतिस्तोषहेतुः ।
तैर्यद्विसृष्टानपि नो वनौकस-श्चकार सख्ये बत लक्ष्मणाग्रजः ॥

(41-42) Let all beings—whether gods, demons, men, or non-humans—worship with heart and soul Sri Rama, who is God in human form, who apprehends the good deeds of all and who gave salvation to all the inhabitants of Uttarakosala. Neither noble birth nor great fortune, neither power of speech nor intelligence nor beautiful appearance—none of these can enable one to obtain the grace of Rama, the Supreme Being incarnate as man. For see how He entered into friendship with us, monkeys, who are without any of the above mentioned qualifications and who are mere inhabitants of the wilds!   (5.19.7-8)

The Devas on the greatness of desireless devotion :

सत्यं दिशत्यर्थितमर्थितो नृणां नैवार्थदो यत्पुनरर्थिता यतः ।
स्वयं विधत्ते भजतामनिच्छता-मिच्छापिधानं निजपादपल्लवम् ॥

(43) It is true that the Lord grants the fulfilment of their prayers to those votaries who approach Him with worldly desires. But by this He does not bestow on them the real fulfilment; for it is found that when one desire is satisfied, they approach Him with new desires. But in regard to those who worship Him without any desire (i.e. with pure love), He, out of His own accord, bestows on them His grace, which roots out all wants (and establishes them in the bliss of Divine communion).   (5.19.27)

Prahlada on the need of solitude for the development of devotion :

तत्साधु मन्येऽसुरवर्य देहिनां सदा समुद्विग्नधियामसद्ग्रहात् ।
हित्वात्मपातं गृहमन्धकूपं वनं गतो यद्धरिमाश्रयेत ॥

(44) O King of Asuras! The right path of spiritual regeneration for men who are distracted in mind by continued involvement in worldly affairs, so fleeting and full of fears, is to devote themselves to the service of Hari, taking themselves to a forest—or a place away from their homes which have imprisoned them as in a dry well and led to their spiritual degradation. (7.5.5)

Note : This does not mean that every one should go to a forest before starting on the path of devotion. It only means that an occasional change from worldly environments and living in the company of holy men are necessary for the generation and development of devotion.

Yama on practice of devotion being the supreme duty of man :

एतावानेव लोकेऽस्मिन्पुंसां धर्मः परः स्मृतः ।
भक्तियोगो भगवति तन्नामग्रहणादिभिः ॥

(45) The scriptures enjoin that man's supreme duty (Dharma) consists in cultivating devotion through hearing and repeating His names and through other devotional practices. (6.3.22)

Samsara (transmigratory existence) cannot be overcome except by dependence on the Lord. This is stated in the words of the Devas :

अविस्मितं तं परिपूर्णकामं स्वेनैव लाभेन समं प्रशान्तम् ।
विनोपसर्पत्यपरं हि बालिशः श्वलांगुलेनाति-तितर्ति सिन्धुम् ॥

(46) There is none who surpasses Him in greatness and could therefore cause Him surprise. He is absorbed in the bliss of His all-comprehending Self and seeks satisfaction from nothing external. He is unaffected by change and He is all peace. The man who abandons Him and seeks shelter in another (for over-

coming Samsara) is silly like one trying to cross the ocean with
the support of a dog's tail.   (6.9.22)

Rudra on the redeeming power of devotion :

नारायणपराः सर्वे न कुतश्चन बिभ्यति ।
स्वर्गापवर्गनरकेष्वपि तुल्यार्थदर्शिनः ॥
वासुदेवे भगवति भक्तिमुद्वहतां नृणां ।
ज्ञानवैराग्यवीर्याणां नेह कश्चिद् व्यपाश्रयः ॥

(47-48) Those who have dedicated themselves to Narayana
(Supreme Being) are free from every fear. They view conditions
like Swarga (heaven), Naraka (hell) and Moksha (liberation) with
equal regard, (as they see the Lord everywhere and in all conditions). Those who have loving devotion to Lord Vasudeva and are
therefore endowed with the strength born of knowledge and dispassion, have no need to depend on any other being.   (6.17.28,31)

*Prahlada on the need for renunciation for the growth of
devotion :*

मतिर्न कृष्णे परतः स्वतो वा मिथोऽभिपद्येत गृहव्रतानाम् ॥
अदान्तगोभिर्विशतां तमिस्रं पुनः पुनश्चर्वितचर्वणानाम् ॥
न ते विदुः स्वार्थगतिं हि विष्णुं दुराशया ये बहिरर्थमानिनः ।
अन्धा यथान्धैरुपनीयमाना वाचीशतन्त्यामुरुदाम्नि बद्धाः ॥

(49-50) Worldly-minded men, slaves to their uncontrolled
senses and confined therefore to the hellish life of ignorance,
repeatedly chew the cud of sensuous experiences (in recurring
cycles of births and deaths). In such persons as are addicted to
worldly life, devotion does not arise either by itself or through
talk with others or from contacts among themselves. (For they
associate themselves only with like-minded worldings, and not
with devotees whose company alone can provide the environment
for the generation of devotion.) Being corrupted by engrossment
in objects of the senses, they cannot know Vishnu who is attained
only by those who have no interest in such objects and seek for

the summum bonum of life within themselves. Being guided by
like-minded teachers (Vedic ritualists whose object is only enjoyment), they resemble blind men guided by the blind, bound as
they are by the Lord's wordy Cord of Bondage, the stout rope of
Vedic ritualism.   (7.5.30-32)

Note : The point stressed here is that spiritual stagnation
is the consequence when people avoid holy company and confine
themselves exclusively to the influence and guidance of worldly
men.   Even the spiritual advisers they seek will be persons versed
in Vedic ritualism or occult practices which promise fulfilment of
desires here and intense sense enjoyments in heavens hereafter.
Vedic ritualism, based on the Vedic Mantras and Brahmana texts,
are described here as 'the Lord's cord of words' for binding Jivas
to worldliness. In modern times, too, we find the same tendency
for worldliness to masquerade under pseudo-spiritual garbs. The
only difference is that occultism has taken the place of ritualism.
Occultists and miracle mongers offer themselves as spiritual
Masters, and worldly minded men find in them congenial spirits
for seeking guidance for the fulfilment of their worldly needs
through occult methods.   This is an absolute erosion of spiritual
values. Occult powers are as irrelevant to spiritual competency as
possession of wealth or political power.

Prahlada on the need of cultivating devotion from early life :

कौमार आचरेत्प्राज्ञो धर्मान् भागवतानिह ।
दुर्लभं मानुषं जन्म तदप्यध्रुवमर्थदम् ॥

(51) Wise people should cultivate the devotional mode of
life from boyhood itself.   For, human birth, in which alone God-
realisation - the supreme end of man's existence—can be had, is
rare and difficult to get; and besides life is short and precarious.

*Prahlada on the ease and naturalness of the practice of
Bhakti :*

न ह्यच्युतं प्रीणयतो ब्रह्वायासोऽसुरात्मजाः ।
आत्मत्वात्सर्वभूतानां सिद्धत्वादिह सर्वतः ॥५२॥

कोऽतिप्रयासोऽसुरबालका हरे-रुपासने स्वे हृदि छिद्रवत्सतः ।
खख्यात्मनः सख्युरशेषदेहिनां सामान्यतः किं विषयोपपादनैः ॥५३॥

(52-53) It is not difficult to please Achyuta (the Immutable
One). He is the innermost self of all beings and is therefore
close to everyone. He is also easy to propitiate, and therefore
attainable to anyone, anywhere. O Children! there is no difficulty in practising devotion to Sri Hari, as He infills the hearts
of one and all like the Akasa (sky). He is the soul of one's soul
and He is the friend of all beings. Of what avail is it to leave
Him and go after sense-enjoyments, which even brute creations
can have?   (7.6.19; 7.7.38)

Prahlada speaks of Bhakti as the highest value.

रायः कलत्रं पशवः सुतादयो गृहा मही कुञ्जरकोशभूतयः ।
सर्वेंऽर्थकामाः क्षणभङ्गुरायुषः कुर्वन्ति मर्त्यस्य कियत् प्रियं चलाः ॥

एवं हि लोकाः क्रतुभिः कृता अमी क्षयिष्णवः साऽतिशया न निर्मलाः ।
तस्माददृष्टश्रुतदूषणं परं भक्त्यैकयेशं भजतात्मलब्धये ॥ ५५ ॥

(54-55) Money, wife, children, domestic animals, house
and other property, accumulated wealth consisting of lands,
elephants, treasury etc.,—what real joy can all such fleeting objects of enjoyment give to man in a life-time that is so short and
transitory? Like the enjoyments of this world, the joys obtaina-
ble in the heavenly regions through the performance of desire-
prompted Vedic rituals (Kamyakarmas) are also temporary,
impure and variable. Therefore, in loving adoration, you worship
the Lord, the Supreme Being, the One unaffected by decay or any
blemish, for the attainment of the highest spiritual fulfilment.
                                                  (7.7.39-40)

Prahlada advocating devotion excluding all other interests :

तस्मादर्थाश्च कामाश्च धर्माश्च यदपाश्रयाः ।
भजता-नीहयात्मान-मनीहं हरिमीश्वरम् ॥ ५६ ॥

(56) Therefore worship Sri Hari, the Supreme Being, who is
above all wants, ridding yourself first of all worldly desires.
Attainment of Dharma (virtue), Artha (wealth) and Kama
(pleasure), are dependent on His will.   (7.7.18)

Note : The idea is that on Him who loves and adores Hari
without any selfish purpose, He may shower worldly fulfilment
also, though they are unsought.   A devotee should be resigned
enough to think that the Lord knows what is good for him.

The sole condition of Divine grace according to Prahlada :

नालं द्विजत्वं देवत्वमृषित्वं वाऽसुरात्मजाः ।
प्रीणनाय मुकुन्दस्य न वृत्तं न बहुज्ञता ॥५७॥
न दानं न तपो नेज्या न शौचं न व्रतानि च ।
प्रीयतेऽमलया भक्त्या हरिरन्यद्विडम्बनम् ॥

(57-58) Neither the status of a Brahmana, nor of a god,
nor of a Rishi ; neither good conduct, nor learning, nor charity,
nor mortification, nor sacrificial rites, nor purificatory observances, nor austere vows can please Sri Hari. He is satisfied only
with pure loving devotion. All other disciplines (mentioned above)
are but show or a mockery (if they are not accompanied by
devotion).   (7.7.51-52)

Prahlada illustrates the above truth with an example :

मन्ये धनाभिजनरूप-तपःश्रुतौज-स्तेजःप्रभाव-बलपौरुषबुद्धियोगाः ।
नाराधनाय हि भवन्ति परस्य पुंसो भक्त्या तुतोष भगवान् गजयूथपाय

(59) Wealth, high birth, beauty, austerity, learning, energy,
impressive personality, power, strength, manliness, intelligence,
Yoga practice—none of these, I deem, is sufficient qualification to
worship Sri Hari and win His grace. (Loving devotion alone gives
that competence); for, the Lord was pleased with Gajendra, the
elephant chief, who had no qualification other than devotion.
                                                         (7.9.9)

Note: The reference is to the episode called Gajendra-moksha in 8th Canto of the *Bhagavata*. A pious king was cursed by a sage for some misdeed to become an elephant. Similarly there was a Gandharva cursed to become a crocodile. As the leader of the elephant herd, the king under curse entered the lake inhabited by the crocodile-become Gandharva. The elephant king was caught by the crocodile and there was a very long struggle, at the end of which the former was about to be dragged down and killed by his opponent. The elephant got the memory of his devotional past and called upon Lord Mahavishnu with all the intensity of his soul as Saranagata (one who has taken complete and unreserved shelter under the Lord). Lord Vishnu came to the scene, cut off the head of the crocodile with his Chakra, and liberated the elephant as also the crocodile from their animal bodies and gave them oneness with His spirit.

If the Lord blessed Gajendra because he was His devotee, is He not showing partiality? This objection is answered in the following verse of Prahlada :

चित्रं तवेहितमहोऽमितयोगमाया-लीलाविसृष्ट-भुवनस्य विशारदस्य
सर्वात्मनः समदृशोऽविषमस्वभावो भक्तप्रियो यदसि कल्पतरुस्वभावः

(60) O Lord, wonderful are Thy deeds! As a mere play Thou hast manifested the whole universe with the inconceivable power of Thy Yoga Maya. And Thou art all-knowing, and Thou residest in everything as its soul, and all beings are alike to Thee. Yet it looks as if Thou art partial in being specially fond of Thy devotees. This, however, is not due to partiality, but because Thou art of the nature of the Kalpataru, the heavenly wish-yielding tree.   (8.23.8)

Note : The Kalpataru grants the wishes of those who approach it and not of those who fail to do so. In this we cannot attribute partiality to the Kalpataru. Even so God blesses all who approach Him and surrender to him. If man fails to, do so and to get His blessings, the blame should go to man and not to God.

Sri Suka on how God is fond of loving devotion :

स्वमातुः स्विन्नगात्राया विस्त्रस्तकवरस्त्रजः ।
दृष्ट्वा परिश्रमं कृष्णः कृपयासीत्स्वबन्धने ॥

एवं संदर्शिता ह्यङ्ग हरिणा भक्तवश्यता ।
स्ववशेनापि कृष्णेन यस्येदं सेश्वरं वशे ॥

नेमं विरिञ्चो न भवो न श्रीरप्यङ्गसंश्रया ।
प्रसादं लेभिरे गोपी यत्तत्प्राप विमुक्तिदात् ॥

नायं सुखापो भगवान् देहिनां गोपिकासुतः ।
ज्ञानिनां चात्मभूतानां यथा भक्तिमतामिह ॥

(61–64) Seeing His mother fatigued with exertion—her hair dishevelled and the floral decorations thereon loosened – Krishna, out of compassion for her, acquiesced in being bound by her with rope. Thus did Hari show how He—the Lord and controller of everything—allows Himself to be subjugated by a devotee. Neither Brahma, nor Siva, nor Sri Devi, who is always associated with the Lord, has been the recipient of such great favour from Him who is the bestower of Mukti, as Yasoda was. Neither philosophers nor contemplatives can attain to the Lord with as much ease as those who are endowed with loving devotion.
(10.9.18-21)

Note : The reference is to an incident in the life of Sri Krishna. As a punishment for the naughtiness of child Krishna, His mother, Yasoda, wanted to tie Him up to a wooden mortar. As she tried to tie Him, the rope she had taken was found to be not of sufficient length, and she got more and more of the rope available nearby, but still the length was found insufficient. She was then at her wit's end and felt exhausted. So Krishna, taking pity on her, submitted Himself to be tied. This is symbolically taken as an illustration of how the Lord subordinates Himself to the devotee in pure personal devotion known as Priti (See Introd.)

Brahmā on devotion as the royal road to the Lord:

श्रेयःसृतिं भक्तिमुदस्य ते विभो क्लिश्यन्ति ये केवलबोधसिद्धये ।
तेषामसौ क्लेशल एव शिष्यते नान्यद्यथा स्थूलतुषावघातिनाम् ॥
पुरेह भूमन् बहवोऽपि योगिन-स्तदर्पितेहा निजकर्मलब्धया ।
विबुध्य भक्त्यैव कथोपनीतया प्रपेदिरेऽञ्जोऽच्युत ते गतिं पराम् ॥

(65-66)   O Lord! Those who abandon the path of pure devotion to Thee, which is the source of all spiritual upliftment, and struggle (through the path of discrimination) for the attainment of unmodified consciousness—their gain is only the pain of thankless labour and nothing else. For they are like persons milling mere husk or chaff that has no grain in it. O Undecaying One, many a Yogi in the past (finding that the discipline of Yoga failed to give him Ananda or spiritual joy) dedicated all his practices to Thee, and by virtue of his past good deeds and by contemplation on Thy glories and attributes, attained pure devotion and, through that, illumination and Thy highest State.   (10.14.4-5)

Uddhava complimenting Nanda for his loving devotion:

तस्मिन् भवन्तावखिलात्महेतौ नारायणे कारणमर्त्यमूर्तौ ।
भावं विधत्तां नितरां महात्मन् किं वावशिष्टं युवयोस्तु कृत्यम् ॥

(67)   O great ones! You two (Nanda and Yasoda, the father and mother of Krishna) are established in the attitude of parental love (Vatsalya-bhava) towards Sri Krishna who is none other than the human embodiment of Narayana, the soul and source of all beings. Having therefore reached life's fulfilment, what other duty have you got to perform?   (10.46.33)

Uddhava on how Bhakti is generated :

दानव्रततपोहोम-जपस्वाध्यायसंयमैः ।
श्रेयोभिर्विविधैश्चान्यैः कृष्णे भक्तिर्हि साध्यते ॥

(68)   Charitable gifts, vows, austerity, worship through divine symbols like fire, repetition of divine names (Japa), scriptu-

ral study, concentration and several such spiritually uplifting
disciplines generate loving devotion to Sri Krishna.   (10.47.24)

*Uddhava's panegyric on tl.e devotion of the Gopis, in whom
the highest form of loving devotion was manifested by the Lord's
grace, even though they had not fulfilled all the above conditions :*

क्वेमाः स्त्रियो वनचरीर्व्यभिचारदुष्टाः
    कृष्णे क्व चैष परमात्मनि रूढभावः ।
नन्वीश्वरोऽनुभजतोऽविदुषोऽपिसाक्षा-
    च्छ्रेयस्तनोत्यगदराज इवोपयुक्तः ॥
नायं श्रियोऽङ्ग उ नितान्तरतेः प्रसादः
    स्वर्योषिता नलिनगंधरुचां कुतोऽन्याः ।
रासोत्सवेऽस्य भुजदण्डगृहीतकंठ-
    लब्धाशिषां य उदगाद्व्रजवल्लवीनाम् ॥
आसामहो चरणरेणुजुषामहं स्यां
    वृन्दावने किमपि गुल्मलतौषधीनाम् ।
या दुस्त्यजं स्वजनमार्यपथं च हित्वा
    भेजुर्मुकुन्दपदवीं श्रुतिभिर्विमृग्याम् ॥

(69-71) How low is the condition of these cowherdesses
(Gopikas) who belong to a group of nomads going from forest to
forest in search of pastures and who are corrupted by loose sex-
relationship prevalent in their society! And how inconceivably
distant from that state is this deep-seated and powerful longing of
the soul for the Supreme Lord Sri Krishna (as we see manifested
in them)! It appears that just as an efficacious medicine cures a
person even if he does not know its value, the Lord also bestows
the Supreme Good on the devotee who loves and serves Him heart
and soul, even though the devotee is uncultured (and is not therefore aware of His greatness and majesty). Neither the heavenly
damsels nor even Sri Devi, who is ever engrossed in Him, got the
blessings of the Lord to the same extent as did these Gopikas of

Vraja who had the rare good fortune to have Sri Krishna rest His arms on their shoulders in the Rasa dance. What then to speak of other devotees! How fortunate would I be to become a grove, a creeper, or a plant in Vrindavana in order to be covered with the dust of the feet of these Gopikas who abandoned their relatives and virtuous conduct as understood in the world, and sought after the feet of Sri Krishna, the quest of even the Vedas! (10.47.59-61)

Note : There is an implication in this verse that the Gopikas did not know Sri Krishna to be Iswara and loved Him as an earthly lover, and yet attained the highest state by virtue of Krishna's transforming power. This is compared to the curative power of a medicine which works even on one who knows nothing about its curative value. This is no doubt an acknowledgement of the redeeming holiness of Sri Krishna. But the view of standard texts on Bhakti like *Narada Bhakti Sutra*, and even of the *Bhagavata* itself as expressed in other contexts in the text, is that the Gopikas had an awareness of Krishna's transcendental nature as Iswara, though it was also mixed up with the attitude towards an earthly lover. What happens in Prema Bhakti of the type represented in the *Bhagavata* is that in addition to a sense of Divine Majesty, the devotee is aware of an intimate personal love for the Lord analogous to human affection for the near and dear ones, because the devotee feels that the Lord is 'one's own'. This sense of closeness and oneness counter-balances the feeling of distance which the sense of Divine Majesty generates. The depiction of Divine love in the *Bhagavata* is noteworthy for the way in which the sense of God as power and the sense of Him as love are harmoniously blended. See Introduction.

Yudhishthira on how God's impartiality is compatible with grace :

न ब्रह्मणः स्वपरभेदमतिस्तव स्यात्
सर्वात्मनः समदृशः स्वसुखानुभूतेः ।
संसेवतां सुरतरोरिव ते प्रसादः
सेवानुरूपमुदयो न विपर्ययोऽत्र ॥

(72) Thou makest no difference between people, looking
upon some as Thy own and on others as aliens. For Thou art
Brahman, the all-inclusive Being, the Soul of all, equal-sighted
and established in Thy own bliss. As with the heavenly tree (the
Kalpataru), Thy blessings fall on all who resort to Thee (but not
on those who persist in not doing so). Rewards are according to
service, not otherwise.   (10.72.6)

Note : The idea is that God is not partial to any one. It is
open to any one to resort to Him. Some do so, and some do not.
If man fails to do so, it is not the fault of the Lord.

Sri Krishna on the potency of pure devotion with no other aid :

मचि भक्तिर्हि भूताना-ममृतत्वाय कल्पते ।
दिष्ट्या यदासीन्मत्स्नेहो भवतीनां मदापनः ॥

(73) Loving devotion to Me enables all beings to attain to
Immortality (Moksha). It is therefore fortunate that you have that
type of devotion leading to Me.   (10.82.45)

*Besides, being a self-sufficient path for salvation, Bhakti is
free from all dangers. This is stated in the following words of
Kavi (one of the Nava-Yogis), giving the quintessence of the Bhagavata Dharma :*

ये वै भागवता प्रोक्ता उपाया ह्यात्मलब्धये ।
अञ्जः पुंसामविदुषां विद्धि भागवतान्हि तान् ॥
यानास्थाय नरो राजन्न प्रमाद्येत कर्हिचित् ।
धावन्निमील्य वा नेत्रे न स्खलेन्न पतेदिह ॥
कायेन वाचा मनसेन्द्रियैर्वा बुद्ध्यात्मनाऽवा-नुसृतस्वभावात् ।
करोति यद्यत्सकलं परस्मै नारायणायेति समर्पयेत्तत् ॥७६॥

(74-76) For aspirants who are not learned (in the Vedas
and other scriptures), the Lord has given the Bhagavata Dharma
(the path of devotion) as an easy way for attaining to Him. A
person following this path never sustains any spiritual fall. Even

if he runs with eyes closed, his feet do not slip and he himself does
not topple down.   Whatever a devotee does with his body, mind,
senses, intellect or spirit—not necessarily scripture-ordained
duties but all activities natural to him—let him consecrate it all
by making an offering of it unto Narayana.   (11.2.34—36)

Prabuddha's statement on the same subject :

इष्टं दत्तं तपो जप्तं वृत्तं यच्चात्मनः प्रियम् ।
दारान् गृहान्सुतान् प्राणान्यत्परस्मै निवेदनम् ॥

(77)   One should give as offering unto the Supreme Being all
one's sacrifices, charities, austerity, Japa and other activities, as
also objects dear to one in life like wife, children, properties and
even life.   (11.3.28)

Kavi on devotion as the means to overcome fear :

भयं द्वितीयाभिनिवेशतः स्यादीशादपेतस्य विपर्ययोऽस्मृतिः ।
तन्माययातो बुध आभजेत्तं भक्त्यैकयेशं गुरुदेवतात्मा ॥

(78)   Those who are averse to the Lord are overpowered by
His Maya (power of ignorance), and consequently they forget
their own nature as spirit and think of themselves as bodies.
Endowed with body-consciousness, they see duality in the shape
of forces opposed to them, and become subject to the fear of destruction. Therefore a man should always serve with single-hearted
and loving devotion, the Supreme Lord who is at once the Teacher
(Guru), the Deity (Devata) and the Self—the Atman who is the
Soul of one's soul.   (11.2-37)

Note: It is taught here that we are in ignorance because of
the Lord's Maya, which we all feel is not within our power or
control. It is stated in the Gita: 'My Maya (creative power),
consisting of the three Gunas, is difficult to overcome. Those who
take shelter in Me with loving devotion overcome it.' So we must
have God's grace if we are to get over Maya and be freed from
the fears and misery arising from ignorance. Grace is bestowed
on one who loves the Lord and resigns oneself to Him; and God

can be loved, because He is the Soul of our souls and not a
stranger. If He were not so, love would have been impossible. As
the Teacher, He comes to instruct us in the path of devotion, and
as the Deity, He enables us to adore Him and to strengthen our
love and devotion to Him. Thus it is maintained that the path
of devotion is sufficient in itself to help man to attain the *summum
bonum*.

Obstacles to devotion in the words of Kama Deva :

त्वां सेवतां सुरकृता बहवोऽन्तरायाः
खौको विलंघ्यपरमं व्रजतां पदं ते ।
नान्यस्य बर्हिषि बलीन् ददतः खभागान्
धत्ते पदं त्वमविता यदि विघ्नमूर्ध्नि ॥

(79) Those devotees of Thine who seek Thy Divine State
meet with many obstructions caused by Devas, who know that
they would be surpassing them and their heavenly regions in
attaining Thy State. But those who give the Devas the offerings
due to them through fire-sacrifices do not meet with such obstacles. Thy devotees, who have Thee as their protector, however
surmount all such obstacles (in the end).   (11.4.10)

Note : The Devas always want men to be their votaries, so
that they may receive the sacrificial offerings. When a devotee
attains to Mukti, the Devas stand to lose these offerings. It is
said that out of this fear of a possible loss to themselves as also
out of jealousy, they obstruct spiritual aspirants and prevent
their higher development by placing temptations before them and
in many other ways. It is, however, maintained here that true
devotees always overcome such obstacles by the Lord's grace,
which always protects them from downfall. From a practical
point of view, we find that these Devas are none other than one's
own nearest kith and kin who often obstruct aspirants in their
spiritual pursuit, for fear of losing the worldly advantages they
expect from them.

Chamasa on the value of dedicated work :

मुखबाहूरुपादेभ्यः पुरुषस्याश्रमैः सह ।
चत्वारो जज्ञिरे वर्णा गुणैर्विप्रादयः पृथक् ॥
य एवं पुरुषं साक्षादात्मप्रभवमीश्वरम् ।
न भजन्त्यवजानन्ति स्थानभ्रष्टाः पतन्त्यधः ॥

(80-81) The four Varnas beginning with Brahmana and the four Ashramas (stages of life) pertaining to them have sprung from the face, arms, thighs and feet of the Supreme Being (the Virat Purusha). This division of the Varnas is based on qualities. Those who do not adore the Supreme Being, their Source, but disregard Him (by failing to do their respective duties as offerings unto Him and to practise devotion in other ways), go down in the scale of evolution.   (11.5.2—3)

Pingala on the supremacy of devotion in Kali Yuga :

घोरे कलियुगे प्राप्ते सर्वधर्मविवर्जिते ।
वासुदेवपरा मर्त्यास्ते कृतार्था न संशयः ॥
संसारकूपे पतितं विषयैर्मुषितेक्षणम् ।
ग्रस्तं कालाहिनात्मानं कोऽन्यस्त्रातुमिहेश्वरः ॥

(82-83) In this degenerate age of Kali, when all religious observances and ethical conduct have disappeared from society, those who are whole-heartedly devoted to Vasudeva will certainly attain the goal of life (Moksha). Who else except Vasudeva, the Supreme Lord, can save the Jivas who have fallen into the well of Samsara, with their eye of discrimination blinded by hankering for sense objects and with the poisonous serpent of Time biting them?   (11.8.41—42)

Krishna on the power of devotion to save even the fallen ones:

बाध्यमानोऽपि मद्भक्तो विषयैरजितेन्द्रियः ।
प्रायः प्रगल्भया भक्त्या विषयैर्नाभिभूयते ॥

8

(84) Even if a devotee of mine, who has not obtained mastery of the senses, happens to be overcome by them, he is rescued from enslavement to them, in the course of time while his devotion becomes mature and strong.   (11.14.18)

The above truth illustrated by Pururavas from his own case :

पुंश्चल्याप्रहृतं चित्तं कोऽन्यो मोचयितुं क्षमः ।
आत्मारामेश्वरमृते भगवन्तमधोक्षजम् ॥

(85) Who else but Vishnu, the Supreme Being, the Self-satisfied, the Lord of all and the Master of the senses, could have saved my mind from the seductive attractions of a harlot (Urvasi), to which it had succumbed?   (11.26.15)

Sri Krishna on devotion as a means to attain Brahman :

भक्त्योद्धवानपायिन्या सर्वलोकमहेश्वरम् ।
सर्वोत्पत्त्यप्ययं ब्रह्म कारणं मोपयाति सः ॥

(86) By means of loving devotion, which is constant and deep-rooted, man attains to Me, the Supreme Master of all the worlds, the First Cause and Brahman, in whom creation, preservation and destruction of the worlds take place.   (11.18.45)

Sri Krishna on Bhakti as the highest purifying agent :

यथाग्निः सुसमृद्धार्चिः करोत्येधांसि भस्मसात् ।
तथा मद्विषया भक्तिरुद्धवैनांसि कृत्स्नशः ॥
न साधयति मां योगो न सांख्यं धर्म उद्धव ।
न स्वाध्यायस्तपस्त्यागो यथा भक्तिर्ममोर्जिता ॥
भक्त्याहमेकया ग्राह्यः श्रद्धयात्मा प्रियः सताम् ।
भक्तिः पुनाति मन्निष्ठा श्वपाकानपि संभवात् ॥

(87-89) Just as the flames of blazing fire burn up all the fuel, even so devotion to Me (Sri Krishna) destroys all sins. Neither Yoga, nor Samkhya, nor Dharma, nor scriptural study, nor austerity, nor renunciation can attract and dominate Me as deep-rooted devotion can. With the help of unswerving devotion coupled with earnest faith, holy men are able to attain to Me, who am as dear to them as their very soul. Deep-rooted devotion to Me purifies even one who is a born sinner.   (11.14.19—21)

Sri Krishna on how, without devotion, other disciplines, though well-pursued, are of little use :

धर्मः सत्यदयोपेतो विद्या वा तपसान्विता ।
मद्भक्त्यापेतमात्मानं न सम्यक् प्रपुनाति हि ॥
कथं विना रोमहर्षं द्रवता चेतसा विना ।
विनाऽनंदाश्रुकलया शुध्येद्भक्त्या विनाऽशयः ॥
वाग्गद्गदा द्रवते यस्य चित्तं हसत्यभीक्ष्णं रुदति क्वचिच्च ।
विलज्ज उद्गायति नृत्यते च मद्भक्तियुक्तो भुवनं पुनाति ॥

(90-92) A Dharma (religious discipline), though inculcating truth, compassion and meditation accompanied with austerity, will not purify the mind, if devoid of devotion. How can the mind be purified without intense devotion expressing itself as horripilation in the body, as melting of the mind with the sentiment of love, and as tears of joy flowing from the eyes? Whose words get choked, whose mind gets melted, who laughs now and next weeps, who dances singing at the top of his voice— all out of intense devotion,—such a devotee of Mine verily purifies the world !   (11.14.22—24)

Note : The first of these verses is a criticism of philosophies like Buddhism and Samkhya which have no place for God, and of certain schools of Advaita in which God has only a nominal place.

How Bhakti gives also Self-knowledge, is described in the words of Sri Krishna :

यथाग्निना हेम मलं जहाति ध्मातं पुनः स्वं भजते च रूपम् ।
आत्मा तु कर्मानुशयं विधूय मद्भक्तियोगेन भजत्यथो माम् ॥

(93)   Just as gold, molten in fire, is rid of dross and assumes its own lustrous form, so by communion through Bhakti (devotion) the Atman attains to Me, being freed from all impurities arising from attachments born of selfish actions.   (11.14.25)

Markandeya on the universal ideal of devotion :

वरमेकं वृणेऽथापि पूर्णात्कामाभिवर्षणात् ।
भगवत्युत्तमा भक्तिस्तत्परेषु तथा त्वयि ॥

(94)   I seek but one boon of Thee who, though Thyself without any desire, bestowest on all the boons that they pray for. May I have devotion to the Supreme Being (Vishnu), to Thy devotees, and to Thee (Siva or one's Ishta Devata).   (12.10.34)

Note :   The prayer is addressed to Siva, and so a distinction is made between 'Thee' and the Supreme Being (here identified with Vishnu). The *Bhagavata* being a Vaishnava text, the Supreme Being for it is Vishnu, and Siva is His manifestation. So freed from the sectarian context, 'Thee' can be taken to mean the Ishta Devata, the Chosen Ideal, who is the manifestation of the Supreme Being.

Devas on why greater importance should be given to Bhakti than to other disciplines :

तथाऽपरे चात्मसमाधियोग-बलेन जित्वा प्रकृतिं बलिष्ठाम् ।
त्वामेव धीराः पुरुषा विशन्ति तेषां श्रमः स्यान्न तु सेवया ते ॥

(95)   There are other sages (followers of the path of Raja Yoga) who control the powerful natural forces through the psychic power generated by the concentration of the mind. They also come to Thee. But their path is full of toil and difficulties (arising from external obstacles and their own weakness), but the path of Thy service (Bhakti Yoga) is free from these.   (3.5.46)

Brahma on why people do not adopt Bhakti in spite of its being an easy path :

अह्न्याप्तार्तकरणा निशि निःश्यना नानामनोरथधिया क्षणभग्ननिद्राः
देवाहृताथैरचना मुनयोऽपि देव युष्मत्प्रसंगविमुखा इह संसरन्ति ॥

(96) Those who are indisposed to contemplate on Thy deeds
and glories are bound to go round and round the cycle of births
and deaths, even if they are learned in philosophies and other
branches of knowledge. For, toiling all through day, they tire
themselves out; at night the agitation of mind caused by various
desires within, disturbs their sleep; and the failure of their worldly
plans and ambitions due to the stroke of destiny, engulfs them in
disappointment. (Thus they will have neither the time nor the inclination to take to the path of devotion.)   (3.9.10)

*Brahma on the nature of Maya, the deluding power of the
Lord :*

येऽभ्यर्थिंगमपि च नो नृगतिं प्रपन्ना
ज्ञानं च तत्त्वविषयं सह धर्म यत्र ।
नाराधनं भगवतो वितरन्त्यमुष्य
संमोहिता विततया बत मायया ते ॥

(97) Birth as a human being is sought after even by us (the
gods). For, in the human birth, one can attain the Knowledge of
spiritual truth and Virtue (Jnana and Dharma). Those who,
having attained to such birth, fail to adore the Lord—they indeed
are persons overpowered by Maya, the beginningless deluding
power of the Lord. (3.15:24)

Brahma's view that devotion overcomes Maya :

विश्वस्य यः स्थितिलयोद्भवहेतुराद्यो
योगेश्वरैरपि दुरत्यययोगमायः ।
क्षेमं विधास्यति स नो भगवांस्त्र्यधीशः
तत्रास्मदीय विमृशेन कियानिहार्थः ॥

(98) Why should we at all worry ourselves with thoughts
of our welfare when we know for certain that we are under the

protection of a Supreme Being—the Master of the three Gunas
and the three aspects of Time—who is the First Cause, the Power
that creates, preserves and dissolves the Universe, and who is
the Controller of Yoga Maya (Cosmic Ignorance) which even the
greatest of Yogis find difficult to overcome.   (3.16.37)

Note : The idea is that if the obstructing power of Maya is
great, the goodness and grace of God are of a much greater
magnitude. So a man who has a settled and unwavering faith in
such a God, never worries about his future, spiritual and secular,
feeling sure that his welfare is assured. That is the characteristic of
one having genuine faith.

Narada on the topic of Divine Grace :

यदाऽयमनुगृह्णाति भगवानात्मभावितः ।
स जहाति मतिं लोके वेदे च परिनिछ्छिताम् ॥

(99) When the Lord bestows His Grace on a person devo-
tedly meditating on Him, that recipient of Divine Grace is freed
from all worldly attachments and adherence to ritualistic duties.
(4.29.46)

Narada on how the Lord is supremely fond of His devotees :

श्रियमनुचरतीं तदर्थिनश्च द्विपदपतीन्विबुधांश्च यः स्वपूर्णः ।
न भजति निजभृत्यवर्गतन्त्रः कथममुमुद्धिसृजेत्पुमान् कृतज्ञः ॥

(100) Neither His consort Sri, ever in association with Him,
nor the votaries like great kings and Devas receive His grace as
His humble servants, the devotees, do ; for He is self-fulfilled and
has nothing to get from anyone else. How can any man, aware of
His abounding grace, keep away from Him even for a while ?
(4.31.22)

Suka on how Bhakti is a higher value than Mukti :

राजन् पतिर्गुरुरलं भवता यदूनां
देवं प्रियः कुलपतिः क्व किंकरो वः ।
अस्त्वेवमंग भजतां भगवान्मुकुन्दो
मुक्तिं ददाति कर्हिचिन्न हि भक्तियोगम् ॥

(101) O King! Lord Krishna has been to you of the Pandu's race and to the Yadavas – master, respected teacher, deity for worship, leader, dear friend, and even a servant sometimes. Indeed, to those who worship Him, the Lord may grant Mukti (liberation), but rarely Bhakti (devotion).   (5,6,18)

Note: The idea is that the Lord subordinates Himself to those who have loving devotion, as He did to the Pandavas by becoming even their servant. Granting liberation does not entail such bondage on Him, and so He liberates Jivas, but hesitates to give them true devotion. This is a poetic and witty way of stating the Bhagavata doctrine of the supreme excellence of devotion. It is on this ground that Bhakti (in the sense of Priti) is considered the fifth Purushartha, higher than Moksha (liberation) even, by the Vaishnavas. See Introduction.

Suka on the excellences of the path of devotion :

सध्रीचीनो ह्ययं लोके पन्थाः क्षेमोऽकुतोभयः ।
सुशीलाः साधवो यत्र नारायणपरायणाः ॥

(102) The path of devotion is indeed excellent, because it contributes to well-being in every way and because it is free from fear of every kind. In this path are to be found innumerable devotees of Narayana who are full of benevolence and holiness.
                                                            (6.1.17)

Yama on the excellence of the path of devotion :

ते देवसिद्धपरिगीत-पवित्रगाथा ये साधवः समदृशो भगवत्प्रपन्नाः ।
तान्नोपसीदत हरेर्गदयाभिगुप्ता-न्नैषां वयं च न वयः प्रभवाम दण्डे ॥

(103) There are devotees whose holiness forms the subject-matter of the songs of gods and demi-gods, who look upon all beings alike, and who have surrendered themselves to Lord Narayana. Do not approach them. They are protected by the divine weapon of the Lord, and are beyond the controlling power of myself (Yama, the God of Death) and of Time.   (6.3.27)

Akrura on the impartiality of God:

न तस्य कश्चिद्दयितः सुहृत्तमो न वा प्रियो द्वेष्य उपेक्ष्य एव वा ।
तथापि भक्तान् भजते यथा तथा सुरद्रुमो यद्वदुपाश्रितोऽर्थदः ॥

(104) None is specially dear, nor friendly, nor inimical,
nor unacceptable to the Lord. If a devotee seeks Him, He blesses
him in a manner suited to his approach, just as the Kalpataru
(heavenly wish-granting tree) confers the desired objects on one
resorting to it. (10.38.22)

Note: God is open to all for adoration. If man fails to take
advantage of it, and consequently fails to obtain His grace, it is
man's fault and not God's.

Sri Krishna on Bhakti as a self-sufficient path:

केवलेन हि भावेन गोप्यो गावो नगा मृगाः ।
येऽन्ये मूढधियो नागाः सिद्धा मामीयुरंजसा ॥

(105) By pure devotion alone the Gopis of Vrindavan attained to Me and reached the *summum bonum* of life. So did even
unintelligent creatures like cows, elephants and snakes. (11.12.8)

Note: The reference is to the cows of Vrindavan, to the
snake Kaliya and to the elephant Gajendra. Though they were
brute creations, Bhakti was generated in them by the Lord's
grace, and they gained liberation. Development of the highest
form of devotion in such apparently unqualified persons is technically called in Vaishnava literature as Pushti—a special growth
due to the influx of Poshana, the spiritual nutrient of Divine
Grace.

Narada on Bhakti being essential for success in all Yogas:

भजन्ति ये विष्णुमनन्यचेतस्-स्तथैव तत्कर्मपरायणा नराः ।
विनष्टरागादि-विमत्सरा-नरा-स्तरन्ति संसार-समुद्रमाश्रमम् ॥
नैष्कर्म्यम-प्यच्युतभाववर्जितं न शोभते ज्ञानमलं निरञ्जनम् ।
कुतः पुनः शश्वदभद्रमीश्वरे न चार्पितं कर्म यदप्यकारणम् ॥

(106-107) Those who devote themselves whole-heartedly to Vishnu and engage themselves entirely in works pertaining to Him, overcome attachments and passions, and easily cross over the ocean of Samsara (even without the help of Sannyasa and Yogic practices). Even the discipline of knowledge, though attended with abstinence from work and freedom from passions, does not fructify in illumination, if it is devoid of devotion to the Supreme Being. That being so, what spiritual potency can be expected in works with a natural element of evil in them, even when performed without desires, unless they are dedicated to the Lord in a spirit of devotion?   (1.5.12)

Note : There are certain types of Advaitic thinkers who rely only on their discriminative power and mastery over the senses as sufficient to attain the knowledge of the unity of the Atman with Brahman. They relegate Iswara (God) to the world of phenomenal appearances, and give a place for the practice of devotion only at an intermediary stage as a means for the purification of the mind and making it fit to be engaged in the discipline of knowledge. Dedicated work as offering to God is also included in early Bhakti discipline. But the *Bhagavata* is throughly opposed to this down-grading of Bhakti, in spite of its metaphysical predilection for non-dualism. It does not tolerate the view that Bhagavan is only a phenomenal appearance. He is the ultimate Reality also. The Jiva finds himself in ignorance not out of his own will, but owing to a power beyond his control. Whatever he may do by his individual power, he cannot root out the force that holds him down. His efforts are only like cutting off the branches and trunk of a tree without removing its roots, because they are beyond his power to reach. From the roots, shoots will again come. His ignorance is due to Maya, the Cosmic Power of the Lord. It is only when the grace of the Lord is bestowed on him, that the power of Maya is neutralised, and it is only through self-surrender and loving devotion that the Jiva comes within the ambit of the Lord's grace. Hence the path of devotion is the one royal road to the spiritual *summum bonum*. The discipline of knowledge is only at best a way that brings certain types of aspirants to this royal

road. It is not, however, essential. Without the influence of Bhakti,
the Jnana discipline will be sterile and self-defeating. As for
Karma, it is only a part of the Bhakti discipline. Even unselfish
action without devotional dedication is not approved here, because
every Karma has got some inherent defect or other. In the words
of the Gita, all action is covered with some evil just as fire is
enveloped by smoke. It is only work done in dedication to the
Lord, as a part of the Bhakti discipline, that makes for real spiritual uplift of man. Thus in the view of the *Bhagavata*, Bhakti is
supreme, both as means and as end, in the spiritual life of man.

Suta on the manifestation of devotion in knowing ones, which
justifies the claim that Bhakti is the fifth Purushartha :

आत्मारामाश्च मुनयो निर्ग्रन्था अप्युरुक्रमे ।
कुर्वन्त्यहैतुकीं भक्तिमित्थं भूतगुणो हरिः ॥

(108) Sages who have been rid of the knots of the heart like
egoism and the rest, and whose minds are always engrossed in the
bliss of the Self, are none the less seen to have motiveless devotion to the Lord. So glorious are Sri Hari's excellences !

(1.7.10)

Vritra on the claim of Bhakti to be the fifth Purushartha :

न नाकपृष्ठं न च सार्वभौमं न पारमेष्ठ्यं न रसाधिपत्यम् ।
न योगसिद्धीरपुनर्भवं वा समञ्जस त्वा विरहय्य काङ्क्षे ॥

(109) I have no hankering after heavenly regions, or the
status of an emperor, or the position of Brahma, or lordship over
Rasatala and other regions, or the psychic powers of Yogis, or
even liberation, if through such attainments I am to be excluded
from Thee, Of Treasure House of all that is good and great !

(6.11.25)

Sri Krishna on the above topic, depicting Bhakti as the highest
value :

तस्मान्मद्भक्तियुक्तस्य योगिनो वै मदात्मनः ।
न ज्ञानं न च वैराग्यं प्रायः श्रेयो भविष्यति ॥

यत्कर्मभिर्यत्तपसा ज्ञानवैराग्यतश्च यत् ।
योगेन दानधर्मेण श्रेयोभिरितरैरपि ॥

सर्वं मद्भक्तियोगेन मद्भक्तो लभतेऽञ्जसा ।
स्वर्गापवर्गौ मद्धाम कथंचिद्यदि वाञ्छति ॥

न किंचित्साधवो धीरा भक्ता ह्येकान्तिनो मम ।
वाञ्छन्त्यपि मया दत्तं कैवल्यमपुनर्भवम् ॥

नैरपेक्ष्यं परं प्राहुः निःश्रेयसमनल्पकम् ।
तस्मान्निराशिषो भक्तिर्निरपेक्षस्य मे भवेत् ॥

न मय्येकान्तभक्तानां गुणदोषोद्भवा गुणाः ।
साधूनां समचित्तानां बुद्धेः परमुपेयुषाम् ॥

एवमेतन्मयादिष्टान् अनुतिष्ठन्ति ये पथः ।
क्षेमं विन्दन्ति मत्स्थानं यद्ब्रह्म परमं विदुः ॥

(110-116) Therefore an aspirant who has devotion to Me and has always his mind centred on Me attains to this highest spiritual realization by Bhakti alone, without any special effort to cultivate knowledge and renunciation, as these come to him naturally with the progress of devotion. Whatever can be attained through Vedic rituals, austerities, knowledge, dispassion, Yoga, charities and other spiritual disciplines—be that the abode of the gods, liberation, or the Vaikuntha (the Eternal Heaven of Vishnu) - all these can be attained by a votary of the path of devotion without any difficulty. But holy men of firm mind, who are endowed with unswerving devotion to Me, do not desire or accept even Moksha, the freedom from the cycle of births and deaths, even if I offer it to them. Nihsreyas (the Supreme Good), also called the highest and unlimited state of Beatitude, is described as a state without any desires. Therefore one who is desireless and without any prayers, attains to pure devotion for me. (In other words, pure and motiveless love of God is real Moksha, and it comes only to one who does not crave even for Moksha as an individual attainment and as freedom from personal sufferings.) Holy men, unswerving in their devotion to Me, even-minded in all situations, and established at a level higher than Buddhi, are not affected by merits and demerits arising from scriptural commandments and prohibitions. Those who follow this path propounded by Me (the path of devotion and self-surrender) attain to My state of Supreme Beatitude, which is also called Supreme Brahman.   (11.20.31–37)

Note : The *Bhagavata* doctrine that Bhakti is a self-sufficient spiritual path and a self-sufficient spiritual End (Purushartha), is firmly established in the above verses. Bhakti may be used as a means for gaining Mukti — freedom from Samsara or the cycle of transmigratory existence. Mukti is generally called the fourth Purushartha and Bhakti is usually included within its scope. But the *Bhagavata* differs from this view and considers Bhakti, understood as Priti, to be distinct from Mukti forming the fourth Purushartha. The Moksha idea is looked upon as a gospel of escapism, predominantly motivated by safety and security for oneself. It is a gospel of selfish salvation. So the true Bhakta does not care for salvation, and is ready to undergo any trials and tribulations to serve the Lord, whose love and service are an end in itself for him. For more detailed discussion, reference may be made to the Introduction.

STRAND 2
SĀDHU-SANGA OR HOLY COMPANY

Sectional Introduction: In the first section a general treatment of devotion and its unique value have been given. Here in the second section the most important condition for the generation of devotion, namely, association with holy personages, is discussed. According to the *Bhagavata*, association with holy men generates Sraddha (Faith) in spiritual matters. Sraddha induces one to practise spiritual disciplines and leads to Rati (attachment to Him and delight in His thought); and Rati matures into Bhakti (loving devotion for God)· Thus association with holy men is at the root of all spiritual development. The explanation of it is that it is only when a person finds God-love and its effect embodied in a living person that he will feel convinced of the reality and possibility of realisation of spiritual values, which were till then accepted only as conventional articles of faith. Only then will man exert himself steadily for the attainment of Bhakti. This change of outlook is what is described as generation of faith. From that all other higher developments follow; for, one who has faith in the real sense, as distinguished from mere belief, will actively strive for higher attainments. Now it must be made clear that it is not every one who wears the garb and emblems of holiness that the *Bhagavata* considers as capable of bringing about this conversion in others. It has in mind only the real Sadhu whose characteristics are described in verses 10–14 and 23-24 and 33-38 of this section. Other standard Bhakti texts like *Narada Bhakti Sutras* and *Sandilya Sutras* also are unanimous in accepting the value of Sadhu-sanga (association with holy men). Such association is, however, very difficult to get. In the absence of it, at least the earnest study of Bhakti literature like the *Bhagavata* or the *Gospel of Sri Ramakrishna* is essential.

Kapila on association with holy men as the source of Bhakti:

सतां प्रसङ्गान्मम वीर्यसंविदो भवन्ति हृत्कर्णरसायनाः कथाः ।
तज्जोषणादाश्वपवर्गवर्त्मनि श्रद्धा रतिर्भक्तिरनुक्रमिष्यति ॥

(1)   The conversations of holy men, proclaiming My glories and greatness, are sweet and ennobling both for the ear and the heart.   By listening to them man develops progressively faith in the path of Moksha (Sraddha), delight in God and spiritual matters (Rati), and deep devotion to the Lord (Bhakti).   (3.25.25)

Note: The genesis and progress of devotion are beautifully analysed and presented here.   The association with holy men and listening to their devotional talks generates the first stage of Bhakti, described here as Sraddha or Faith.   It is a state of mind in which the truths of religion are taken. very seriously and an effort is made to realise them in one's consciousness.   Such a person goes to an authentic teacher (Guru), takes initiation and practises spiritual disciplines.   Long practice of disciplines takes him to the stage of Rati, or delight in God.   This stage is distinguished by the fact that a person's mind begins to remain fixed in God even without practice of disciplines.   When Rati is deepened it is called Bhakti.   A more detailed treatment of this very important part of the teaching will be found in the Introduction.

The Divine announcement regarding Narada cited as an example of this :

सत्सेवयाऽदीर्घयापि जाता मयि दृढा मतिः ।
हित्वाऽवद्यमिमं लोकं गन्ता मज्जनतामसि ॥

(2)   Even with a short association with, and service of, holy men, your (Narada's) mind got fixed in Me.   And on abandoning your present body of impure origin, you will attain the status of one of My heavenly associates.   (1.6.24)

Note :   The great sage Narada was of lowly origin and had to work as a servant boy in his previous birth.   But he got the opportunity to serve very holy sages, and cultivated the spirit of devotion in their company.   He then took to a life of exclusive contemplation and devotion.   In the course of his austerities he got the Divine commandment that on casting off his present body, he would become an eternal servant of God, carrying the gospel of devotion far and wide.

Saunaka glorifies holy association as the greatest blessing :

तुलयाम लवेनापि न स्वर्गं नाऽपुनर्भवम् ।
भगवत्सङ्गिसङ्गस्य मर्त्यानां किमुताशिषः ॥

(3) We do not consider heaven or Moksha — not to speak of
any earthly felicity — as equal to even a brief period of association
with holy men.   (1.18.13)

The Rishis sing the praise of holy association :

यत्पादसंश्रयाः सूत मुनयः प्रशमायनाः ।
सद्यः पुनन्त्युपस्पृष्टाः स्वर्धुन्यापोऽनुसेवया ॥

(4) Holy men, who are resigned to the Lord and are over-
flowing with peace, purify those who go near them immediately,
while even the holy Ganga can do this only gradually, through the
daily ablutions in it.   (1.1.15)

Note : The heart of a holy man is the drawing room of the
Lord, says Sri Ramakrishna. God is manifest in holy personages
more than anywhere else and hence they sanctify the people who
contact them. The river Ganga is considered holy, because it is
believed to flow from the feet of Vishnu. Its purifying effect is
confined to people who have this faith, and the effect is felt only
gradually.

Suka on the unfailing efficiency of holy association :

नष्टप्रायेष्वभद्रेषु नित्यं भागवतसेवया ।
भगवत्युत्तमश्लोके भक्तिर्भवति नैष्ठिकी ॥

(5) When the sinful tendencies that obstruct the dawning of
devotion are eliminated by the constant service of holy men, there
arises firm and unswerving devotion to the Lord.   (1.2.18)

*Suta's words are cited to show how holy association elevates
even the low-born and the uncultured :*

अहो वयं जन्मभृतोऽद्य हास्म वृद्धानुवृत्त्यापि विलोमजाताः ।
दौष्कुल्यमाधिं विधुनोति शीघ्रं महत्तमाना-मभिधानयोगः ॥

(6) How wonderful is this! Though I was born in a low and
fallen family, my life has become fruitful today because of my
association with holy sages like you! For, conversation with such
great and holy personages quickly erases the stigma of low birth
and the sense of diffidence and worry arising from it.   (1.18.18)

Note : Suta, the narrator cf the *Bhagavata* and other
Puranas, belonged to a caste originating from a forbidden mixed
marriage. Though low-born, he was learned and devoted, and
so narrated the holy text to great sages. Here he pays compli-
ments to the sanctifying power of the holy men with whom he is
conversing.

Parikshit's words on the sanctifying influence of holy men :

येषां संस्मरणात्पुंसां सद्यः शुद्ध्यन्ति वै गृहाः ।
किं पुनर्दर्शनस्पर्श-पादशौचासनादिभिः ॥

(7) Even by the remembrance of holy men, the very houses
where they are remembered get purified. How much more sanctifying it will be if they are seen, contacted and served !   (1.19.33)

Vidura's words on the rarity of holy association :

दुरापा ह्यल्पतपसः सेवा वैकुण्ठवर्त्मसु ।
यत्रोपगीयते नित्यं देवदेवो जनार्दनः ॥
तत्सेवया भगवतः कूटस्थस्य मधुद्विषः ।
रतिरासो भवेत्तीव्रः पादयोर्व्यसनार्दनः ॥

(8-9) Holy men, who are always talking and singing about
the Lord, are men's guides to Vaikuntha, the Divine State beyond
sorrow and fear. Opportunities of serving them are difficult to
get, unless men have practised great austerities (for making them
worthy of it). By serving holy ones (and thereby hearing their

elevating spiritual talks and observing their pious mode of life)
one gets intense and abounding love for the Supreme Being—the
eternal and the changeless One – which erases ignorance, the
cause of all fear and sorrow.   (3.7.20,19)

Kapila on the characteristic of truly holy men :

प्रसंगमजरं पाशमात्मनः कवयो विदुः ।
स एव साधुषु कृतो मोक्षद्वारमपावृतम् ॥

तितिक्षवः कारुणिकाः सुहृदः सर्वदेहिनाम् ।
अजातशत्रवः शान्ताः साधवः साधुभूषणाः ॥

मय्यनन्येन भावेन भक्तिं कुर्वन्ति ये दृढाम् ।
मत्कृते त्यक्तकर्माण-स्त्यक्तस्वजनबान्धवाः ॥

मदाश्रयाः कथा मृष्टाः शृण्वन्ति कथयन्ति च ।
तपन्ति विविधास्तापा नैतान्मद्गतचेतसः ॥

त एते साधवः साध्वि सर्वसङ्गविवर्जिताः ।
सङ्गस्तेष्वथ ते प्रार्थ्यः सङ्गदोषहरा हि ते ॥

(10-14) Wise men say that intense attachment to objects is
a bondage for the soul. But when such attachment is felt for holy
men, it becomes an open gate to liberation. Holy men are persons
endowed with equanimity in all the ups and downs of life. They
are full of kindness and they are friendly to all beings. They
are serene in temperament, and they have no enemies. Goodness is
their only ornament. They practise unswerving devotion to Me,
without looking for any support other than Me. They consecrate
all their actions to Me, and they abandon all relatives and clansmen for my sake. They engage themselves in hearing of, and
discoursing on, My glories, attributes and actions which purify
all who hear them. Those who are devoted to Me are never
worried by the various ills of life. Persons who have abandoned
all worldly attachments are holy men. Association with them is
always desirable, because it helps one to liberate oneself from the
bondage of worldly attachments.   (3.25.20–24)

9

Dhruva on the sanctifying effect of holy company :

भक्ति मुहुः प्रवहतां त्वयि मे प्रसङ्गो भूयादनन्तमहता-ममलाश्रयानाम्
येनाञ्जसोल्बणमुरुव्यसनं भवाब्धिं नेष्ये भवद्गुणकथामृत-पानमत्तः
ते न स्मरन्त्यतितरां प्रियमीश मर्त्यं ये चान्वदः सुतसुहृद्गृहवित्तदाराः
ये त्वब्जनाभ भवदीयपदारविन्द-सौगन्ध्यलुब्धहृदयेषु कृतप्रसङ्गाः ॥

(15-16) O Infinite One, may I always have close association with Mahatmas of great holiness and purity, from whom the
stream of devotion is constantly flowing ! In their company I
shall be inebriated with divine love, hearing the recital of Thy
glory and majesty, and shall easily get across the turbulent ocean
of Samsara which is full of great sorrows and sufferings. O Lord,
those who keep company with Thy devotees, who have their minds
ever engrossed in inhaling the fragrance of Thy holy feet (like
bees inhaling that of flowers), get detached in mind from their
own dear bodies as also from all objects associated with them
like wife, children, friends, property etc.   (4.9.11 – 12)

*Emperor Prithu glorifies the sanctifying effect of holy
company :*

तेषामहं पादसरोजरेणुं आर्या वहेयाधिकिरीटमायुः ॥
यं नित्यदा विभ्रत आशु पापं नश्यत्यमुं सर्वगुणा भजन्ति ॥

(17) As long as I live, I shall bear the dust of the feet of
holy men on my crown; for the sins of those who do this every day
shall be washed off and all virtues shall take root in them.

(4.21.43)

Sanatkumara on the beneficial effect of holy company :

सङ्गमः खलु साधूनामुभयेषां च संमतः ।
यत्संभाषणसंप्रश्नः सर्वेषां वितनोति शम् ॥

(18) Meeting with holy men is joyous to both the parties
concerned. The questions put to them (at such meetings) and

their conversations by way of answers benefit all (who listen to
them).   (4 22.19)

Rudra teaches the Prachetas to pray for holy company :

अथानघाङ्घ्रेस्तव कीर्तितीर्थयो-रन्तर्बहिः स्नानविधूतपाप्मनाम् ।
भूतेष्वनुक्रोशसुसत्वशीलिनां स्यात्संगमोऽनुग्रह एव नस्तव ॥

(19) O Lord, Thou whose worshipful feet dispel the sins of
devotees ! May we have association with holy ones who have been
purified internally through contemplation on Thy attributes and
externally by bath in the holy Ganga (which has its source at Thy
feet),—holy ones in whom love of all beings, purity of mind and
virtuous qualities are present. This is the blessing we seek of
Thee.   (4.24.58)

The Prachetas describe the attractiveness of holy company :

यत्रेड्यन्ते कथा मृष्टास्तृष्णायाः प्रशमो यतः ।
निर्वैरं यत्र भूतेषु नोद्वेगो यत्र कश्चन ॥
यत्र नारायणः साक्षान्न्यासिनां परमा गतिः ।
प्रस्तूयते सत्कथासु मुक्तसंगः पुनः पुनः ॥
तेषां विचरतां पद्भ्यां तीर्थानां पावनेच्छया ।
भीतस्य किन्न रोचेत तावकानां समागमः ॥

(20–22) Holy men engage themselves always in the recital
of the Lord's sanctifying attributes. Their company effaces worldly desires, enmity to others, and restlessness of mind. In their
midst one always hears talks and hymns in praise of Narayana,
the resort of all men of renunciation, articulated with a mind free
from all worldly attachments. They go from one holy place to
another to sanctify those places. Who is there among men afflicted
with the world's woes that will not feel overjoyed by the company
of such devotees of the Lord !   (4.30.35—37)

*Sage Rishabha draws a contrast between the effects of holy and
evil company :*

महत्सेवां द्वारमाहुर्विमुक्ते-स्तमोद्वारं योषितां सङ्गिसङ्गम् ।
महान्तस्ते समचित्ताः प्रशान्ताः विमन्यवः सुहृदः साधवो ये ॥
ये वा मयीशे कृतसौहृदार्थाः जनेषु देहम्भरवार्तिकेषु ।
गृहेषु जायात्मजरातिमत्सु न प्रीतियुक्ता यावदर्थाश्च लोके ॥

(23-24)   It is said that association with holy men is the gate-
way to Moksha (liberation), even as the company of uxorious
persons is to spiritual darkness. Holy men are persons who are
even-minded, serene, free from anger, friendly to all, and good by
nature. They consider the cultivation of love for Me, the Lord
of all, to be the purpose of life. They entertain no liking for the
company of men who are interested only in catering to their own
physical needs or are always engrossed in their household affairs,
in wife, children and wealth. They are satisfied with such worldly
goods as are required for bare subsistence.   (5.5.2—3)

Sage Rishabha on who is one's real friend :

गुरुर्न स स्यात्स्वजनो न स स्या-त्पिता न स स्याज्जननी न सा स्यात् ।
दैवं न तत्स्यान्न पतिश्च स स्या-न्न मोचयेद्यः समुपेतमृत्युम् ॥

(25)   In the case of a person travelling in the path of death
(Samsara consisting of births and deaths), he alone deserves to be
called a friend and well-wisher who helps him out of that path.
Any one who does the contrary does not deserve to be called his
teacher if he be his teacher, his relative if he be related to him,
his father if he be his father, his mother if she be his mother,
his deity if he be his deity, and (in respect of a woman) her husband if he be her husband.   (5.5.18)

Note :   The implication is that only holy men are helpful
in the spiritual path, and therefore they are the only friends and
relatives to whom a devotee could look up to.

Prahlada's words on holy company :

मागारदारात्मजवित्तबन्धुषु संगो यदि स्यादभगवत्प्रियेषु नः ।
यः प्राणवृत्त्या परितुष्ट आत्मवान् सिध्यत्यदूरात् न तथेन्द्रियप्रियः ॥

(26) If we are to have attachment, let it be for the devotees of the Lord, and not for house, wife, children and wealth. He who is self-controlled and is satisfied with the bare requirements for the sustenance of life, attains to realisation quickly, but not those who are fond of sensuous indulgences. (5.18.10)

King Rahugana on the effect of holy company for even short duration :

अहो नृजन्माखिलजन्मशोभनं किं जन्ममिस्त्वप्यरैरप्यमुष्मिन् ।
न यद्धृषीकेशयशः कृतात्मनां महात्मनां वः प्रचुरः समागमः ॥
नैवाङ्गृतं त्वच्चरणाब्जरेणुभिः हतांहसो भक्तिरधोक्षजेऽमला ।
मौहूर्तिकादस्य समागमान्मे दुस्तर्कमूलोऽपगतोऽविवेकः ॥

(27-28) Indeed human birth is the most excellent birth. Embodiment in heavenly rigions is futile, for there association with holy men, whose minds have been purified by the practice of devotion to God, is hard to get. There is nothing astonishing in the fact that devotion to the Lord is generated in the minds of persons whose sins have been destroyed by the dust of the feet of holy men. For it is seen that even my brief association with you (Jadabharata) has removed from me my ignorance born of perversity of thought. (5.13.21—22)

Note : Jadabharata was an illumined sage who went about as an able-bodied dumb idiot. A king named Rahugana was passing in a palanquin borne on the shoulders of bearers. Being short of one bearer, the king's men caught hold of the able-bodied idiot, Jadabharata, and put him in the team of bearers. Not being accustomed to bearing palanquins, the new bearer was walking awkwardly causing great discomfort to the king. The king thereupon severely reprimanded the offending bearer. The palanquin stopped, and the apparent idiot began to speak for the first time in life. He gave an inspiring discourse to the king on knowledge and devotion, which had a transforming effect on the king. The reference in the passage is to this incident.

The following additional verse is given in some editions:

रहूगणैतत्तपसा न याति न चेज्यया निर्वपणाद्गृहाद्वा ।
न च्छन्दसा नैव जलाग्निसूर्यै-विना महत्पादरजो'भिषेकम् ॥

(28a) O Rahugana ! Neither austerities, nor sacrifices, nor
an ascetic mode of life, nor Vedic studies, nor worship of various
deities, can generate devotion in one. Only by bathing in the
dust of the feet of holy men can one attain to devotion. (5.12.12)

The dust of the feet of holy men is praised in the words of
Prahlada :

नैषां मतिस्तावदुरुक्रमाङ्घ्रिं स्पृशत्यनर्थापगमो यदर्थः ।
महीयसां पादरजोभिषेकं निष्किंचनानां न वृणीत यावत् ॥

(29) So long as man does not bathe in the dust trodden by
the feet of holy men who have none but Thee to depend upon, his
mind fails to obtain communion with Thy feet as also relief from
the afflictions of life, which forms the special virtue of such
communion.   (7.5.32)

Prahlada on the effect of holy company :

तस्मादमूस्तनुभृतामहमाशिषो ऽज्ञ
आयुः श्रियं विभवमैन्द्रियमाविरिंश्यात् ।
नेच्छामि ते विलुलितानुरुविक्रमेण
कालात्मनोपनय मां निजभृत्यपार्श्वम् ॥
एवं जनं निपतितं प्रभवाहिकूपे
कामाभिकाममनु यः प्रपतन् प्रसङ्गात् ।
कृत्वात्मसात् सुरर्षिणा भगवन् गृहीतः
सोऽहं कथं नु विसृजे तव भृत्यसेवाम् ॥
यत्सङ्गलब्धं निजवीर्यवैभवं तीर्थं मुहुः संस्पृशतां हि मानसम् ।
हरत्यजोऽन्तः श्रुतिभिर्गतोमलं क वै न सेवेत मुकुन्दविक्रमम् ॥

(30-32)　Knowing as I do, that Thou wouldst, as Time, destroy everything, I do not desire for anything conducive to sense-bound life like prosperity, longevity, psychic powers and other objects of enjoyment open to embodied beings in spheres up to that of Brahma. May the Lord be gracious to direct me to His devotees! O Lord, there is the well of Samsara with the serpent of births and deaths in it, and men going after sense-enjoyments fall into it. I too was about to fall into it owing to association with men of that type, but have been saved by the sage Narada who made me his own. How then can a person like me ever abandon the service of Thy devotees? Through the sanctifying recitals of the Lord's attributes and excellences, which a person takes in through the ears in holy company, the Lord Himself gains entry into his heart and destroys his sinful tendencies. Whosoever will then be averse to hearing the Lord's excellences!　　(7.9.24,28&5.18.11)

Sri Krishna on the greatness of his devotees :

अहं भक्तपराधीनो ह्यस्वतन्त्र इव द्विज ।
साधुभिर्ग्रस्तहृदयो भक्तैर्भक्तजनप्रियः ॥

नाहमात्मानमाशासे मद्भक्तैः साधुभिर्विना ।
श्रियं चात्यन्तिकिं ब्रह्मन् येषां गतिरहं परा ॥

ये दारागारपुत्राप्तान् प्राणान्वित्तमिमं परं ।
हित्वा मां शरणं याताः कथं तांस्त्यक्तुमुत्सहे ॥

मयि निर्बद्धहृदयाः साधवः समदर्शिनः ।
वशं कुर्वन्ति मां भक्त्या सत्स्त्रियः सत्पतिं यथा ॥

मत्सेवया प्रतीतं च सालोक्यादि चतुष्टयम् ।
नेच्छन्ति सेवया पूर्णाः कुतोऽन्यत् कालविप्लुतम् ॥

साधवो हृदयं मह्यं साधूनां हृदयं त्वहम् ।
मदन्यत्ते न जानन्ति नाहं तेभ्यो मनागपि ॥

(33–38) O Sage, it is as if I am not free, subject as I am to
my devotees. Being fond of my devotees, my heart is under their
sway. I do not value Myself or even Sri who is ever associated
with Me, as I do these holy men who have accepted Me as their
supreme goal. How can I abandon these men who have sought
refuge in Me, abandoning their wives, children, relatives, house,
wealth and even life itself? The holy men who have deep-rooted
love for me and are benevolent to all beings, win Me over as a
faithful wife does a dutiful husband. Having attained to life's
fulfilment in My service, they do not care for the four forms of
Mukti (liberation) like Salokya (attainment of the Divine sphere)
and the rest, which are theirs by virtue of their service of Me.
How little then would they care for the perishable attainments of
the world? Holy men are verily My heart, and I verily am the
heart of holy men. They do not know of anything but Me,
and I, of anything but them.   (9.4.63-68)

Note : The passages given above are a complete and con-
vincing statement of the reasons for the very important place
given to the service of holy men in the discipline of Bhakti.
Stated briefly, the Bhakta and the Bhagavan are one. In this
connection it is worth while to remember the great vision that Sri
Ramakrishna had at the conclusion of his adoration of Sri
Krishna through Madhura Bhava (sweet loving relationship). He
saw a bright ray of light emanating from the feet of Sri Krishna,
touching the *Bhagavata* (the scripture revealing the Lord's glory),
and himself (the Bhakta), and forming a triangle as it were. The
vision remained steady for long. And he declared on the basis
of this vision, that the Bhagavan, *Bhagavata* and Bhakta—these
are one in three and three in one. He also declared that the heart
of the Bhakta is the drawing room of the Lord, i.e., the place
where He could be seen, served and communed with.

Sri Krishna to Akrura on the special merit of holy company:

भवद्विधा महाभाग्म निषेव्या अहसत्तमाः ।
श्रेयस्कामैर्नृभिर्नित्यं देवाः स्वार्था न साधवः ॥

(39) Men who care for their own spiritual welfare must resort to such worshipful ones like you. For even gods are moved by selfish considerations, but never so the holy ones.   (10.48.30)

The royal sage, Muchukunda, on holy company :

भवापवर्गो भ्रमतो यदा भवे-ज्जनस्य तर्ह्यच्युत सत्समागमः ।
सत्संगमो यर्हि तदैव सद्गतौ परावरेशे त्वयि जायते मतिः ॥

(40) O Indestructible One ! When the time has come for an individual to attain liberation from Samsara, he gains the company of holy men, and in consequence his mind is soon drawn to Thee, the Lord of all spheres and the ultimate goal of all pious men.   (10.51.54)

Sri Krishna speaks of the superiority of holy company to all other devotional aids :

न ह्यम्मयानि तीर्थानि न देवा मृच्छिलामयाः ।
ते पुनन्त्युरुकालेन दर्शनादेव साधवः ॥

(41) It is not that holy waters (*Tirthas*) are not altogether holy. It is not also that divine images made of clay and stone are not divine. While these take a very long time to purify the mind of man, holy men accomplish it by their very Darsan (meeting).
                                (10.48.31)

Note: This verse occurs twice in the *Bhagavata* (10-48-31 and 10-84-11). In both the places it is put in the mouth of Sri Krishna, but is addressed to different persons. The first line of the verse, if literally interpreted, will amount to a denial of the sanctity of *Tirthas* and of holy images. This will be contrary to the general import of the *Bhagavata*. So it has to be interpreted to mean the opposite of the literal, in accordance with the rhetorical usage, *Kaku Dhwani*. The translation follows this rule.

Sri Krishna on the supreme excellence of holy company :

अहो वयं जन्मभृतो लब्धं कात्स्न्र्येन तत्फलम् ।
देवानामपि दुष्प्रापं यद्योगेश्वरदर्शनम् ॥

किं स्वल्पतपसां नृणामर्चायां देवचक्षुषाम् ।
दर्शन-स्पर्शन-प्रश्न-प्रह्व-पादार्चनादिकम् ॥

(42-43) It is difficult even for gods (Devas) to have association with Yogis of great holiness. It is therefore a rare good
fortune indeed that human beings like us, possessed as we are of
so little of merit accruing from austere practices (Tapas), and
given to the worship of God only through images, can meet, touch,
converse and worship such holy ones. We have thereby attained
to the final fruit of embodied existence.   (10.84.9-10)

Sri Krishna on the supreme importance of holy company :

नाग्निन सूर्यो न च चन्द्रतारका न भूर्जलं खं श्वसनोऽथ वाङ्मनः ।
उपासिता भेदकृतो हरन्त्यघं विपश्चितो घ्नन्ति मुहूर्तसेवया ॥
यस्यात्मबुद्धिः कुणपे त्रिधातुके स्वधीः कलत्रादिषु भौम इज्यधीः ।
यत्तीर्थबुद्धिश्च जले न कर्हिचित् जनेष्वभिज्ञेषु स एव गोखरः ॥

(44-45) Fire, sun, moon, stars, earth, water, sky, air,
speech, mind and all such entities worshipped by men cannot
efface their sinful tendencies (which obstruct the growth of devotion). For, all such worship is prompted by self-centred motives
generated by the sense of difference of oneself from others. But
even a brief contact with enlightened ones destroys these sinful
tendencies. He who considers this corpse-like body composed of
the three humours as the Atman, he who thinks of his wife and
other close relatives as his own, he who looks upon clay and stone
as objects of worship and water-pools as holy waters—but never
sees any divinity in the wise and holy men—he is to be termed as a
varitable 'ass for conveying grass for cattle'.   (10.84.12-13)

Note : Here and in other passages the object is not to
condemn the worship of holy images and the resort to sacred
Tirthas. The object is to emphasise that God is manifest in a
holy man in a more real sense. As Sri Ramakrishna said, the
heart of a holy man is God's drawing room, i.e., the place where
He can be met face to face. A person who is insensate to the

Divine present in a holy man, but makes a show of worshipping the Divine in images and holy waters, is a mere pretender. He has no real devotional sense.

King Bhagiratha tells Ganga why holy men are to be adored:

साधवो न्यासिनः शान्ता ब्रह्मिष्ठा लोकपावनाः ।
हरन्त्यघं तेऽङ्गसङ्गात् तेष्वास्ते ह्यघभिद्धरिः ॥

(46) Holy men who have renounced all possessions, who are peaceful and who are established in God-consciousness, purify all the worlds. Their very contact removes sins, for in them dwells Sri Hari who is the dispeller of all sins.   (9.9.6)

Vasudeva speaks to Narada about the special excellences of holy men:

भूतानां देवचरितं दुःखाय च सुखाय च ।
सुखायैव हि साधूनां त्वादृशा-मच्युतात्मनाम् ॥
भजन्ति ये यथा देवान् देवा अपि तथैव तान् ।
छायेव कर्मसचिवाः साधवो दीनवत्सलाः ॥

(47-48) From relationship with gods through Vedic rituals man derives both good and bad results—good results when they are done correctly according to prescribed procedures, and bad when done otherwise. But association with holy men, whose minds are entirely given to the Lord, ends only in good. Devas bless men according to what they are given as offerings in rituals. Just as the shadow of a form corresponds to the shape of the form, the favour of the Devas corresponds to the ritual performed. But holy men bless the afflicted out of love, and not from consi-derations of any selfish gain for themselves.   (11.2.5&6)

Here are Janaka's words on the subject:

दुर्लभो मानुषो देहो देहिनां क्षणभङ्गुरः ।
तत्रापि दुर्लभं मन्ये वैकुण्ठप्रियदर्शनम् ॥

(49) Human birth is rare to obtain. It is of short duration
too. Even in this rare human birth, it is only very seldom that
one meets great devotees dear to the Lord.   (11.2.29)

*Sri Krishna on the universal applicability and power of holy
company:*

न रोधयति मां योगो न साङ्ख्यं धर्म एव च ।
न स्वाध्याय-स्तपस्त्यागो नेष्टापूर्तं न दक्षिणा ॥

व्रतानि यज्ञश्छन्दांसि तीर्थानि नियमा यमाः ।
यथावरुन्धे सत्सङ्गः सर्वसंगापहो हि माम् ॥

सत्सङ्गेन हि दैतेया यातुधानाः खगाः मृगाः ।
गन्धर्वाप्सरसो नागाः सिद्धाश्चारणगुह्यकाः ॥

विद्याधरा मनुष्येषु वैश्याः शूद्राः स्त्रियोऽन्त्यजाः ।
रजस्तमः प्रकृतयस्तस्मिंस्तस्मिन् युगेऽयुगे ॥

बहवो मत्पदं प्राप्ता-स्त्वाष्ट्रकायाधवादयः ।
वृषपर्वा बलिर्बाणो मयश्चापि विभीषणः ॥

सुग्रीवो हनुमान् ऋक्षो गजो गृध्रो वणिक्पथः ।
व्याधः कुब्जा व्रजे गोप्यो यज्ञपत्न्यस्तथापरे ॥

ते नाधीतश्रुतिगणा नोपासितमहत्तमाः ।
अव्रतातप्ततपसः सत्सङ्गान्मामुपागताः ॥

(50-56) Practice of Yoga, study of philosophy, performance
of ritualistic works, recital of the Vedas, practice of austerities,
work without desire for fruits, performance of philanthropic and
sacred works, giving of liberal sacrifical gifts, observance of vows
and fasts, worship of the Devas, performance of secret rites, bath
in holy waters, practice of self-control within and without—none
of these attract and bind Me as the association with holy ones,
which has the power to efface all attachments. In different ages
many beings with Rajas or Tamas (passion or dullness) predomi-

nating in them—Asuras, Rakshasas, beasts, birds, Gandharvas, Apsaras, serpents, Siddhas, Charanas, Guhyakas, Vidyadharas, and among humans, unqualified ones like women, Vaisyas, out-castes,—have all attained to My being by the power of holy association alone. Examples of this are Vritrasura, Prahlada, Vrishaparva, Mahabali, Banasura, Maya, Vibhishana, Hanuman, Jambavan, Gajendra, Jatayu, Dharmavyadha, Kubja, Gopikas, and the wives of the Brahmana priests. None of these had studied the Vedas, nor attended on Vedic teachers (as students under them do). They had not observed any spiritual disciplines or austerities. By the power of holy association alone they attained to Me.

Note : Regarding the various devotees mentioned here, their lives and teachings are expounded in the narratives of the *Bhagavata.* No explanation of the allusions is attempted here.(11.12.1–7)

Sri Krishna and Kapila draw a contrast between the benefits of holy company and the degrading effects of unholy association:

ततो दुःसङ्गमुत्सृज्य सत्सु सज्जेत बुद्धिमान् ।
सन्त एवास्य छिंदन्ति मनोव्यासङ्गमुक्तिभिः ॥
यदसज्जिः पथि पुनः शिश्नोदरकृतोद्यमैः ।
आस्थितो रमते जन्तुस्तमो विशति पूर्ववत् ॥
सत्यं शौचं दया मौनं बुद्धिः श्रीः ह्रीयशः क्षमा ।
शमो दमो भगश्चेति यत्सङ्गाद्याति संक्षयम् ॥
तेष्वशान्तेषु मूढेषु योषित्क्रीडामृगेषु च ।
संगं न कुर्याच्छोच्येषु खंडितात्मखसाधुषु ॥

(57-60) An intelligent man should avoid evil company and seek the association of holy men. Through instructions, holy men remove the tendencies that obstruct the growth of devotion. A person who associates with, and delights in, the company of purely worldly-minded men, who live solely for the satisfaction of the stomach and the sex instinct, enter again into the world of darkness. Truth, purity, kindness, restraint in speech, discrimination, intelligence, auspiciousness, modesty,

reputation, forbearance, control of mind, control of the senses and
all other virtues perish through association with purely worldly-
minded men. These worldlings are evil in disposition, body-
minded, restless and undiscriminating. They are mere pet animals
of their womenfolk. Do not associate with them.

(11.26.26 & 3.31.32-34)

*Sri Krishna's advice on how holy company saves a man, is given
below :*

यथोपश्रयमाणस्य भगवन्तं विभावसुम् ।
शीतं मयं तमोऽप्येति साधून्संसेवतस्तथा ॥
निमज्जोन्मज्जतां घोरे भवाब्धौ परमायनम् ।
सन्तो ब्रह्मविदः शान्ता नौर्दृढेवाप्सु मज्जताम् ॥
अन्नं हि प्राणिनां प्राण आर्तानां शरणं त्वहम् ।
धर्मो वित्तं नृणां प्रेत्य सन्तोऽर्वागृबिभ्यतोऽरणम् ॥
सन्तो दिशन्ति चक्षूंषि बहिरर्कः समुत्थितः ।
देवता बान्धवाः सन्तः सन्त आत्माहमेव च ॥

(61-64) Just as a man resorting to fire (on a cold and dark
night) gets relief from cold, fear and darkness, so one resorting
to holy company is saved from all obstacles in the spiritual path.
Holy men who know Brahman and are tranquil in mind, form a
firm support for one caught in the terrible sea of Samsara, just as
a well-built boat does to one drowning in the sea. Food constitu-
tes the strength of living beings.   I (Iswara) am the support of
afflicted persons.   For dead persons, the good work they had done
in life is their wealth.   And holy men constitute the refuge for
those who are afflicted by the transmigratory cycle (Samsara).
The rising sun is like an eye revealing all things aronnd. The
holy ones, by their devotional instructions, consitute the eye
that reveals the truths of spiritual life.   Verily, the holy ones are
(to an aspirant) deity, friend, soul and the Lord.   (11.26.31-34)

STRAND 3

THE NINE MODES OF BHAKTI

Introduction : This section provides a general treatment of the nine forms or modes which Bhakti (devotion) takes, namely, hearing, singing, remembering, service worshipping, prostrating, servitude, loving intimacy, and surrender. In the very first verse of this section these are enumerated. While the contact with holy ones, described in the earlier section, is the cause of the genesis of devotion, the disciplines mentioned now lead to the enhancement of devotion and its fulfilment. It must be noted that while these are, on the one hand, the Sadhanas (practices) for the development of devotion, they are also, on the other hand, the expressions of devotion. The first six disciplines take more of the nature of Sadhana, and may be considered preparatory, from the point of view of the beginner. The practice may be of all the disciplines together, or of a few or of a single one of them, according to the capacity and inclination of the aspirant. As preliminary devotional disciplines, they come under what is technically called as Vaidhi Bhakti or devotion according to scriptural injunctions. The last three, namely servitude, loving intimacy and surrender, are devotional attitudes which develop gradually even from the early preparatory stages, but become established and manifest in their distinctiveness only in the maturity of devotional life. Of course, a little of love and surrender is there in all stages of the disciplines. These attitudes are therefore characteristics of Prema Bhakti or loving devotion of a spontaneous nature. But they become established only when the devotee begins to look upon God as his 'own', and recognizes that God is not mere 'power' but primarily 'Love'. Even in the life of advanced devotees, the first six modes of devotion too can be found, but then it is more as the expression of their sentiment of Divine Love than as a means of cultivating devotion. Thus we come across cases of exalted devotees listening to scriptures like the *Bhagavata*, hearing and singing hymns of the Lord, worshipping and decorating His images, feeding Him, dancing before Him and so on. Such devotional activities on their part, unlike in the case of beginners, are the result of the perception of the very presence of the Lord in the image and are therefore the spontaneous expression of their loving sentiment. More explanation of this topic is given in the Introductions to the ensuing sections dealing with each of these modes of devotion.

The practice of devotion in its ninefold form is stated in the words of Prahlada :

श्रवणं कीर्तनं विष्णोः स्मरणं पादसेवनम् ।
अर्चनं वन्दनं दास्यं सख्यमात्मनिवेदनम् ॥
इति पुंसार्पिता विष्णौ भक्तिश्चेन्नवलक्षणा ।
क्रियते भगवत्यद्धा तन्मन्येऽधीतमुत्तमम् ॥

(1–2) The practice of devotion takes the following nine forms : hearing about God, singing about His greatness, remembering Him always, serving Him (through consecrated images, holy men and all living beings), worshipping Him (in holy images), paying obeisance to Him, practising the attitude of a servant towards Him, cultivating loving intimacy with Him, and surrendering one's body, mind and soul to Him. A person who offers this ninefold offering of devotion to the Lord, in truth and in spirit, is indeed a well-educated person.   (7.5.23–24)

Sri Suka gives the example of king Ambarisha as an ideal devotee :

स वै मनः कृष्णपदारविन्दयो-र्वचांसि वैकुण्ठगुणानुवर्णने ।
करौ हरेर्मन्दिर-मार्जनादिषु श्रुतिं चकाराच्युतसत्कथोदये ॥
मुकुन्दलिङ्गालयदर्शने दृशौ तद्भृत्यगात्रस्पर्शेऽङ्गसङ्गमम् ।
घ्राणं च तत्पादसरोजसौरभे श्रीमत्तुलस्या रसनं तदर्पिते ॥
पादौ हरेः क्षेत्रपदानुसर्पणे शिरो हृषीकेशपदाभिवन्दने ।
कामं च दास्ये न तु कामकाम्यया यथोत्तमश्लोकजनाश्रया रतिः ॥

(3–5) He (king Ambarisha) had his mind engaged in the contemplation of Krishna's feet; his speech in describing the

Lord's excellences; his hands in cleaning the temples of Hari; his ears in hearing the elevating narratives about the Lord; his eyes in seeing temples with consecrated images of the Lord; his sense of touch in contacting the feet of His devotees; his sense of smell in breathing the fragrance of Tulasi leaves used for His worship; and his tongue in tasting the food offered to him. With his feet he went on pilgrimage to places where Sri Hari is worshipped and with his head he made prostrations to Him everywhere. His one desire was to serve Him whole-heartedly without desire for anything in return. He lived in a way that would generate deep-seated love for the Lord and His devotees. (9.4.18-20)

Here are Narada's words on the ninefold expression of devotion :

श्रवणं कीर्तनं चास्य स्मरणं महतां गतेः ।
सेवेज्यावनति-दास्यं सख्य-मात्मसमर्पणम् ॥

(6) Hearing about Him, singing His praise, remembering Him always, attending on Him, worshipping Him, saluting Him, practising the attitude of servitude towards Him, developing loving intimacy with Him, and surrendering oneself to Him— these are the nine forms of devotion to the Lord, the refuge of all holy men. (7.11.11.)

Sri Suka on the consequence of the practice of such devotion :

श्रुतः सङ्कीर्तितो ध्यातः पूजितश्चाद्रतोऽपि वा ।
नृणां धुनोति भगवान् हृत्स्थो जन्मायुताशुभम् ॥

(7) When a devotee hears of Him, hymns on Him, meditates on Him, worships Him and devotes himself to Him, the Lord, who dwells in his heart, destroys his sins of countless past births. (12.3.46.)

Kunti on the result of the above practice :

शृण्वन्ति गायन्ति गृणन्त्यभीक्ष्णशः स्मरन्ति नन्दन्ति तवेहितं जनाः ।
त एव पश्यन्त्यचिरेण तावकं भवप्रवाहोपरमं पदाम्बुजम् ॥

(8) Devotees who hear about Thee, sing hymns on Thee, speak about Thee, remember Thee, and feel joy in Thee—they quickly attain to Thy holy feet which put an end to transmigratory existence.   (1.8.36)

Vritra on the attitude of a true devotee :

अहं हरे तव पादैकमूल-दासानुदासो भविताऽस्मि भूयः ।
मनः स्मरेताऽसुपतेगुणांस्ते गृणीत वाक् कर्म करोतु कायः ॥

(9) Lord, may I be born again and again as the servant of Thy devotees! May my mind always be engaged in the remembrance of the excellences of Thee who art the support of life's energies; my speech, in singing Thy glories; and my body, in works of service to Thee.   (6.11.24)

How the sufferings of embodied existence do not affect a devotee, is stated in the words of Maitreya :

अशेषसंक्लेशशमं विधत्ते गुणानुवादश्रवणं मुरारेः ।
कुतः पुन-स्तच्चरणारविन्द-परागसेवारति-रात्मलब्धा ॥

(10) Merely listening to the excellences of the Lord obliterates in itself the sufferings of transmigratory existence. How much more efficacious it would be if one feels delight in the contemplation of His holy feet in one's inmost heart!   (3.7.14)

Suta on how devotion overcomes fear of death :

नोत्तमश्लोकवार्तानां जुषतां तत्कथामृतम् ।
स्यात्संभ्रमोऽन्तकालेऽपि स्मरतां तत्पदांबुजम् ॥

(11) A devotee who keeps up constant remembrance of the Lord through the recital and contemplation of His excellences is never agitated and overcome by fear even at the time of death.
                    (1.18.4)

Suka on the excellence of the Path of devotion :

मर्त्यस्तयानुसवमेधितया मुकुन्द-श्रीमत्कथाश्रवण-कीर्तन-चिन्तयैति ।
तद्धाम दुस्तरकृतान्तजवापवर्गं ग्रामाद्वनं क्षितिभुजोऽपि ययुर्यदर्थाः ॥

(12) Through contemplation, intensified by the constant hearing and recital of the Lord's excellences, the aspirant attains to the Divine State beyond the sphere of decay and death. It was for this attainment that even kings abandoned their kingdoms (prized so highly from the worldly standpoint) and took to the solitude of forests.   (10.90.50)

Suka on how Bhakti is generated :

यानीह विश्वविलयोद्भव-वृत्तिहेतुः-कर्माण्यनन्तविषयाणि हरिश्चकार ।
यस्त्वङ्ग गायति शृणोत्यनुमोदने वा भक्तिर्भवेद्भगवति ह्यपवर्गमार्गे

(13) In the creation, preservation and dissolution of the universe, the Supreme Being has expressed Himself in activities that are unique and infinite in magnitude. Whoever hears and sings about these divine attributes and majesty and feels a delight in the same, attains to supreme devotion.   (10.69.45)

Sanaka on devotion as the safeguard from all fears :

कामं भवः स्ववृजिनैर्निरयेषु नः स्या-
च्चेतोऽलिवद्यदि नु ते पदयो रमेत ।
वाचस्तु नस्तुलसिवद्यदि तेऽङ्घ्रिशोभाः
पूर्येत ते गुणगणैर्यदि कर्णरन्ध्रः ॥

(14) If our minds would always be set on the lotus of Thy feet like a beetle, if our words would always reflect Thy glory like the Tulasi leaves made lustrous by Thy feet, if our ears were always filled with hymns and recitals of Thy excellences, then we would not in the least mind even if our sins take us to lowly births or even to hell.   (3.15.49)

Note : The *Bhagavata* doctrine is that salvation (Mukti) consists not in attaining to any heavenly region or to the dissolution of individuality, but in the development of delight and absorption in the thought of the Lord, which is designated by the term Priti. With Priti for the Lord welling from the heart, hell and heaven lose their distinction.

Narada on the involvement of the whole man in devotion :

मनसो वृत्तयो नः स्युः कृष्णपादांबुजाश्रयाः ।
वाचोऽभिधायिनी-र्नाम्नां कायस्तत् प्रह्वणादिषु ॥

(15) May our minds be engaged in the contemplation of
Krishna, our speech in uttering His holy names, and our body in
prostrating before His form.   (10.47.66)

Yama on the superiority of God's name over penances :

शृण्वतां गृणतां वीर्याण्युद्दामानि हरेर्मुहुः ।
यथा सुजातया भक्त्या शुद्ध्येन्नात्मा व्रतादिभिः ॥

(16) Observance of vows does not purify the mind of man so
effectively as devotion, which is generated easily by listening to,
and singing of, the wonderful excellences of Sri Hari.   (6.3.32)

Sri Krishna on how devotion ends in spiritual experience :

यथा यथात्मा परिमृज्यतेऽसौ मत्पुण्यगाथा-श्रवणाभिधानैः ।
तथा तथा पश्यति वस्तु सूक्ष्मं चक्षुर्यथैव-अांजनसंप्रयुक्तम् ॥

(17) Just as a defective eye treated with medicines gains
the capacity to see minute things, so a mind purified by devotion
resulting from the contemplation of My divine attributes, develops
the power to perceive the subtle spiritual truths.   (11.14.26)

Parikshit on the quick fruition of Hearing :

शृण्वतः श्रद्धया नित्यं गृणतश्च स्वचेष्टितम् ।
कालेन नातिदीर्घेण भगवान् विशते हृदि ॥

(18) Soon does the Lord enter into the heart of one who
hears and speaks every day in faith and devotion about His glories
and attributes.   (2.8.4)

Suka on the transforming effect of devotion :

सङ्कीर्त्यमानो भगवाननन्तः श्रुतानुभावो व्यसनं हि पुंसाम् ।
प्रविश्य चित्तं विधुनोत्यशेषं यथा तमोऽर्कोऽभ्रमिवातिवातः ॥

(19) The Lord, who is unlimited and whose greatness is
manifest everywhere, enters into the mind of one who always
thinks of Him with devotion, and puts an end to all sorrows of that
person, just as the sun shatters darkness and a strong wind, the
clouds.   (12.12.47)

Śuka on the supreme importance of devotional practice :

तस्माद्भारत सर्वात्मा भगवान् हरिरीश्वरः ।
श्रोतव्यः कीर्तितव्यश्च स्मर्तव्य-श्चेच्छताऽभयम् ॥

(20) Therefore, all who want freedom from fear should
always hear of, sing about, and remember Sri Hari, who is the
soul and the lord of all.   (2.1.5)

Dhruva on devotion as the supreme value in life:

या निर्वृति-स्तनुभृतां तव पादपद्म-
  ध्यानाद् भवज्जनकथाश्रवणेन वा स्यात् ।
सा ब्रह्मणि स्वमहिमन्यपि नाथ मा भूत्
  किं त्वन्तकासिलुलितात् पततां विमानात् ॥

(21) The bliss that can be had by contemplating on Thee
and hearing the recital of Thy glories by Thy devotees cannot be
had even by dwelling in the impersonal infinite Being, Brahman,
who is the self of all, not to speak then of the joys of heavenly
life, which are ever threatened by the sword of Time!   (4.9.10)

Note: According to the *Bhagavata*, Bhajanananda (bliss of
Divine service) is superior to Brahmananda (bliss of union with
Impersonal Brahman). So Bhakti, which alone can produce
Bhajananda, is considered superior to Mukti. Here Bhakti is
not a means to Mukti (salvation', but the end itself.

*Kavi, one of the Navayogis, on the ideal of a devotee engrossed
in Bhajanananda :*

शृण्वन्सुभद्राणि रथाङ्गपाणे-र्जन्मानि कर्माणि च यानि लोके ।
गीतानि नामानि तदर्थकानि गायन् विलज्जो विचरेदसङ्गः ॥

(22) There are the highly sanctifying accounts of the Lord's, incarnations and of His cosmic activities; there are also His Names and hymns on Him revealing His nature and excellences. Singing and hearing about these, one should wander about without any attachments and fear of criticism or ridicule. (11.2.39)

Sri Suka condemns the places where the Lord is not worshipped

न यत्र श्रवणादीनि रक्षोघ्नानि खकर्मसु ।
कुर्वन्ति सात्वतां भर्तु-र्यातुधान्यश्च तत्र हि ॥

(23) Where the recital of the Lord's names and His glories so potent in driving away evil influences, is not heard, there the demonesses of cruelty, fraud, oppression etc. thrive. (10.6.3)

Yama on the dire consequences of leading an unspiritual life

जिह्वा न वक्ति भगवद्-गुणनामधेयं
चेतश्च न स्मरति तच्चरणारविन्दम् ।
कृष्णाय नो नमति यच्छिर एकदापि
तानानयध्व-मसतोऽकृत-विष्णुकृत्यान् ॥

(24) You may fetch to Naraka (hell) such wicked persons as have eschewed worship of Vishnu from their lives—persons whose tongues have never uttered the names of the Lord indicative of His attributes, and whose minds have never kept remembrance of the holy feet of the Lord, and whose heads have never bowed down to Him. (6.3.29)

Saunaka on how human life is meaningless without devotion

बिले बतोरुक्रमविक्रमान् ये न श्रृण्वतः कर्णपुटे नरस्य ।
जिह्वाऽसती दार्दुरिकेव सूत न चोपगाय-त्युरुगायगाथाः ॥
भारः परं पट्टकिरीटजुष्ट-मप्युत्तमाङ्गं न नमेन्मुकुन्दम् ।
शावौ करौ नौ कुरुतः सपर्यां हरेर्लसत् काञ्चनकङ्कणौ वा ॥
बर्हायिते ते नयने नराणां लिङ्गानि विष्णोर्न निरीक्षितो ये ।
पादौ नृणां तौ द्रुमजन्मभाजौ क्षेत्राणि नानुव्रजतो हरेर्यौ ॥

जीवञ्छवो भागवताङ्घ्रिरेणुं न जातु मर्त्योंऽभिलमेत यस्तु ।
श्रीविष्णुपद्या मनुजस्तुलस्याः श्वसन् शवो यस्तु न वेद गन्धम्

(25-28) The human ears that have not listened to recitals
of Divine glory are mere caves, and the voices of men who have
not sung of it are mere croakings of frogs. A man's head, though
decorated with a silken turban, is a mere burden to bear, if it is
not accustomed to bowing down to the Lord; his arms, though
wearing shining golden ornaments, are purposeless like those of a
corpse, if they are not used in the service of the Lord. The eyes
that are not accustomed to seeing Divine images are equal to the
eyes of a peacock feather, and the legs of people who do not walk
to, and go round, holy places are comparable to trees. A man
who has never touched the holy dust sanctified by the feet of the
devotees of the Lord is indeed a living corpse; and he who has not
smelt the fragrance of Tulasi leaves from the feet of the holy
images of Vishnu, is a veritable breathing corpse.　　(2-3-20-23)

Parikshit on how devotion alone makes life meaningful :

सा वाग्यया तस्य गुणान् गृणीते करौ च तत्कर्मकरौ मनश्च ।
स्मरेद्वसन्तं स्थिरजङ्गमेषु शृणोति तत्पुण्यकथाः स कर्णः ॥
शिरस्तु तस्योभयलिङ्गमाने-त्तदेव यत्पश्यति तद्धि चक्षुः ।
अङ्गानि विष्णोरथ तज्जनानां पादोदकं यानि भजन्ति नित्यम् ॥

(29-30) That alone is real faculty of speech which is used
for reciting the Lord's attributes and His glories; those alone
are real hands which are used for the service of the Lord; that
alone is the real mind which contemplates on the Lord as dwelling
in everything; and that alone is the real power of hearing which
is utilised for listening to the description of the Supreme Being.
Again, that alone is the real head which bows down before the two
symbols of the Lord, His image and His devotees; they alone are
the real eyes which see them both (the images and the devotees);
they alone are the real limbs which become purified by the waters
with which the feet of holy images and holy men are washed.

(10.80.3-4)

The same idea is repeated in Maitreya's words :

एकान्तलाभं वचसोनुपुंसां सुश्लोकमौले-गुणवादमाहुः ।
श्रुतेश्च विद्वद्भि-रुपाकृतायां कथासुधाया-मभिसंप्रयोगम् ॥

(31)   The Supreme purpose of man's power of speech is to
sing hymns in praise of the attributes of Sri Hari, the most
glorious of all beings. And the purpose of man's power of hearing
is to listen to the recitals of His glories as described in the compositions of holy and learned men.   (3.6.37)

The section concludes with a verse of Narada from Hari-
bhaktisudhodaya which summarises the theme of the chapter :

तस्माद् गोविन्दमाहात्म्य-मानंदरससुन्दरम् ।
शृणुयात्कीर्तयेन्नित्यं स कृतार्थो न संशयः ॥

(32)   Whoever hears and recites the blissful and attractive
accounts of God's attributes and majesty, verily attains to the
supreme fulfilment of life.   There is no doubt about this.

(H. B., 8.6.)

STRAND 4

SRAVANA OR HEARING

Introduction: Sravana or 'hearing', the first of the nine modes of devotion, is dealt with in this section. 'Hearing' can mean hearing the scriptural expositions, listening to songs on Divine excellences and participation in collective singing called Bhajan or Sankirtan. In fact the disciplines of 'hearing' and that of 'singing' usually go together in many devotional gatherings, unless it be that a musical piece of devotional import is sung by a technically trained musician. However 'hearing' is a distinctive discipline when it is concerned with matters like exposition of devotional scriptures or the chanting of Stotras (verses of praise), Sahasranama (thousand names of the Lord) etc. Here some one speaks or recites, and the others hear. Thus Sravana (hearing) looks passive, but it is most potent in filling the mind with lofty thoughts and with devotional traditions so necessary to build an enduring edifice of devotional life. Its potency is all the greater when we have the good fortune of hearing the discourses or songs of great devotees whose hearts, being the dwelling place of God, are full of devotional sentiment. The *Bhagavata* is powerful, because it was given out by Suka. The subject matter of 'hearing' derives a real transforming power from the person who speaks. Therefore it is maintained in the verses IV, 20-26 of this Anthology that real 'hearing' consists in hearing the devotional talks and songs of men whose mind is steeped in devotion. Such 'hearing' is a much more powerful aid than our self-effort. Reading of devotional scriptures may also be included in this discipline, as it means absorbing devotional ideas through another sense, the eye. In olden days for want of literacy and scholarship, only a few could read. They had to depend on expositions by scholars. Today printed literature is the most potent means of spreading ideas.

Suta on the purifying effect of ' Hearing ' (Sravana) :

शृण्वतां स्वकथां कृष्णः पुण्यश्रवणकीर्तनः ।
हृदन्तःस्थो ह्यभद्राणि विधुनोति सुहृत्सताम् ॥

(1)   Sri Krishna dwells in the hearts of all. He is the special
friend of holy men.   His name sanctifies all who hear or utter it.
He removes all impurities from the minds of people who listen to
accounts of His deeds in His Divine play as the Incarnate.

(1.2.17)

Suka on the same theme :

पिबन्ति ये भगवत आत्मनः सतां कथामृतं श्रवणपुटेषु संभृतम् ।
पुनन्ति ते विषयविदूषिताशयं व्रजन्ति तच्चरण-सरोरुहान्तिकम् ॥

(2)   Whosoever fills the cup of his ears with the nectar
consisting in the narratives of the excellences of the Lord, the
life and soul of devotees, and quaffs off the same, such a person,
though corrupted by many worldly tendencies, will become purified, and he will attain to the feet of the Lord.   (2.2.37)

*The Vedantas declare that discharge of duties (Swadharmanush-
thana) is the means for purifying the mind and attaining Mukti.
What then is the place af Sravana in this scheme? This is stated
in Suta's words :*

धर्मः स्वनुष्ठितः पुंसां विष्वक्सेनकथासु यः ।
नोत्पादये-द्यदि रतिं श्रम एव हि केवलम् ॥

(3)   If the proper performance of Swadharma (duties enjoined on a person) fails to bring about interest in hearing about, and
contemplating on, the glories of the Lord, then that performance
of it is mere fruitless labour.   (1.2.8)

Note: Duty (Dharma) is a moral discipline that can be both
worldly and transcendental in its significance. Today, for example, we have large numbers of people who are interested only in
matters having a social concern, and in their view also duty has
a great place in life. For them, however, it is only a social value.
The *Bhagavata* differs from this view. Duty receives its sanction
from God and not from any worldly authority. So duty properly
done should ultimately generate love of God. If this does not
happen, duty has failed in its real purpose. The *Bhagavad Gita*

says : 'He, from whom this creation has come forth and who
pervades all objects, by adoring Him by one's Swadharma (duty),
man attains to spiritual competence' (18.46). As for the Vedan-
tin's contention that it is an aid to Jnana (knowledge of God)
the *Bhagavata* holds that while it is undoubtedly so, its immediate effect is to generate devotion, and to one who has devotion,
Jnana comes automatically by God's grace. No separate discipline
of Jnana is needed.

*Self-sufficiency of Bhakti as a spiritual discipline in Brahma's
words :*

ज्ञाने प्रयासमुदपास्य नमन्त एव
जीवन्ति सन्मुखरितां भवदीयवार्ताम् ।
स्थाने स्थिताः श्रुतिगतां तनुवाङ्मनोभि-
र्येप्रायशोऽजित जितोऽप्यसितैस्त्रिलोक्याम् ॥

'4) Those devotees who, avoiding the difficulties of ascetic
life associated with the path of Jnana, remain in their homes,
resigning themselves to Thee fully in body, mind and speech, and
hearing the recitals of Thy narratives from the mouth of holy
men,—such devotees will conquer even Thee, O Thou the Invincible
in all the three worlds ! (They attain to Jnana also automatically
with the development of Bhakti.)   (10.14.3.)

Sanaka on how the bliss of Sravana excels liberation :

नात्यन्तिकं विगणयन्त्यपि ते प्रसादं
किन्त्वन्यदर्पितभयं ध्रुव उन्नयैस्ते ।
येऽङ्ग त्वदङ्घ्रिशरणा भवतः कथायाः
कीर्तन्यतीर्थयशसः कुशला रसज्ञाः ॥

(5) There are some intelligent persons who take refuge at
Thy feet, having understood how great is the bliss that could be
derived from the hearing and recital of the sanctifying and world-
renowned accounts of Thy divine manifestations. Immersed in the

bliss of 'hearing' and 'recital', they care little even for liberation,
the highest of Thy blessings, much less for any of the worldly and
heavenly attainments which are subject to destruction at the
movement of Thy eyebrows.   (3.15.48)

Rishi on the purifying effect of Sravana :

को वा भगवतस्तस्य पुण्यश्लोकेड्यकर्मणः ।
शुद्धिकामो न श्रृणुया-द्यशः कलिमलापहम् ॥

(6) Holy men always sing in praise of Thy divine sportive
activities. The accounts of Thy glory destroy the evils of the age
of Kali. Who, indeed, that wants to be purified of all his sinful
tendencies, will refuse to listen to the recital of such accounts?
                                                       (1.1.16)

Parikshit on the purifying effect of Sravana :

प्रविष्टः कर्णरन्ध्रेण खानां भावसरोरुहम् ।
धुनोति शमलं कृष्णः सलिलस्य यथा शरत् ॥

(7) Entering (in the shape of recitals of His excellences)
the hearts of devotees through their ears, Krishna soon cleanses
them of all impurities, just as the autumn season clears the
waters of rivers and tanks of their dirt.   (2.8.5)

Note : When water in a pot is purified by any purifying
chemical agent, the dirt only settles down, and can come up again
when stirred. The purifying effect of penances is only like that
in so far as they cannot destroy sinful tendencies. But when God
enters into the heart and manifests as devotion, these very sinful
tendencies are destroyed. This radical effect of devotion is compared to that of the autumn season when the turbidity of water
in rivers completely subsides due to all mud being washed away.
Afterwards only clear water flows.

Further elucidation of the same in the words of the Devas :

शुद्धिर्नृणां न तु तथेड्य दुराशयानां विद्याश्रुताध्ययन-दानतपःक्रियाभिः
सत्त्वात्मनामृषभ ते यशसि प्रबुद्ध-सच्छ्रद्धया श्रवणसंभृतया यथा स्यात्

(8)   O Lord, the Support of pure and holy ones! Learning, charities, teaching, austerities and the like cannot purify the corrupted hearts of men in as effective a way as that sanctifying faith developed by listening to accounts of Thee and Thy excellences.   (11.6.9)

Parikshit on the all-comprehensive relevancy of Sravana:

निवृत्ततर्षै-रुपगीयमानाद्-भवौषधाच्छ्रोत्रमनोऽभिरामात् ।
क उत्तमश्लोकगुणानुवादा-त्पुमान्निवर्ज्येत विना पशुघ्नात् ॥

(9)   Who except killers (i.e. inhuman persons) would not feel interested in hearing the recitals of the Lord's glories and excellences coming from the mouths of holy men free from all worldly desires (i.e. Jivanmuktas)—recitals that are so delightful to the ear and are possessed of the power of curing the ailment of Samsara like a potent medicine?   (10.1.4)

Note: The implication is that according to the *Bhagavata,* practice of devotion has relevance to people at all levels of spiritual evolution and is not meant only for under-developed minds (Mandabuddhis), as some types of Advaitins maintain. Jivanmuktas like Narada sing the Lord's praise out of love and awareness of His immediate presence everywhere. Men who feel the bondage of Samsara and seek release resort to it as sick men take medicine. Even ordinary worldly-minded people hear devotional recitals, firstly because they are delightful to hear, and next because those people have the belief that such recitals may be helpful in warding off calamities in the world. It is only the most perverse type of men that will eschew all devotional contacts from their lives. So the *Bhagavata* calls them 'killers', brutes.

Rishis on how even spiritually perfect ones resort to Sravana:

को नाम तृप्येद्रसवित् कथायां महत्तमैकान्तपरायणस्य ।
नान्तं गुणानामगुणस्य जग्मु-र्योगेश्वरा ये भवपाद्ममुख्याः ॥

(10)   Where is the connoisseur of spiritual values who has attained to satiety in respect of hearing the accounts of the ex-

cellences of the Lord, the sole refuge of holy men? Even beings
with great Yogic powers like Brahma and Siva have failed to dive
deep into the auspicious qualities of the Lord, who is beyond the
the qualities of Prakriti.   (1.18.14)

Note: Brahman is described in the *Taittiriycpanishad* as
Rasa or Bliss (*Raso vai sah*). This Bliss manifests as the highest
type of devotion. So according to the teachings of the *Bhagavata*,
the perfect Jnani or knower of God, is also the most exalted type
of Bhakta, and vice versa. Examples of this are Suka, Narada
and others in the Puranas. In modern times Sri Ramakrishna is
the best-known example of the *Bhagavata* teaching that Jnana
and Bhakti are not opposed, but are rather complementary in all
persons of spiritual development, including Jivanmuktas.

Sri Suka on the very wide scope of Sravana :

ज्ञानं यदा प्रतिनिवृत्तगुणोमिचक्र-मात्मप्रसाद उभयत्र गुणेष्वसङ्गः ।
कैवल्यसंमतपथ-स्त्वथ भक्तियोगः को निर्वृतो हरिकथासु रतिं न कुर्यात्

(11) Which spiritual aspirant, engrossed in the accounts of
the Lord's excellences, will cease to be delighted with them, the
knowledge of which establishes one in serenity here and hereafter
by freeing the mind from the sway of passions, and gives one
detachment from the qualities (Gunas) of Prakriti and thereby
carries one along the path of devotion to the goal of liberation?
                                                            (2.3.12)

*Saunaka in condemnation of absence of interest in the Lord's
name :*

आयुर्हरति वै पुंसामुद्यन्नस्तं च यन्नसौ ।
तस्यर्ते यत् क्षणो नीत उत्तमश्लोकवार्तया ॥
तरवः किं न जीवन्ति भस्त्राः किं न श्वसन्त्युत ।
न खादन्ति न मेहन्ति किं ग्रामपशवोऽपरे ॥
श्वविड्वराहोष्ट्रखरैः संस्तुतः पुरुषः पशुः ।
न यत्कर्णपथोपेतो जातु नाम गदाग्रजः ॥

(12-14) Except in the case of those who spend at least a little of their time in contemplating on the Lord, the life-span of men is meant only to be swallowed up by Time, symbolised by the rising and setting sun. For do not the trees also live like men? Do not the bellows also inhale and exhale air like them? Do not the domestic animals also eat and mate like them? He into whose ear the Lord has not found entrance through the recitals of His excellences, is verily an animal — a dog or a pig, a camel or an ass.

(2.3.17 19)

NOTE: The sole purpose of human life, according to the *Bhagavata* and according to great Teachers like Sri Ramakrishna, is the practice of devotion and attainment of knowledge and love of God. If man eschews this spiritual value, his life, however advanced it may be in the matter of material power and opportunities for sensuous enjoyments, is little different from that of animals. This is a point that modern man, who boasts so much of science, technology and social advancement, should ponder over.

Vidura on the purposelessness of a life without spiritual interest:

तान् शोच्यशोच्यानविदोऽनु शोचे हरेः कथायां विमुखानघेन ।
क्षिणोति देवोऽनिमिषस्तु तेषा-मायुर्वृथावादगतिस्मृतीनाम् ॥

(15) I feel sympathy for those extremely pitiable and ignorant people who, out of their sinful tendencies, abhor the recitals of the Lord's excellences. Their lives, spent in vain disputations, actions and thoughts, are consumed by the winkless spirit of Time.

(3.5.14)

Brahma on the evil consequences of abandoning spiritual values:

यन्न व्रजंत्यघभिदो रचनानुवादा-
च्छृण्वंतियेऽन्यविषयाः कुकथा मतिघ्नीः ।
यास्तु श्रुता हतभगैर्नृभिरात्तसारा-
स्तांस्तानुक्षिपंत्यशरणेषु तमःसु हंत ॥

(16) There are worldings who do not like to listen to devotional scriptures dealing with the excellences and the cosmic

manifestations of the Lord, the destroyer of all sins, but on the other hand, resort to, and absorb, unspiritual thoughts and teachings which corrupt the mind and destroy the higher susceptibilities (by rousing up lust, greed and other passions). It is indeed sad to contemplate how such unfortunate persons are hurled, by the very thoughts and teachings they imbibe, into blinding darkness (i.e. the hell-life of ignorance) from which there is no easy escape.   (3.15.23)

Devas on Sravana as a supreme discipline :

पानेन ते देव कथासुधायाः प्रवृद्धभक्त्या विशदाशया ये ।
वैराग्यसारं प्रतिलभ्य बोधं यथाञ्जसान्वीयुरकुण्ठविष्ण्यम् ॥

(17) O Lord, with the devotional sentiment enhanced by listening to Thy nectarine excellences, pure-minded persons become endowed with the power of detachment from all worldly objects, and thereby attain easily to spiritual illumination and to the state from which there is no fall.   (3.5.45)

Brahma on the effectiveness of devotion:

ये तु त्वदीयचरणाम्बुजकोशगन्धं
जिघ्रंति कर्णविवरैः श्रुतिवातनीतम् ।
भक्त्या गृहीतचरणाः परया च तेषां
नापैषि नाथ हृदयाम्बुरुहात् स्वपुंसाम् ॥

(18) Devotees absorb the fragrance of the lotus of Thy feet wafted to their ears by the wind of the discipline of 'hearing'. Thou dost never leave the heart-lotus of such devotees, who consider themeselves as Thine, being held fast to Thy feet through the ardour of their intense devotion.   (3.9.5)

The Siddhas put the bliss of Sravana (Bhajanananda) on a par with Brahman-intuition (Brahmananda):

अयं त्वत्कथामृष्टपीयूषनद्धां मनोवारणः क्लेशदावाग्निदग्धः ।
तृषार्तोऽवगाढो न संसार दावं निष्क्रामति ब्रह्मसंपन्नवस्तः ॥

(19) The wild elephant of our mind, scorched and rendered
thirsty by the forest-fire of Samsara, has gone deep into, and got
immersed in, the nectarine stream of Thy sanctifying excellences.
Immersed in it, it has forgotten the fire, but it refuses to come
out, like one united with the bliss of Brahman.   (4.7.35)

*Emperor Prithu on the superiority of Sravana over even
Kaivalya:*

वरान् विभो त्वद्वरदेश्वराद् बुधः कथं वृणीते गुणविक्रियात्मनाम् ।
ये नारकाणामपि सन्ति देहिनां तानीश कैवल्यपते वृणे न च ॥
तदप्यहं नाथ न कामये क्वचित् न यत्र युष्मच्चरणाम्बुजासवः ।
महत्तमान्त-हृदयान्मुखच्युतो विधत्स्व कर्णायुतमेष मे वरः ॥
स उत्तमश्लोक महन्मुखच्युतो भवत्पदाम्भोज-सुधाकणानिलः ।
स्मृतिं पुनर्विस्मृत-तत्त्ववर्त्मनां कुयोगिनां नो वितरत्यलं वरैः ॥
यशः शिवं सुश्रव आर्यसङ्गमे यदृच्छया चोपशृणोति ते सकृत् ।
कथं गुणज्ञो विरमेद्विना पशुं श्रीयैत्प्रवत्ते गुणसंग्रहेच्छया ॥

(20-23) O Lord, Thou all-pervading Being! Who, endowed
with wisdom, will seek petty worldly boons of Thee who art capable of bestowing liberation itself and who art looked upon as their
Master by the boon-giving gods like Brahma, to whom men
resort for worldly favours? Let worldlings grovelling in body-consciousness and living satisfied with the foolish life of the senses,
available even to inhabitants of hell, do so, but I (who approach
Thee with pure devotion) shall not do that. I do not seek even
Kaivalya (Moksha which Thou alone canst give); for in that state
one cannot hear the recital of Thy excellences, which is the
expression, through the mouth, of loving devotion—the sweet
honey of Thy bliss lodged in the hearts of great devotees. So if I
am to seek a boon at all, it is that I may have a thousand ears to
listen to the recitals of Thy excellences. O Thou, the most auspicious and glorious Being! The words coming out of the mouths
of holy ones (concerning Thy excellences) are like the winds

11

carrying the globules of ambrosia residing in the lotus of Thy feet.
Even fallen Yogis who, out of their perversity, have forgotten,
and deviated from, the path of Truth, are brought back to the
right path (by listening to Thy excellences).   So what boon shall
I seek (other than the opportunity to listen to these, Thy glories)?
O Thou of abounding auspiciousness! How can a human being,
(naturally endowed with the capacity to grasp the idea of God and
His attributes), abstain from listening to the glorification of these
auspicious attributes, even if he has heard it only once casually
in the company of holy ones, unless he be a brute by nature
(though human in form)? Even Sri Devi chose Thee, attracted by
Thy excellences, which include all that is good and great.

(4.20.23-26)

NOTE: The third verse reminds us that devotion is the most
potent corrective force in spiritual life and that it can restore
even a man who had a fall in his spiritual life, to the height he fell
from.   There are many obstacles in the path of the aspirant, and
these can be overcome only by the grace of God.   Hence the
supreme importance of devotion.

Narada answers how Sravana can equal Moksha:

तस्मिन्महन्मुखरिता मधुभिश्चरित्र-
पीयूषशेषचरितः परितः स्रवन्ति ।
ता ये पिबन्त्यवितृषो नृप गाढकर्णै-
स्तान्न स्पृशन्त्यशन-तृड्भयशोकमोहाः ॥
एतैरुपद्रुतो नित्यं जीवलोकः स्वभावजैः ।
न करोति हरेर्नूनं कथामृतनिधौ रतिम् ॥

(24-25) Flowing around holy men is the purest stream of
ambrosia constitued of the recitals of Divine excellences coming
out of their mouths. Those who drink deep of this ambrosial stream
with their ears again and again without satiety, are unaffected by hunger, thirst, fear, sorrow and grief. It is due to the
disturbance of these natural urges that men generally fail to
evince any delight in the excellences of Sri Hari.   (4.29.40-41)

NOTE: It is maintained that the bliss of devotion (Bhajana-nanda) is equal, if not superior, to the bliss of Moksha, as physical and mental infirmities of man like hunger, fear, etc., are drowned in that joy, and man thus gets above the limitations of body and mind. In our age, the lives of Sri Ramakrishna and his disciples bear witness to this. It is well known how Sri Rama-krishna became oblivious of the torturing pain of cancer when his mind was stimulated by the joy and fervour of devotional sing-ing. In the lives of his disciples also we see how they spent days in devotional singing or in meditation, taking only a little, or even no, food on many days.

But it may be objected that ordinarily when we read of God from books and hear recitals of songs about His excellences, nothing happens to us. The explanation is that this overcoming of hunger, fear etc. happens only when 'hearing' is done from, and in the company of, men of very high devotional attainments. Only through their words do the ambrosial waters of devotion, residing in their hearts, flow out in a stream and fill the heart of the hearers. In other words real Sravana (hearing) consists not in one's own reading something of scriptures or one's hearing the talks of some ordinary exponents of devotional thought, but in listening to words as they come out from the mouths of holy ones who have true loving devotion to God. Such 'hearing' can pro-duce a bliss equal to that of Moksha itself. It should however be noted that there should be spiritual hunger in the 'hearer'. Otherwise nothing will happen by 'hearing' even a saintly person. Hence a devotee of the highest order does not care for Moksha. This is a doctrine maintained in the *Bhagavata* in several places. It is also implied that devotion can be cultivated effectively only in the company of other devotees, and not merely by one's efforts, however valuable these may be in themselves. Development of devotion is like one fire lighting another fire. So 'Satsanga', contact with the holy ones, is considered the first requisite for cultivating devotional life. Of course it is taken for granted that the wick or firewood is not too wet; if so, it will not be lighted quickly. There are many verses devoted to this subject in the earlier sections.

The above-mentioned truth is illustrated from the example of Parikshit:

नैषातिदुःसहा क्षुन्मां त्यक्तोदमपि बाधते ।
पिबन्तं त्वन्मुखाम्भोज-च्युतं हरिकथामृतम् ॥

(26) Though I have given up even the drinking of water, this unbearable hunger does not overpower me, as I am inbibing the ambrosia of Divine excellences flowing out of your mouth.(10.1.13)

Parikshit says how devotion helps one overcome fear of death:

तं मोपयातं प्रतियन्तु विप्रा गङ्गा च देवी धृतचित्तमीशे ।
द्विजोपसृष्टः कुहकस्तक्षको वा दशत्वलं गायत विष्णुगाथाः ॥

(27) May the holy men and Goddess Ganga know me, whose mind is fixed on the Lord, as one who has surrendered myself wholly unto Him. Induced by the Brahmana, let the treacherous serpent Takshaka bite me. (I am unconcerned about it). Sing for me the glories of Hari's excellences.   (1.19.15)

NOTE : The allusion is to the well-known story of Raja Parikshit who was, for some misdeed, cursed by a sage that he would die within seven days, bitten by the serpent Takshaka. So the king prepared himself for death, abandoning every worldly concern including food and drink, and resigned himself to the Lord. The *Bhagavata* is the narrative of the sportive Divine manifestations and Divine excellences given by Sri Suka to Parikshit in this situation, with a view to inspiring in him supreme devotion and resignation. This Note is applicable to the earlier verse also.

Suka on Sravana as a source of unending joy:

अन्येषां पुण्यश्लोकाना-मुदामयशसां सताम् ।
उपश्रुत्य भवेन्मोदः श्रीवत्साङ्कस्य किं पुनः ॥

(28) Even on hearing accounts of saintly devotees of the Lord, far-famed for their holiness and virtuous lives, we derive great joy. Then how much more should be the joy derived from hearing about the excellences of the Lord Himself!   (3.19.34)

Janaka on the great merit of Sravana;

तस्माद्वीमन्कथां पुण्यां गोविन्द चरिताश्रिताम् ।
महत्पुण्यप्रदां यस्माच्छृणुष्वनृपसत्तम ॥
नानुतृप्ये जुषन्युष्म-द्वचो हरिकथामृतम् ।
संसारतापनिस्तप्तो मर्त्यस्तत्तापभेषजम् ॥

(29-30) O King, hear this narrative which is full of the
holy and divine excellences of Govinda, the hearing of which bestows great merit on the listener.   One is never tired of hearing
your words conveying the most blissful accounts of Sri Hari; such
hearing is the best curative for one like me who is subject to the
sufferings of Samsara (cycle of births and deaths).   (11.3.2)

Suta on the supreme importance of Sravana:

संसारसिंधु-मतिदुस्तर-मुक्तितीर्षो-र्नान्यः प्लवो भगवतः पुरुषोत्तमस्य ।
लीलाकथारस-निषेवणमन्तरेण पुंसो भवेद्विविधदुःखदवार्दितस्य ॥

(31) For men caught between afflictions of the forest fire of
worldly miseries and the dangers of the sea of Samsara, there
is no other means to go across that sea than the boat of absorbing
accounts of the Lord's excellences as displayed in His sportive
manifestations.   (12.4.40)

*According to the Vedanta the cessation of Samsara can take
place only on the removal of ignorance.   How then can Sravana,
the 'hearing' of the Divine excellences, effect this?   The reply is
given in the words of Yudhishthira:*

कुतोऽशिवं त्वच्चरणाम्बुजासवं महन्मनस्तो मुखनिःसृतं क्वचित् ।
पिबन्ति ये कर्णपुटैरलं प्रभो देहंभृतां देहकृदस्मृतिच्छिदम् ॥

(32) How can there be any downfall for those who absorb,
through their ears, the inebriating nectar residing at the lotus of
Thy feet and emerging from the minds of holy ones through the
medium of their speech (in the form of hymns and narratives of
Thy excellences)?   Such 'hearing' destroys that forgetfulness

(ignorance) which effaces in embodied beings the memory of the Supreme Iswara (who is their source and to whom they are intimately related by bonds of love).   (10.83.3)

NOTE : Ignorance is, according to all systems of Indian thought, the cause of bondage, though there are differences among them about the nature of that ignorance. One of the ways in which ignorance operates is by bringing about a forgetfulness of the real nature of oneself and everything else. Thus the Jiva has forgotten his own nature as Spirit and thinks of himself as a limited perishable body. So also he is ignorant about the existence of God and his relationship with God. Instruction in devotional disciplines brings enlightenment and restores the memory about the Truth of God and one's relationship with Him.

How Sravana destroys ignorance, is stated in the words of the Devas:

बिभ्व्यस्तवामृत-कथोदवहा-त्रिलोक्याः
पादावनेजसरितः शमलानि हन्तुम् ।
आनुश्रवं श्रुतिभिरङ्घ्रिजमङ्गसङ्गे-
स्तीर्थद्वयं शुचिषदस्त उपस्पृशंति ॥

(33) There are two agents capable of purifying the three worlds—the nectarine waters of the stream constituted of narratives and hymns about Thy excellences, and the holy river Ganga flowing from Thy feet. Of these two, the narratives and hymns purify a devotee by entering into his soul through the ear, and the sacred river, by its contact with the body.   (11.6.19)

NOTE : The idea is that if the mind of man is purified, the knowledge of one's spiritual nature must immediately dawn on it. Between such purification and the dawn of knowledge there is no need for assuming an intermediary stage, and saying that devotion and such disciplines can lead one only up to that lower intermediatry stage called purificational, and that thenceforth one has to adopt the specific discipline of the path of knowledge for gaining illumination. This is only a way of lowering the

status of devotion adopted by the advocates of the path of know
ledge. The doctrine of Bhakti, however, maintains that through
preparatory disciplines, Bhakti becomes firmly established and
this mature Bhakti is in itself a self-sufficient means of salvation.
God's grace is bestowed on such devotees, and they thereby gain
enlightenment and freedom from ignorance. God's grace obtained
through mature devotion and self-surrender alone can bring this
divine state. Says the Gita: 'To such as are ever united with Me
in loving devotion, I bestow that communion through understanding, by which they attain to me. Out of mercy for these, I
destroy the darkness of ignorance in these by lighting the luminous lamp of wisdom in their hearts by abiding as their very self.'
No mere effort of the Jiva called Jnana Vichara (process of dis-
criminatien) can give that illumination. It comes only as a result
of the grace of God, and the path of devotion is the most suitable
path for attaining that grace. Bhakti is thus a self-sufficient
means of illumination and liberation.

Uddhava on how Sravana destroys ignorance:

तव विक्रीडितं कृष्ण नृणां परममङ्गलम् ।
कर्णपीयूषमास्वाद्य त्यजत्यन्यस्पृहां जनः ॥
वयं त्विह महायोगिन् भ्रमन्तः कर्मवर्त्मसु ।
त्वद्वार्तया तरिष्याम-स्तावकैर्दुस्तरं तमः ॥

(34-35) Man gives up desire for everything else, having enjoyed through his ears the nectarine accounts of Thy sportive
activities, so conducive to the highest good. O Lord, Thou
Supreme Yogin! We who are wandering about the paths of worldly
activities, shall, by virtue of 'hearing' about Thy excellences in
the company of Thy devotees, overcome the blinding darkness of
ignorance so difficult to transcend.   (11.6.44,48)

*Sri Krishna says that interest in Sravana is a measure of man's
spiritual progress:*

तावत्कर्माणि कुर्वीत न निर्विद्येत यावता ।
मत्कथाश्रवणादौ वा श्रद्धा यावन्न जायते ॥

(36) So long as a man has not attained to dispassion for worldly things and so long as a deep-rooted interest in 'hearing' about My excellences has not arisen in him, he has the obligation to work.   (11.20.9)

NOTE : According to Indian spiritual tradition, it is sinful for a man to abandon his wordly duties and obligations until he has developed a whole-hearted longing for God. If he has that longing, he can abandon works of the nature of duties for undertaking an exclusive pursuit of spiritual disciplines. According to this verse the development of a deep-rooted interest in 'hearing' is one of the signs of this spiritual maturity; for thus can man be fully occupied with the thought of God.

Superiority of devotion over ritualism according to Rishi Saunaka:

कर्मण्यस्मिन्ननाश्वासे धूमधूम्रात्मनां भवान् ।
आपाययति गोविन्द-पादपद्मासवं मधु ॥

(37) These sacrificial rites worry our minds by the uncertainty of their fruits and blacken our bodies through continued exposure to smoke (and heat) of the sacrificial fires. We who are so placed, are now being fed by you (to our great relief) with the nectar taken from the lotus of Krishna's feet (consisting in the narrative of His sportive activities and His excellences).

(1.18.12)

The discipline of 'Hearing' includes not only the praise of the Lord but also the accounts of His devotees, as they are conducive to the growth of devotion. The lives of devotees reflect the glory and excellence of the Lord. Their heart is the drawing room of the Lord. This is put in the words of Vidura:

श्रुतस्य पुंसां सुचिरश्रमस्य नन्वञ्जसा सूरिभिरीडितोऽर्थः ।
यत्तद्गुणानुश्रवणं मुकुन्द-पादारविन्दं हृदयेषु येषाम् ॥

(38) Wise men have declared that the ultimate purpose of all scriptural study assiduously cultivated, is the attainment of delight

in hearing devotional recitals dealing with the holy ones who feel the presence of the Lord within.   (3.13.4)

Through Maitreya's description of the state of the royal sage Prithu before his death, the importance of hearing devotional recitals even to Yogis is stressed:

छिन्नान्यधी-रधिगतात्मगति-निरीह-
स्तत्तत्यजेऽछिनदिदं वयुनेन येन ।
तावन्न योगगतिभि-र्यतिरप्रमत्तो
यावद् गदाग्रजकथासु रतिं न कुर्यात् ॥

(39) The mind might have been restrained from running to external objects; one's nature as spirit might have been understood; the desire for psychic powers might have disappeared; even the ego of having attained to spiritual perfection might have been abandoned. Still the spiritual aspirant should be assiduous in the practice of disciplines until he has developed delight and absorption in (the hearing and contemplation of) Divine excellences.
                    (4.23.12)

NOTE: He (Prithu), having attained to the knowledge of the Self, was without desires, had no identification with the body, and felt no more need for any spiritual practice. He could be like that, because his mind had attained to complete absorption and delight in the Lord's glories and excellences. Until a spiritual aspirant is established in such a state, he is prone to the temptations of psychic powers arising from Yoga.

The Gopis on zeal in 'hearing' about the Lord:

तव कथामृतं तप्तजीवनं कविभिरीडितं कल्मषापहम् ।
श्रवणमङ्गलं श्रीमदाततं भुवि गृणन्ति ते भूरिदा जनाः ॥

(40) The accounts of Thy sportive manifestation are like life-giving ambrosia to those who are being burnt in the fire of worldly life. Sages sing in praise of them. They wash off the sins of men. The very hearing of them (irrespective of any action

following or not following) is conducive to the highest good. They
confer serenity. To preach them far and wide is the greatest gift
(that one can make to mankind).   (10.31.9)

*Chitraketu on why it is so meritorious to preach the glory of
God's name:*

न हि भगवन्नघटितमिदं त्वद्दर्शनान्नृणा-मखिलपापक्षयः ।
यन्नाम सकृच्छ्रवणात् पुल्कसकोऽपि विमुच्यते संसारात् ॥

(41) It is no exaggeration to say that man is freed from all
sins by seeing Thee. For even the lowest of the low is immediately,
and in this very birth, purified by even once listening to Thy
name and excellences.   (6.16.44)

NOTE :   Reference may be made to Section V, verse 2 to 30
for an elaborate treatment of this topic, the potency of the Divine
Name in purifying even sinners.

*It is now stated that the virtue of devotion is not merely the
negative one of removing sins. It is a positive value. This value
is the highest that man can realise in life. This is stated in Maitreya's words:*

को नाम लोके पुरुषार्थसारवित् पुराकथानां भगवत्कथासुधाम् ।
आपीय कर्णाञ्जलिभिर्भवापहा-महो विरज्येत विना नरेतरम् ॥

(42) Only a beast in the form of man, and never a person
having a grasp of the true meaning of life, will ever turn away
from   hearing   the   delightful   descriptions   of Divine excellences given in the narratives of the Puranas, which are capable
of destroying man's entanglement in Samsara.   (3.13.50)

Kapila's condemnation of the pursuit of sensual values:

नूनं दैवेन निहता ये चाच्युतकथासुधाम् ।
हित्वा श्रृण्वन्त्यसद्गाथाः पुरीषमिव विड्भुजः ।

(43) Those who abandon the ambrosia of Divine excellences
and go after sensuous entertainments like pigs after excreta, have

indeed been stricken down by their own evil fate (or Prarabdha).
                                                        (3.32.19)

Sri Suka's words of exhortation :

यस्तूत्तमश्लोकगुणानुवादः संगीयतेऽभीक्ष्णममङ्गलघ्नः ॥
तमेव नित्यं शृणुयादभीक्ष्णं कृष्णेऽमलां भक्तिमभीप्समानः ॥

(44) Therefore let those who aspire for pure and steady
devotion to Sri Krishna constantly hear the sanctifying narratives
of the Lord's excellences from the mouths of holy men.   (12.3.15)

Sri Suka's summary of the topic of this section :

इत्थं परस्य निजवर्त्मरिरक्षयात्त-लीलातनो-स्तदनुरूप-विडम्बनानि ।
कर्माणि कर्मकषणानि यदुत्तमश्य श्रूयादमुष्य पदयोरनुवृत्तिमिच्छन् ॥ ।

(45) A person who desires to serve Sri Krishna, the Supreme Being, and attain to His feet, should listen to the narratives
of the Lord's activities in His sportive manifestation as the Divine
Incarnate,—activities appropriate to His mission and destructive
of the Karmic bondage of devotees, and undertaken by Him for the
preservation of the Bhagavata Dharma, the path of spiritual
redemption established by Himself.   (10.90.49)

STRAND 5
KIRTANA OR HYMNING

[Introduction : The fifth section deals with Kirtana, which means 'Hymning' or 'Praising'. In Sravana, 'Hearing', the devotee is a passive factor, but in Kirtana he is active. What are technically called Kirtanas in the devotional-cum-musical tradition of India, consist of compositions of great devotee-musicians like Tyagaraja. They are sung by highly trained artistes with musical accompaniments. Though they are devotional, the science of music dominates them. Music has always been considered a natural ally of devotion in India. But there are various other forms of devotional songs, not requiring high musical training, used commonly for collective singing called Bhajan and Sankritan, which consist mainly of recitals of Divine names and Divine attributes, and of brief references to the sportive activities of Divine Incarnations. Choral singing in simple tunes is the purpose for which these are used. These Bhajans and Sankirtans, sometimes accompanied with simple rhythmic dancing, have always played the most dominant part in the life of the Indian people whenever devotional cults became mass movements. Kirtana in this sense is essentially a collective affair, and devotees gather in groups, big or small, for this kind of devotional service. As distinguished from these, there are Stotras or Praises and Prayers, which draw more on the poetic art than on music for their enrichment. In fact the *Bhagavata* itself is noted for many such Stotras or Stutis (Praises of God) couched in sublime language and rendered deeply meaningful and attractive by the harmonious combination of poetry and philosophy. Vocal prayers in prose, of the type we find among Christians, can also come under this head. Swadhyaya of the Hindus consisting of loud chanting or recitals of devotional and scriptural texts, and chanting of Sahasranama, Ashtottara and such other holy texts also come under this head. All these can come under 'Hearing' as well, as they can be both heard and chanted. Next there is the silent repetition of a Divine Name or a Mantra, which stands as a class by itself. It may be justifiable to bring it under Smarana or Remembrance. In fact the nine disciplines of the practice of devotion, though distinguishable up to a certain extent, do overlap, each one helping the advancement of the other.]

Narada on absorption in the recital of Divine excellences as the object of all forms of spiritual practice.

इदं हि पुंसस्तपसः श्रुतस्य च शिष्टस्य सूक्तस्य च बुद्धिदत्तये: ।
अविच्युतोऽर्थः कविभिर्निरूपितो यद् उत्तमश्लोकगुणानुवर्णनम् ॥

(1) Wise men have ascertained after due deliberation that the ultimate purpose of austerities, Vedic study, sacrifices, power of speech, intellectual ability, and practice of charity consists in the attainment of delight and absorption in the description of, and contemplation on, the excellences of the Lord.   (1.5.22)

NOTE : In other words it is only through continuous practice of these disciplines, perhaps for lives, that man attains to delight in devotional practices. An impure mind cannot have that delight.

According to Suta only literature associated with the Lord is beneficial:

मृषा गिरस्ता ह्यसतीरसत्कथा न कथ्यते यद्भगवानधोक्षजः ।
तदेव सत्यं तदुहैव मङ्गलं तदेव पुण्यं भगवद्गुणोदयम् ।
तदेव रम्यं रुचिरं नवं नवं तदेव शश्वन्मनसो महोत्सवम् ।
तदेव शोकार्णवशोषणं नृणां यदुत्तमश्लोक-यशोऽनुगीयते ॥

(2-3) Vain are the words and purposeless the narratives that are not concerned with the Supreme Being. That indeed is true, that auspicious and virtuous, which brings into prominence the excellences of the Lord. (3) Only such words and writings as do proclaim the glory of God can assuage the sorrows of men, enthuse their minds perpetually with joy, and stimulate them with ever-renewing interest.   (12.12.48-49)

Narada on the same theme:

न यद्वचश्चित्रपदं हरेर्यशो जगत्पवित्रं प्रगृणीत कर्हिचित् ।
तद्वायसं तीर्थमुशन्ति मानसा न यत्र हंसा निरमन्त्युशिक्क्षयाः ॥
तद्वाग्विसर्गो जनताघविप्लवो यस्मिन् प्रतिश्लोक-मबद्धवत्यपि ।
नामान्यनन्तस्य यशोंऽकितानि यत् शृण्वन्ति गायन्ति गृणन्ति साधवः ॥

(4–5) Compositions, even though they be couched in beautiful words, are like ponds provided for crows to bathe, if they do
not exalt the glory of God who purifies all the worlds. As the swan
accustomed to living in the Manasa lake does not like to swim in
such ponds (used by crows), great sages, who are ever engrossed
in the bliss of Brahman, do not feel any joy in such writings (that
have no devotional import).　Though containing mistakes, if every
sentence in a composition reflects the glory and greatness of God,
such a composition can revolutionise the sinful life of man.　Holy
men use such compositions for their own study and for reciting or
expounding to others.　　　　　　　　　　　　　　(1.5.10-11)

Saunaka describes the power of the Lord's Name:

आपन्नः संसृतिं घोरां यन्नाम विवशो गृणन् ।
ततः सद्यो विमुच्येत यद्बिभेति स्वयं भयम् ॥

(6) Man caught in this terrible cycle of worldly existence
(Samsara), does indeed attain to instantaneous release, if he
resorts to the Name of the Lord, with a feeling that one is forlorn
and helpless without Him.　For His name is a terror even to the
God of Death, who is the terror of all.　　　　　　　(1.1.14)

Narada on the efficacy of chanting the Name:

ततोऽन्यथा किञ्चन यद् विवक्षतः पृथग्दृशः तत्कृतरूपनामभिः ।
न कर्हिचित् क्वापि च दुःस्थिता मतिर्लभेत वाताहतनौरिवास्पदम् ।

(7) A man whose spirit is alien to the thought of God and
who engages himself in worldly concerns alone, feels distressed
in mind by the various fancies that the mind so engaged calls

forth, and finds no shelter or resting place, like a ship caught in
a storm.   (1.5.14)

Narada again on the same theme:

प्रगायतः खवीर्याणि तीर्थपादः प्रियश्रवाः ।
आहूत इव मे शीघ्रं दर्शनं याति चेतसि ॥

(8) God, the fountain-head of holiness, the far-famed centre
of charming Divine excellences, reveals Himself in my mind like
one called by name, as I sing about His glories.   (1.6.34)

Suta on the importance of praising the Lord:

या याः कथा भगवतः कथनीयोरुक्रमणः ।
गुणकर्माश्रयाः पुम्भिः संसेव्यास्ता बुभूषुभिः ॥

(9) Those who desire freedom from fear should resort to the
narratives dealing with the excellences and the deeds of the Lord,
whose mighty works (of creation, preservation etc.) are worthy of
praise.   (1.18.10)

Suka's words on the same are quoted:

एतन्निर्विद्यमानाना-मिच्छतामकुतोभयम् ।
योगिनां नृप निर्णीतं हरेर्नामानुकीर्तनम् ॥

(10) It is an established fact that the chanting of Hari's
Name is the panacea for all fears for all men, be they renouncers,
Yogis or men with desires.   (2.1.11)

Narada on the effectiveness of chanting the Lord's Name:

एतद्ध्यातुरचित्तानां मात्रास्पर्शेच्छया मुहुः ।
भवसिन्धुप्लवो दृष्टो हरिचर्यानुवर्णनम् ॥

(11) For men who have become afflicted and miserable by
the repeated and recurring desire for sense enjoyments, the
recounting of Sri Hari's deeds and excellences forms a veritable
boat for crossing the ocean of Samsara.   (1.6.35)

Brahma on the merit of remembering the Lord's Name at the time of death:

यस्यावतार-गुणकर्म-विडम्बनानि नामानि येऽसुविगमे विवशा गृणन्ति ।
तेऽनेकजन्मशमलं सहसैव हित्वा संयान्त्यपावृतमृतं तमजं प्रपद्ये ॥

(12) Those who resort at the time of death, in a mood of helpless supplication, to the Names of the Lord dealing with His incarnations, actions and attributes, quickly overcome the sins of many births and attain to Him who is the Truth uncovered. I salute that Eternal Being.   (3.9.15)

The truth mentioned above about the potency of the Divine Name uttered at the time of death is elaborated in the following thirteen verses by the emissaries of Vishnu, in connection with the Ajamila episode:

अयं हि कृतनिर्वेशो जन्मकं ह्यंहसामपि ।
यद् व्याजहार विवशो नाम खस्त्ययनं हरेः ॥

एतेनैव ह्यघोनोऽस्य कृतं स्यादघनिष्कृतम् ।
यदा नारायणायेति जगाद चतुरक्षरम् ॥

स्तेनः सुरापो मित्रधुक् ब्रह्महा गुरुतल्पगः ।
स्त्रीराजपितृगोहन्ता ये च पातकिनोऽपरे ॥

सर्वेषामप्यघवतामिदमेव सुनिष्कृतम् ।
नामव्याहरणं विष्णोर्यतस्तद्विषया मतिः ॥

न निष्कृतैरुदितै-र्ब्रह्मवादिभि-स्तथा विशुद्ध्यत्यघवान् व्रतादिभिः ।
यथा हरे-र्नामपदैरुदाहृतै-स्तदुत्तमश्लोक-गुणोपलंभकम् ॥

नैकान्तिकं तद्धि कृतेऽपि निष्कृते मनः पुनर्धावति चेदसत्पथे ।
तत् कर्मनिर्हारमभीप्सतां हरे-र्गुणानुवादः खलु सत्त्वभावनः ॥

अथैनं माऽपनयत कृताशेषाघनिष्कृतम् ।
यदसौ भगवन्नाम म्रियमाणः समग्रहीत् ॥

साङ्केत्यं पारिहास्यं वा स्तोभं हेलनमेव वा ।
वैकुण्ठनामग्रहण-मशेषाघहरं विदुः ॥

पतितः स्खलितो भग्नः सन्दष्टस्तप्त आहतः ।
हरिरित्यवशेनाह पुमान्नार्हति यातनाम् ॥

गुरूणां च लघूनां च गुरूणि च लघूनि च ।
प्रायश्चित्तानि पापानां ज्ञात्वोक्तानि महर्षिभिः ॥

तैस्तान्यघानि पूयन्ते तपोदानव्रतादिभिः ।
नाधर्मजं तद्‌हृदयं तदपीशांघ्रिसेवया ॥

अज्ञानादथवा ज्ञाना-दुत्तमश्लोकनाम यत् ।
संकीर्तितमघं पुंसो दहेदेधो यथाऽनलः ॥

यथागदं वीर्यतममुपयुक्तं यदृच्छया ।
अजानतोऽप्यात्मगुणं कुर्यान्मन्त्रोऽप्युदाहृतः ॥

(13-25) Having uttered (at the time of death) in a mood of helplessness and supplication the Name of Hari, which is the means for liberation, he (Ajamila) has atoned for the sins of a thousand life-times. (14) By uttering the four syllables Nā-rāya-na 'Narayana!' (O Narayana, come!) this sinful man has done expiation for all his sins. (15-16) For thieves, drunkards, betrayers of friends, slayers of men, seducers of women; for murderers of women, rulers, parents and holy beings; and for all other types of sinners—the best expiation is the utterance of the Names of Vishnu. For, by calling the Lord by name His attention is directed to the supplicant and his prayer. (17) The expiations prescribed by Vedic scholars do not purify the sinners so effectively as the Names of the Lord reflecting His great attributes. (18) Even when penances have been done in expiation of sinful acts, the mind still goes after the same sinful indulgences. So these expiations do not really purify the sinner. Those who want to root out the tendencies of sinful actions should chant the Names of Hari indicating His excellences. For, such chanting

12

purifies the mind.   (19) As he (Ajamila) has done expiation for all his sins by whole-heartedly resorting to the Lord's Name at the time of death, do not lead him to hell (the regions of sinners). (20) Whether it be in addressing one by name, or in ridicule, or in anger, or by way of completing a tune, or in contempt—the utterance of the Names of Vishnu destroys all sins.   (21) If a man cries out in a mood of helplessness "O Hari!"—be this done when falling down from a height, or when slipping down, or when being cut up, or when bitten, or burnt, or belaboured—he does not deserve the punishments of hell.   (22) Great sages have, with due discrimination, prescribed difficult expiations for heinous sins and light ones for minor sins.   (23) These expiations, consisting of austerities, charities and vows, no doubt cleanse one of the particular sins committed, but not of the sinful tendency of the heart (responsible for their commission). Even that tendency is effaced by the service of the Lord. (24) The Names of the Lord, be they uttered with or without the knowledge of their power and holiness, destroy the sins of man, as fire consumes fuel.   (25) A potent drug, even when used casually without any awareness of its powers, manifests its inherent curative quality; even so does the utterance of a Mantra (the Lord's Name).   (6.2.7-19)

NOTE :   This passage is a piece of advice given by the emissaries of Vishnu to those of Yama, the God of Death, who came to carry away the soul of Ajamila, the wicked Brahmana, to hell. Though born a Brahmana with all the facilities needed for leading a holy life, Ajamila turned into a brigand and led a wicked life given to greed, cruelty and debauchery.   At the last moment of his life he was overcome with great fear as the terror-inspiring emissaries of Yama came to carry him away to hell, and in great distress he called out to his son named Narayana, "O Narayana!". Narayana is the Name of Vishnu, the Supreme Being, and on His Name being invoked, the emissaries of Vishnu appeared on the scene and warded off the ferocious attendants of Yama.   The verses given above, addressed by the emissaries of Vishnu to those of Yama, set forth the justification for the interference of the former on behalf of this wicked man whose proper place should have been in hell in the ordinary course.

The justification is that Ajamila took the name of Vishnu at the time of death in utter fear and helplessness. That he had in mind only his son when he uttered 'Narayana', does not detract from the saving power of the divine Name, according to the *Bhagavata* doctrine. It is contended that just as a potent medicine has its effect on a man swallowing it, irrespective of his knowledge or ignorance of its potency, or of his attitude towards it, the Divine Name exerts its inherent saving power on one who utters it. It attracts the Lord's attention to the utterer. Besides, its power being inherent, its effectiveness is not dependent on any extraneous factor. This uncompromising *Bhagavata* doctrine of the complete objective efficacy of the Name, without any reference to the knowledge, faith or attitude of the utterer, may be a great hurdle to a rational devotee. He may be prepared to accept its claim as an Arthavada—a eulogy or exaggeration to prompt people to the devotional path with the thought that if the Name could save even a man like Ajamila by a casual utterance, how much more effective would it indeed be in the case of good men calling on God in faith and sincerity !

There is an implication of this kind in the verse 28, coming hereafter, but some of the commentators of the *Bhagavata* hold that this doctrine is not a eulogy or exaggeration, but a literal truth, and any doubt on this point is only a sign of lack of faith in, and understanding of, the greatness of God and His Divine Name. Such a doubting attitude is technically called *Nāmā-parādha* or offence to the sanctity of the Divine Name, and is considered highly sinful. There are, however, some commentators who seek to reconcile the points of view of reason and faith with regard to the power of the Name by holding that the word *Vivasa*, 'in helplessness and supplication', used in the text to refer to Ajamila's attitude at the time of death, indicates that the thought of the Supreme Being as his only Saviour must have come to his mind at the moment. Another point to be remembered is that Ajamila was, according to the *Bhagavata* text, leading a holy life

before he took to sinful ways, and that is pointed out as the
justification for the sacred Name of God with saving power coming to his mind, be it by chance, at his last moment. Besides,
Ajamila survived this incident, and lived for some time more,
reconverted to the ways of holy living that he had once abandoned. This note has to be read along with the succeeding verses
on the same subject.

The significance of the Ajamila episode and the power of the
Name in Sri Suka's words:

एवं स विप्रावितसर्वधर्मा दास्याः पतिः पतितो गर्ह्यकर्मणा ।
निपात्यमानो निरये हतव्रतः सद्यो विमुक्तो भगवन्नाम गृह्णन् ॥
नातः परं कर्मनिबन्धकृन्तनं मुमुक्षतां तीर्थपदानुकीर्तनात् ।
न यत्पुनः कर्मसु सज्जते मनो रजस्तमोभ्यां कलिलं ततोऽन्यथा ॥

(26-27) This man (Ajamila), the paramour of a courtesan,
who had transgressed all the dictates of Dharma, indulged in
heinous acts, degraded himself and lived without any restraints,
was to be consigned to hell. But he was saved without the least
delay, because he resorted to the Name of the Lord. For those
who seek salvation (Moksha), there is nothing so effective in up-
rooting the sinful tendencies of the heart as the chanting of the
Names of the supremely holy Lord. For a mind, purified by the
Lord's Name, is never more drawn to evil deeds, whereas other
purificatory rites are likely to taint one's mind with the qualities
of Rajas and Tamas (which prompt one again to evil deeds).

(6.2.45-46)

NOTE: The idea conveyed in the second part of verse 27 is
this: The expiatory rites prescribed in Smritis for emancipation
from sins often involve hard ascetic practices and also rituals involving much effort and materials. All these are likely to make a
man egotistic and also make him do unethical actions for collect-
ing wealth and materials for rites. Thus the value of such rites
is superficial, and they may even be the cause of new sins by in-
creasing Rajas and Tamas in man. Repetition of God's Name

has none of these adverse effects and will also root out sinful tendencies.

The idea here is reminiscent of an instruction of Sri Rama-krishna to one of his Sannyasin disciples. Yogen, who became Swami Yogananda afterwards, asked the Master how one could overcome the hold of the sex urge. He expected that the Master would instruct him to practise some difficult Yogic exercise, give him a strict regimen of dieting, and prescribe some rare herbal medicaments. But to his surprise the Master asked Yogen only to repeat the Name of Hari. Yogen went unconvinced as he thought that the prescription was too simple and commonplace, but he found gradually that this was the only remedy.

Any doubt about this doctrine is warded off in the words of Suka:

त्रियमाणो हरेर्नाम गृणन् पुत्रोपचारितम् ।
अजामिलोऽप्यगाद्धाम किं पुनः श्रद्धया गृणन् ॥

(28) Ajamila, while dying, uttered the Name of the Lord, though indirectly, by referring to his son. Yet he attained to the supreme state. What to speak then of those who utter it with faith!

(6.2.49)

NOTE : This verse indicates that, unlike some of its com-mentaries, the *Bhagavata* is not intolerant of the view that takes this episode as a eulogy, though its sympathy is more with literalism, as indicated in the succeeding verses. It should, however, be carefully noted that the intention of the *Bhagavata* text in stressing the unqualified holiness of the Name is not to encourage wrong doing in the hope of effecting easy expiation through uttering the Divine Name afterwards, knowingly or un-knowingly. It is firmly held by the Vaishnava savants that noth-ing can be a more unpardonable insult to the Name (Nama-paradha) than entertaining such a light attitude towards the Name as to consider it a cheap remedy available at one's choice, and to sin in anticipation. Remembrance of God's Name at death takes place only in the case of men whose whole life has been having a devotional trend. Or, Ajamila's is an exceptional case, probably an instance of Divine Grace. It also highlights the un- qualified greatness of the Name even in a purely objective sense. In pure grace there can be no law or regulatory principle as in justice. Or, as is stated by Ajamila himself in a later verse, his good deeds in a previous life might have been the cause of this unexpected good fortune. In this view grace is tempered with justice.

What the emissaries of Vishnu told those of Yama regarding the holiness of the Name is confirmed by Yama in his subsequent instruction to those very emissaries of his:

नामोच्चारणमाहात्म्यं हरेः पश्यत पुत्रकाः ।
अजामिलोऽपि येनैव मृत्युपाशादमूमुचत् ॥
एतावताऽलमघनिर्हरणाय पुंसां
संकीर्तनं भगवतो गुणकर्मनाम्नाम् ।
विक्रुश्य पुत्रमघवान् यदजामिलोऽपि
नारायणेति म्रियमाण इयाय मुक्तिम् ॥

(29-30) Dear boys, see the greatness of the Divine Name! By uttering it alone Ajamila was released from the noose of Death! The recital of the Names of the Lord indicative of His deeds and excellences, is not merely a means for expiation of sins. For, what Ajamila attained by simply shouting 'Narayana!' to call his son at the time of death, was Mukti, liberation from the cycle of births and deaths. (The merit of steady devotional practice must then be certainly much more). (6.3.23-24)

NOTE: In these two verses the *Bhagavata* seems to prefer to accept the power of the Name as such, though it is tolerant of the view that considers the claim to be a eulogy. But at the same time it answers the question: What then is the need of long and sustained devotional practices? This question is posed in verse 30. The commentator Sridhara answers this question by saying that sinful tendencies of the mind will be eliminated only

by the long practice of devotional disciplines. Only then will
Divine Love as a deep-rooted and unshakable sentiment of the
heart be generated. According to the Bhakti Sastra, Mukti or
liberation is not the highest gift of God to man; Bhakti is
the highest gift. It is therefore called the fifth Purushartha (end
to be realised). In verse 1.101 the Lord says that He gives Mukti
liberally, but not Bhakti. The superiority of Bhakti over Mukti
is emphasised in several places in these selections. See verses
1.20-24 ; 1.101 ; 1.113 ; 2.34 38 ; 3.21 ; 4.20-23 etc. It is said
that merely by dying at Kasi one obtains Mukti. So also Mukti
may be had by uttering the Divine Name. But Bhakti is
generated only through constant practice of devotional disciplines
and the attainment thereby of not merely expiation from sin but
effacement of sinful tendency itself. Reference may be made
also to the note on verses 1.33-35 for further information on this
topic.

*The question may be asked why, when there is such a simple
way of expiation for sins, the Law Codes of Manu and Vedic
ritualistic codes lay down very arduous and expensive forms of
penances, rituals and expiatory rites, and again why, when there is
the simple devotional practice of repetition of Divine Names for
attaining Mukti, difficult Yogic and Jnana disciplines have been
laid down by various authoritative teachers. This is answered in the
following two verses of Yama:*

प्रायेण वेद तदिदं न महाजनोऽयं
देव्या विमोहितमतिर्बत माययाsलम् ।
त्रय्यां जडीकृतमति-र्मधुपुष्पितायां
वैतानिके महति वर्मणि युज्यमानः ॥

एवं विमृश्य सुधियो भगवत्यनन्ते
सर्वात्मना विदधते खलु भावयोगम् ।
ते मे न दण्डमर्हन्त्यथ यद्यमीषां
स्यात्पातकं तदपि हन्त्युरुगायवादः ॥

(31-32) The so-called great sages, with their minds in-
fatuated by the Lord's Maya (delusive power), with their intelligence rendered dull by sweet and flowery Vedic texts (offering
promises of attractive rewards and heavenly felicities), and with
their attention fixed on elaborate Vedic rites (for the achievement
of such ends), were not generally aware of this (saving gospel of
devotion). (32) Therefore, after due deliberation, let all men
practise whole-hearted devotion to the Lord, the Supreme Being
and the Indweller of all. Such devotees do not come under my
(Yama's)sway. Even if they have sins, they are all dispelled by
taking the Names of the Lord.   (6.3.25-26)

NOTE : The doubt naturally arises how such an easily
accomplished discipline like the repetition of the Lord's Name
could remove heinous sins and even give liberation. As against
this simple recipe, there are the Dharma Sastras of great sages
which prescribe elaborate forms of expiation (Prayaschittas) for
freeing oneself from the effects of sinful deeds. There are also
difficult forms of Sadhana laid down in Yogic and Vedantic texts
for the attainment of the spiritual *summum bonum*. It is more
credible to accept these as more true than this very simple devotional prescription of taking the Divine Name ; for it is natural
to believe that difficult disciplines are superior and more effective.
The verses 31 and 32 form the answer of the Bhaki cult to persons with the above outlook. The answer is that even the so-
called great sages were ignorant of the path of devotion, and they
blindly and dogmatically adhered to Vedic ritualism and ascetic
practices. Further, it may be added that it is wrong to assume
that complexity in itself is a virtue and simplicity a deficiency. It
may be just the other way. It is sometimes seen that a simple
herbal prescription cures a disease that does not yield to very
complicated and costly treatments.

Not only for the expiation of sins but for the attainment of
union with God also, the devotional doctrine, it is claimed, has
outmoded the Yogic and the Jnana methods of discipline. For
on one who loves the Lord with his whole being, the Lord bestows
knowledge of the unity of all existence also. But while the Bhakta

may have this awareness of unity, he retains his individuality, as he considers it better to love the Lord and serve Him than be merged in Him. This has been discussed in the note to verses 5.29.30 and the references given there.

Historically speaking this verse is a distant echo of the controversy between the Pancharatrins, known also as Bhagavatas, Ekantins, Sattvatas etc., and the Vedic ritualists known familiarly as the Purva-mimamsakas who looked down upon the Pancharatrins as heterodox and non-Vedic. As the hold of Vedic ritualism declined, the rituals and religion of the Pancharatra and other Agamas gained dominance. They also came to be accepted as not inconsistent with Vedic Philosophy through the writings of great Vaishnava sages and savants like Yamuna, the grand preceptor of Ramanuja. Today this controversy has completely subsided, but here and there we get in texts like this echoes of the issues that were once hotly debated among the theologians of this country. Just as ritualism was criticised, the extreme intellectualism of Jnana Yoga was also subjected to criticism by the Bhagavatas.

An explanation of the good fortune that befell Ajamila, reconciling the glory of the Name and the necessity of meritorious acts, is given in the words of Ajamila himself:

अथापि मे दुर्भगस्य विबुधोत्तमदर्शने ।
भवितव्यं मृष्टलेन येनात्मा मे प्रसीदति ॥

अन्यथा म्रियमाणस्य नाशुचेर्वृषलीपतेः ।
वैकुंठनामग्रहणं जिह्वा वक्ष्यमिहार्हति ॥

क्वाहं कितवः पापो ब्रह्मघ्नो निरपत्रपः ।
क्व च नारायणेत्येतद्भगवन्नाम मङ्गलम् ॥

(33-35) Though a sinner (in this life), I must have had some meritorious Karma of previous births to my credit to have had the vision of these divine personages (i.e. emissaries of Vishnu) and the serenity of mind arising from it. Otherwise, an impure man, paramour of a low-born woman, could not have uttered, at the time of death, 'Narayana!', the attractive name of Lord Vishnu. What am I—a cheat, a sinner, a murderer and an unregenerate rogue ! And how great is the Lord's holy Name,' Narayana'! (But for some past merits, or the Lord's unconditioned grace, how could that holy Name come to my mouth?)   (6.2.32-34)

NOTE : Here the *Bhagavata* itself gives an answer reconciling the power of the Name and the apparently undeserving nature of Ajamila. The answer is, that man must have great merits coming from past lives, if not from the present life, to be fortunate enough to utter the Name of the Lord with its inherent saving power. Sri Ramakrishna illustrates the special effect of the Name uttered at the time of death by a simile. If an elephant is washed immediately before being confined to the stable, it remains clean, as it cannot put dust on its body any more. But if it is washed earlier and let loose, it covers itself with dust in no time. So in ordinary life men utter the Name, and yet they are found unregenerate, because they still continue to act in the world with their sinful tendencies still unerased. But if purified by the Name at the time of death, there is no more chance of sinning, as illustrated by the example of the elephant. It is, however, to be remembered that it is by continuous devotional practice alone that deep and abiding love of God is established and sinful tendency of the mind erased and man rendered sinless in the fullest sense of the term, even while living. It can also occur, though rarely, without all this, by the Lord's grace.

Rishis on the purifying potency of the Name :

ब्रह्महा पितृहा गोघ्न मातृहाऽचार्यहाऽघवान् ।
श्वादः पुल्कसको वापि शुद्ध्येरन् यस्य कीर्तनात् ॥

(36) By singing His praise even heinous sinners like murderers of holy men and parents and teachers, as also men of low and impure birth, are redeemed.   (6.13.8)

NOTE : It is to be specially noted that this is not an exhortation to people to commit such sins in the hope that they can be easily absolved from them afterwards. The object of the verse is to impress on man the utter holiness and power of the Name and to show that it offers a means of purification for those who are sincerely repentant. The sign of true repentance is that man feels intense pain in the heart for the past sinful deeds and turns his face away from them once for all, seeking refuge in the Lord.

Devahuti extols the greatness of the Name :

अहो बत श्वपचोऽतो गरीयान् यज्जिह्वाग्रे वर्तते नाम तुभ्यम् ।
तेपुस्तपस्ते जुहुवुः सस्नुरार्या ब्रह्मानूचुर्नाम गृणन्ति ये ते ॥

(37)   A dog-eater (i.e. a man of low birth and unclean habits) is more worthy of honour than a man of high birth, if the former is always uttering Thy holy Name. For only such noble ones as have undergone austerities, performed sacrifices, bathed in holy waters, and learnt and taught the Vedas (in previous births) repeat Thy holy Name always.   (3.33.7)

NOTE : The idea seems to be that only those who have earlier undergone the disciplines enumerated, can gain that purity, faith and devotional fervour that would enable them to repeat the Lord's Name always and remember Him. So the continuous repetition of the Name involves the efficacy of all those disciplines and much more, the latter being only parts of Apara Bhakti (preparatory devotion) while the former is a mark of Para Bhakti (perfected devotion).

Sri Krishna on the path of devotion being open even to house-holders :

गृहेष्वाविशतां चापि पुंसां कुशलकर्मणाम् ।
मद्वार्तायातयामानां न बंधाय गृहा मताः ॥

(38)   The home does not become a cause of bondage to house-holders who have entered that state of life and are engaged in useful works dedicated to Me, and who devote their time to devotional practices (consisting of My worship, repetition of My Names and glorifying of My deeds and excellences).   (4.30.19)

NOTE : The *Bhagavata* religion, while it respects asceticism, is primarily the religion for the ordinary man. Attachment to home and engagement in work are natural to him. He need not condemn himself for this and feel that spiritual progress is impossible for him. If he calls upon the Lord earnestly, offers the fruits of all works to Him, and every day devotes some time to devotional practice his progress is assured.

Prahlada illustrates the above doctrine by his own example :

तस्मादहं विगतविक्लव ईश्वरस्य
सर्वात्मना महि गृणामि यथा मनीषम् ।
नीचोऽजया गुणविसर्गमनुप्रविष्टः
पूयेत येन हि पुमाननुवर्णितेन ॥

(39) Though born in a sinful line, I adore the Lord without any doubt or hesitation by whole-hearted praise of His Divine majesty and greatness, according to my capacity and understanding. For such praise purifies a man even if he be entangled in worldly life, which Maya, the Lord's mysterious power, has created.

(7.9.12)

NOTE : This verse specially inculcates that no man should hesitate to take to devotional life from any sense of unworthiness or sinfulness. None is too low or sinful to be acceptable to God. It is also to be pointed out here that worship and praise of God are not done to bribe and flatter Him, as some critics of devotional practices sometimes remark. Through worship and praise we commune with Him, and the Divine Spirit purifies the worshipper even as water purifies a man who submerges himself in it.

Prahlada states how the above-mentioned devotional discipline of 'Hearing' and 'Praising' takes a man to spiritual perfection :

सोऽहं प्रियस्य सुहृदः परदेवताया लीलाकथास्तव नृसिंह विरिश्चगीताः
अञ्जस्तितर्म्यनुगृणन् गुणविप्रमुक्तो दुर्गाणि ते पदयुगालयहंससंगः ॥

(40) O Lord, I shall easily get over all obstacles and get released from the hold of the qualities of Prakriti (material Nature) by taking to the recital of the glorious accounts emanating from Brahma and the exalted sages regarding the sportive manifestations of Thine—the Friend, the Dear One and the Supreme Lord of all —, and by associating myself with the Swans, the Paramahamsas, having their abode at the lotus of Thy feet.

(7.9.18)

Sri Suka on the purifying effect of the Lord's name on rituals and worship :

मन्त्रतस्तन्त्रतः छिद्रं देशकालार्हवस्तुतः ।
सर्वं करोति निश्छिद्रं नामसङ्कीर्तनं तव ॥

(41) Whatever imperfections there may be in rituals and acts of worship in regard to the utterance of Mantras, the observance of procedure and the choice of the place, the time, the recipient of gifts etc.—all such deficiencies and defects are removed by the utterance of Thy Name.   (8.23.16)

NOTE : It is customary to conclude rites and ceremonies with the invocation : 'Whatever omissions have been caused knowingly or unknowingly, may all of them be made good and the ceremony made perfect by the utterance of the Lord's Name— Sri Hari, Sri Hari.'

Praise by the women of Mathura for the Gopikas who always thought and sang of Sri Krishna and His greatness :

या दोहनेऽवहनने मथनोपलेप-प्रेह्रेह्रनामेरुदितोक्षणमार्जनादौ ।
गायन्ति चैनमनुरक्तधियोऽश्रुकण्ठ्यो धन्या व्रजस्त्रिय उरुक्रमचित्तधानाः ॥

(42) Fortunate indeed were the milk-maids of Vraja who always thought of, and sang about, the Lord with minds full of love and throats choked with feeling—whether they were engaged in milking or pounding, churning or rubbing, attending to babies or cleansing vessels.   (10.44.15)

Gopikas on the attractiveness of the Lord's excellences :

क उत्सेहत सन्त्यक्त-मुत्तमश्लोकसंविदम् ।
अनिच्छतोऽपि यस्य श्रीरङ्गान्न च्यवते क्वचित् ॥

(43) Who can forget the Lord and His deeds? He is so attractive that Sri Devi never leaves Him, although He does not care for her in the least!   (10.47.48)

Uddhava declares that men with true discrimination always engage themselves in the recital of the Lord's excellences. The references are to the exploits of Sri Krishna :

गायन्ति ते विशदकर्म गृहेषु देव्यो राज्ञां स्वशत्रुवधमात्मविमोक्षणं च ।
गोप्यश्च कुञ्जरपतेर्जनकात्मजायाः पित्रोश्च लब्धशरणा मुनयो वयं च ॥

(44) The wives of the kings imprisoned by Jarasandha, while engaged in their household duties, are singing songs about (the forthcoming) destruction of their enemy (Jarasandha) and about the early liberation of their imprisoned husbands, just as the Gopikas and also the holy men and devotees like us, who have sought shelter in Thee, are singing about Thy exploits like the saving of the elephant king, the rescuing of Sita and the liberation of Thy own parents from the prison of Kamsa.   (10.71.9)

Hymning is extolled indirectly by a verse of Narada (selected not from the Bhagavata but the Haribhaktisudha) :

जिह्वां लब्ध्वापि यो विष्णुं कीर्तनीयं न कीर्तयेत् ।
लब्ध्वापि मोक्षनिःश्रेणीं स नारोहति दुर्मतिः ॥

(45) He who, in spite of being endowed with the vocal organ, does not sing the excellences of the worshipful Vishnu, is like the fool who, having got the ladder for scaling the tower of Moksha, fails to ascend it.

The futility of having the power of speech that is never used for taking the Name of the Lord is stated in Sri Krishna's words :

गां दुग्धदोहा-मसतीं च भार्यां देहं पराधीन-मसत्प्रजां च ।
वित्तं त्वतीर्थीकृतमङ्ग वाचं हीनां मया रक्षति दुःखदुःखी ॥

यस्यां न मे पावनमङ्ग कर्म स्थित्युद्भवप्राणनिरोधमस्य ।
लीलावतारेप्सितजन्म वा स्याद् वन्ध्यां गिरं तां बिभृयान्न धीरः ॥

(46-47) He indeed is a miserable man who possesses a milk-
less cow, an adulterous wife, an enslaved body, a wicked offspring,
tainted wealth, or power of speech that is never used in praise of
Me. A man of wisdom should not allow his literary powers to
become fruitless by failing to use them for glorifying My works of
creation, preservation, re-absorption and redemption, and for
describing the highly attractive deeds performed by Me in My
sportive manifestations as Incarnations.   (11.11.19-20)

Karabhājana on Kirtana as the special discipline for Kali Yuga:

कलिं सभाजयन्त्यार्या गुणज्ञाः सारभागिनः ।
यत्र सङ्कीर्तनेनैव सर्वः स्वार्थोऽभिलभ्यते ।
न ह्यतः परमो लाभो देहिनां भ्राम्यतामिह ।
यतो विन्देत परमां शान्तिं नश्यति संसृतिः ॥

(48-49) Wise men who know what is good and what is
essential, speak very highly of the iron age of Kali. For in this
age man attains to the supreme state by merely singing the praise
of Krishna (Sankirtana). For Jivas caught in Samsara there is
nothing so valuable as this discipline of Sankirtana which can
bring supreme peace and freedom from Samsara (cycle of births
and deaths).   (11.5.36-37)

*Suka extols the duty of propagating the Divine Name in Kali
Yuga:*

ते सभाग्या मनुष्येषु कृतार्था नृप निश्चितम् ।
स्मरन्ति सारयन्तो ये हरेर्नाम कलौ युगे ।

(50) In this age of Kali they indeed are the fortunate and
blessed ones who themselves remember the Name of Hari and
also help others to remember the same.

Suka glorifies Kali for making salvation easy through Sankir-tana:

कलेर्दोषनिधे राजन् अस्ति ह्येको महान् गुणः ।
कीर्तनादेव कृष्णस्य मुक्तसङ्गः परं व्रजेत् ॥
कृते यद् ध्यायतो विष्णुं त्रेतायां यजतो मखैः ।
द्वापरे परिचर्यायां कलौ तद्धरिकीर्तनात् ॥

(51-52) The age of Kali, though abounding in evil, has one great advantage about it. For in this age, even by Kirtana alone man can gain release and attain to Krishna. What an aspirant attains in the Krita Yuga through meditation on Vishnu, in the Treta Yuga through sacrifices to Him, and in the Dwapara Yuga through worship of Him, is attained in the Kali Yuga through hymning the praise of Hari (Sankirtana).   (12.3.51-52)

NOTE: Krita Yuga, Treta Yuga, Dwapara Yuga and Kali Yuga are the four ages of time, and from the first to the last of them, the process is one of progressive deterioration of man's spiritual, ethical and physical stature and capacities. In Kali, the most degenerate of all ages, the easiest form of discipline, namely, Sankirtana, is sufficient for spiritual upliftment. Knowing that man's physical and mental powers are very limited in this age, the Lord has provided an easy discipline which every one can practise. This is the view of the *Bhagavata*. The present times are supposed to come within the early period of the Kali Age.

To the question what attributes of Hari are to be praised, a reply is given in the words of Brahma to the effect that His attri-butes are endless and so man may select whatever he likes:

विष्णोर्नु वीर्यगणनां कतमोऽर्हतीह
यः पार्थिवान्यपि कविर्विममे रजांसि ।
चस्कंभ यः स्वरंहसाऽस्खलता त्रिविष्टं
यस्मात् त्रिसाम्यसदनादुरुकंपयानम् ॥

नान्तं विदाम्यहममी मुनयोऽग्रजास्ते
मायाबलस्य पुरुषस्य कुतोऽपरे ये ।
गायन् गुणान् दशशतानन आदिदेवः
शेषोऽधुनापि समवस्यति नास्य पारम् ॥

(53-54) To compute the glories and attributes of Sri Hari
is impossible even for a wise man who is supposed to possess the
power to calculate the number of particles of dust comprising the
earth. So wonderful are His powers that as the Vamana covering
the worlds with His three steps, He held together through His
puissance, the whole cosmos from Satyaloka down, as it trembled
and whirled under the speed of the movement of His feet.
[An alternative translation: See how by His puissance He held
together the whole universe in Himself, while everything in it
(from Pradhana, the rudimentary state of Prakriti up to Satyaloka, the most highly evolved state moved at terrific speed by)
the irresistible might of His feet.] Though I am Brahma, the
creator, I have no understanding of the extent of the mysterious
power of the Lord. Nor do your elders, the foremost among the
Munis, know. Adisesha, the first of all the divinities, has ever
been singing about His glories with all his thousand mouths, and
yet is nowhere near exhausting them.   (2.7.40-41)

*Drumila on the childishness of limitng His greatness by our
worldly calculation:*

यो वा अनन्तस्य गुणाननन्ता-ननुक्रमिष्यन् स तु बालबुद्धिः ।
रजांसि भूमेर्गणयेत्कथंचित् कालेन नैवाखिलसत्त्वधाम्नः ॥

(55) He who tries to exhaust by calculation the excellences
of the Infinite Being is indeed a childish mind. Perhaps in the
course of ages it may be possible to count how many particles of
dust constitute the earth, but not so to determine exhaustively
the attributes and glories of the Lord, who is the source of
infinite power.   (11.4.2)

13

In Akrura's words it is stated that the presence of even a little of the Divine sentiment in an otherwise secular literary production, would make it acceptable:

यस्याखिलामीवहमिः सुमङ्गलै-र्वाचो विमिश्रा गुणकर्मजन्मभिः ।
प्राणन्ति शुम्भन्ति पुनन्ति वै जगद्द्यास्तद्विरक्ताः शवशोभना मताः ॥

(56) If literary productions are at least partially mixed with the description of the attributes and the workings of the Lord, the most auspicious, sinless and sanctifying Entity, then they purify the world and give it light and life. Otherwise they (the so-called fine literary pieces) are like decorations on a corpse.   (10.38-12)

Suka on Sravana and Kirtana being the essential part of the path of devotion :

इत्थं हरेर्भगवतो रुचिरावतार-वीर्याणि बालचरितानि च शन्तमानि ।
अन्यत्र चेह च श्रुतानि गृणन् मनुष्यो भक्तिं परां परमहंसगतौ लभेत ॥

(57) A person who resorts to the auspicious and enthralling accounts of the Lord's incarnations and of His exploits and His doings in childhood, as given in this work and in others (like the Vishnu Purana), will progress in the path of the Paramahamsas, attaining supreme devotion in this life and liberation hereafter.
          (11.31.28)

STRAND 6

SMARANA OR REMEMBRANCE

[**Introduction :** This section deals with Smarana or Remembrance of the Lord, which forms the third of the devotional disciplines. But it must be noted that these disciplines are not watertight compartments. They impinge on, and supplement, one another. In fact Hearing and Praising, the disciplines treated earlier, as also some of the others that follow, are mainly intended to create a vivid consciousness of God at all times. So the success in one's practice of these disciplines is to be measured by the capacity they develop in one to keep up an undercurrent of Smarana (Remembrance) of the Lord even when one is engaged in other occupations of life. We may feel this is impossible; but it becomes possible to the extent that a longing, a hunger, for God is generated in us. Sri Ramakrishna illustrates this by the instance of a man with a toothache. He may be doing his daily duties, but the consciousness of the pain never leaves him. It is indeed a great achievement in devotional life to keep up Smarana, Remembrance, at all times. The silent repetition of a Divine Name or a Mantra is one of the effective ways of practising Remembrance. Japa or repetition of a Mantra is done at fixed times in a ceremonial way. But in the pure path of devotion it can be done always and anywhere. There are Hindu devotees whose lips always move in the silent repetition of such holy Names as Rama, Krishna, Narayana etc. This is the most effective way of keeping up Remembrance.]

Uddhava on Smarana as illustrated in the Gopikas :

अहो यूयं स्म पूर्णार्था भवत्यो लोकपूजिताः ।
वासुदेवे भगवति यासामित्यर्पितं मनः ॥

(1) You (the Gopikas) have attained to the highest fulfilment in life indeed, and have become worthy of worship by all the

worlds.   For you.have your minds constantly fixed on Vasudeva,
the Supreme being.   (10.47.23)

*The same idea is emphasized by Sri Krishna in His advice to
Uddhava:*

एतावान् योग आदिष्टो मच्छिष्यैः सनकादिभिः ।
सर्वतो मन आकृष्य मय्यद्धावेश्यते यथा ॥

(2)   I have instructed my disciples like Sanaka and others to
the effect that Yoga consists in disciplining the mind in such a way
that it is drawn away from all objects and fixed in remembrance
of Me.   (11.13.14)

The purifying power of Smarana in the words of Sri Suka:

सकृन्मनः कृष्णपदारविन्दयो-निवेशितं तद्गुणरागि यैरिह ।
न ते यमं पाशभृतश्च तद्भटान् स्वप्नेपि पश्यन्ति हि चीर्णनिष्कृताः ॥

(3)   If a person fixes his mind on Krishna's feet even once
with a fervent appreciation of His excellences, that person would
have atoned for all his sins of the past, and neither Yama nor his
emissaries with noose in hand would ever approach him even in a
dream.   (6.11.9)

The pervasive effect of Smarana in the words of Brahma:

न भारती मेऽङ्ग मृषोपलक्ष्यते न वै क्वचिन्मे मनसो मृषा गतिः ।
न मे हृषीकाणि पतन्त्यसत्पथे यन्मे हृदौत्कण्ठ्यवता धृतो हरिः ॥

(4)   Because I hold Sri Hari in my heart with the ardour of
intense devotion, my words never turn untrue, my thoughts
always become effective and my senses never go into the paths of
sin.   (2.6.33)

Suka on Smarana as the end of all Sadhana:

एतावान् सांख्ययोगाभ्यां स्वधर्मपरिनिष्ठया ।
जन्मलाभः परः पुंसामन्ते नारायणस्मृतिः ॥

(5)   This much is the purpose of practising the paths of
Jnana, Yoga and Karma—that man may have the remembrance

of Narayana at the time of death. This, indeed, is the highest
gain in life.   (2.1.6)

NOTE: The last thought at the time of death is given the
greatest importance by the Hindus, as it determines the further
course of evolution. In order that men may not misunderstand
this, it is hinted in this verse that it is continued devotional
practice all through life that will generate the thought of God at
the time of death. This comes as a corrective to any misunderstanding one may have from the example of Ajamila narrated in
the earlier section (V.13-12) that one can live a merry life and at
the last moment utter the name of Narayana and get salvation.
Ajamila's case is to be understood in the light of the good works
done by him in some previous birth, the effects of which were
lying in abeyance, or as an act of the Lord's unconditioned grace.

The same truth emphasized in the words of Sri Suka:

तस्मात्सर्वात्मना राजन् हृदिस्थं कुरु केशवम् ।
म्रियमाणो ह्यवहितः ततो यासि परां गतिम् ॥
म्रियमाणैरभिध्येयो भगवान् परमेश्वरः ।
आत्मभावं नयत्यंग सर्वात्मा सर्वसंश्रयः ॥

(6-7) Therefore, O King, you being at the end of your life,
fix your mind on Sri Hari, in a firm and steady way. You shall
attain to the supreme state thereby. The Supreme Lord, the soul
and support of all, draws into Himself one who meditates on Him
at the time of death.   (12.3.49-50)

*The Vedanta says that only Jnana can give Moksha. How then
can Smarana or Remembrance be said to give liberation? The
reconciliation is to be had in these words of Suta :*

अविस्मृतिः कृष्णपदारविन्दयोः क्षिणोत्यभद्राणि च शं तनोति ।
सत्त्वस्य शुद्धिं परमात्मभक्तिं ज्ञानं च विज्ञानविरागयुक्तम् ॥

(8) The constant Remembrance of Krishna renders a man
sinless. It purifies and pacifies his mind, and generates in him

devotion and knowledge (Jnana), accompanied by Vairagya (dispassion) and Vijnana (Special Knowledge).

(12.12.45)

NOTE: The teaching of the *Bhagavata* is that devotion is in itself a self-sufficient spiritual path. One who always remembers Krishna attains to everything through His grace. This is the view upheld by Sri Ramakrishna also. The distinction hinted at between Jnana and Vijnana in the verse is very significant, and is reminiscent of Sri Ramakrishna's teaching. Jnana is the knowledge of the Unity of all existence sought to be obtained in Samadhi by the elimination of all multiplicity as mere illusion, a Maya. But it is realised as Lila or sportive manifestation of the Unity (i.e. of the Supreme Being) by one who gets the ego of Vidya after the Samadhi, by the Divine will. Such a person is a Vijnani as contrasted with a Jnani. It must be noted that the perception of multiplicity by a man without Jnana and the perception of it by one with Vijnana are basically different in significance. The ordinary ignorant man has no apprehension of the Base or Ground of multiplicity. The Jnani apprehends the Base or Ground only, and the many as its expression. The Vijnani experiences both the Base or Ground and the multiple manifestation, the One and the many, simultaneously. So his knowledge is more complete and he is therefore called Vijnani (one endowed with specialised knowledge). The Jnani describes the many as Maya, illusion, and the Vijnani as Lila, playful manifestation. In the Vijnani knowledge and devotion manifest themselves without any contradiction. Sri Ramakrishna describes such a spiritual state in a poetic way as the simultaneous existence of the lunar light and the solar light. The *Bhagavata* seems to stand for this very same philosophical and devotional doctrine.

Suka on Smarana as the most important of spiritual disciplines.

विद्यातपः प्राणनिरोधमैत्री तीर्थाभिषेक-व्रतदानजप्यैः ।
नात्यन्तशुद्धिं लभतेऽन्तरात्मा यथा हृदिस्थे भगवत्यनन्ते ॥

(9) Learning, austerities, regulation of breath, kindliness, pilgrimages, gifts, repetition of Mantras—none of these practices

can purify the mind so efficiently as the constant Remembrance
of the Lord (i.e. the installation of Him in the heart).   (12.3.48)

The same he emphasizes again :

पुंसां कलिकृतान् दोषान् द्रव्यदेशात्मसंभवान् ।
सर्वान्हरति चित्तस्थो भगवान् पुरुषोत्तमः ॥
यथा हेम्नि स्थितो वह्निर्दुर्वर्णं हन्ति धातुजम् ।
एवमात्मगतो विष्णुर्योगिनामशुभाशयम् ॥

(10-11) Owing to the evil influence of the Iron Age of Kali
men are likely to commit many sins arising from the use of prohi-
bited materials, residence in undersirable surroundings and indulgence in evil ways with the body and the mind.   The Lord dispels
such sins and sinful tendencies when He manifests in the heart of
a devotee through constant Remembrance.   Just as fire removes
the stain found in gold owing to contact with other metals, so
Vishnu, by His presence, removes all the evil tendencies in the
Yogis.   (12.3.45-47)

NOTE : The purport of the first verse is not to give a licence
to commit sin.   It is applicable only to the sincerely repentant
person who wants to turn a new leaf in life.   Constant Remembrance is possible only at an advanced stage of devotional life
attained through long practice of other disciplines mentioned
earlier and hereafter.   Similarly the second verse describes how
Remembrance purifies a sinful heart.   It is to be noted that
it is the Lord who purifies the heart of the Yogi and not his practices, as
one might think, just as it is the fire, and not the water etc., used for
dipping the gold, that purifies the gold.

Uddhava on how Smarana purifies even the enemies of God :

मन्येऽसुरान् भागवतांस्त्र्यधीशे संरम्भमार्गाभिनिविष्टचित्तान् ।
ये संयुगेऽचक्षत तार्क्ष्यपुत्र-मंसे सुनाभायुधमापतन्तम् ॥
एनः पूर्वकृतं यत्तद्राजानः कृष्णवैरिणः ।
जहुस्त्वन्ते तदात्मानः कीटः पेशस्कृतो यथा ॥

(12-13) I consider as devotees even the Asuras who, in a mood of anger and confrontation, fixed their mind on the Lord, the Master of the worlds. For they could see with their naked eyes the Lord Mahavishnu, the wielder of the discus, rushing at them on the neck of His eagle vehicle. Being united with Krishna in mind through enmity, these kings overcame their earlier sins, just as the larva abandons its old form and becomes a Pesakrit (a kind of wasp) by constant thought of it through fear.   (3.2.24); (7.10.39)

NOTE : That just as God could be approached through love, He could also be reached through a form of intense antagonism born of mortal fear, is a special doctrine of the *Bhagavata.* The principle underlying this doctrine is that, whatever the motivation, if the mind could be fixed on Him firmly and with the whole energy of one's being, His grace descends on one in a form appropriate to the mood in which such a fixing is made. One can approach Him through prayer and supplication, as all devotees usually do, and He blesses them appearing before them as their protector. But there are some titanic spirits, Asuras like Hiranyaksha, Hiranyakasipu, Ravana, Kumbhakarna, Sisupala etc (the like of whom we come across only in the Puranas and not in actual life), who lived in mortal dread of Mahavishnu and, in consequence, kept themselves always in a mood of alertness and confrontation, thinking of Him with intense fear and hatred. The Puranas describe how in good time He appeared before them in appropriate forms of a terrible nature and destroyed them in battle. They were physically destroyed, but spiritually regenerated, the blows He delivered on them being His blessings appropriate to the mood of the Asuras. Also see notes on verse 6.15. The verse 13 describes how fear and antagonism effect this transformation. A larva is imprisoned in a hole or muddy crust by a certain type of wasp (*pesakrit*) which goes on buzzing, hovering about or sitting on the spot. Poetic fancy attributes the gradual transformation of the larva to its constant thought of the wasp generated by fear. Intense and constant fear fixes one's attention on the foe as much as love does on the beloved. As these Asuras fixed their mind on Vishnu or His incarnations, though it might be through fear, this act had a transforming effect, irrespective of the nature of the motivating emotion. The relevant fact is that the mind was fixed intensely on Vishnu. This rather strange way of approaching the Divine is called Vidvesha-Bhakti, communion through confrontation. As these Asuras and Asuric kings perished at His hands and attained salvation immediately, they did not live to exemplify of what nature the transformation that came over them was, unlike the Gopikas who also approached Krishna through another dubious passion, carnal love of woman for man, but got transformed by the contact with Krishna (see notes on verse 6-16, 17) and lived to illustrate what the highest form of Divine love means.

This is probably why the Prema Bhakti (loving devotion) of the Gopikas has played an important part in devotional traditions and in the discussion of the theorizers of the gospel of devotion like Narada and Sandilya in the Bhakti Sutras attributed to them, unlike the concept of Vidvesha-Bhakti. In calling a sentiment Bhakti (loving devotion), there are two pre-suppositions: The devotee must have *tadiyata*, a feeling of 'belonging' to Him, and God must be conceived of as having *anukulya*, favourable responsiveness, when approached. Both these are absent in Vidvesha-Bhakti or habitual antagonism and confrontation, and it is therefore very difficult to bring it under the concept of Bhakti. This together with its practical uselessness to ordinary man, is probably why Narada and Sandilya do not take it up for discussion, in spite of the definite place given to it in the *Bhagavata*. It has perhaps application only to some titanic spirits like Hiranya-kasipu, Ravana etc., and even these are not, according to the Puranas, ordinary Jivas working out their spiritual evolution, but divine spirits under a curse, awaiting redemption by meeting with destruction at the hands of the Lord as the Incarnate, as stated in a succeeding verse. (See notes on verse 6-15). One point, however, has to be clarified here. No one should mistake this idea of 'communion through confrontation' with atheism and agnosticism. In such attitudes there is no concentration on God in any sense. They are superficial intellectual doctrines. They

are the result of an attitude of indifference to God and extreme
concern with worldly enjoyments, which are hostile to the generation of a purposeful philosophic enquiry.

The above idea is further emphasized in the words of Narada:

वैरेण यं नृपतयः शिशुपालपौण्ड्र-
शाल्वादयो गतिविलासविलोकनाद्यैः ।
ध्यायन्त आहतधियः शयनासनादौ
तत्साम्यमापुरनुरक्तधियां पुनः किम् ॥

(14) Kings like Sisupala, Paundra, Salva and others thought
of the Lord always (in mortal dread) as their enemy—be it while
walking, playing, sleeping or sitting. Their minds, being thus
directed to Him, meditated on Him always and they attained
union with Him. What to speak then of those who have loving
devotion to Him!

(11.5.48)

NOTE: Remembrance of the Lord, with all the energy of
one's being, whatever might be the motive or passion directing
that energy, will result in His manifesting Himself to the person
concerned. Antagonism, accompanied by mortal fear, can be
such a driving passion in some exceptional souls. This seems to
be the teaching.

*The spiritual background of some of these cases of Vidvesha
Bhakti is given in the words of Jaya and Vijaya, two famous examples of this brand of devotion in the Bhagavata :*

भूयादघोनि भगवद्भिरकारि दण्डो
यो नौ हरेत सुरहेलनमप्यशेषम् ।
मा वोऽनुतापकलया भगवत्स्मृतिघ्नो
मोहो भवेदिह तु नौ व्रजतोरधोऽधः ॥

(15) You sages (Sanaka and the other Kumaras) have right-
ly punished us, offenders against holy ones. May it for ever
efface from us the tendency to insult holy sages. But taking pity

on us who are being expelled from the supreme heavenly state to a life of darkness and degradation, bless us so that we may not have that forgetfulness of ignorance resulting in the effacement of Remembrance of the Lord.   (3.15.36)

NOTE : Jaya and Vijaya, who address the above prayer, were the gate-keepers of Vaikuntha, the heavenly abode of Vishnu. When Sanaka and the holy Kumaras (the eternal Boy Devotees) went to see the Lord, these gate-keepers refused them admission and thus insulted them. Though the sages were not mentally hurt by their indiscreet behaviour, they felt that these emissaries of Vaikuntha were not fit to be in their exalted position but required further purification. So they cursed them to the effect that they would be degraded as creatures in the lower scales of evolution. The repentant emissaries prayed for remission from the curse and the sages offered them a way of release. Taking birth as Asuras, they would be endowed with a born antagonism to ·Vishnu and intense dread of Him. The intensity of these feelings would make them focus their mind always on Him. Thus through Remembrance they could exhaust their evil Karma in three births, in every one of which they would be killed by the Lord in His incarnations in forms appropriate to the attitudes of confrontation they assumed. Accordingly they took three successive births as fraternal pairs,—Titanic souls noted for their power and antagonism to God, known in Hindu mythology as Hiranyaksha and Hiranyakasipu, Ravana and Kumbhakarna, and Sisupala and Dantavaktra. Maha-vishnu destroyed them in turn in His Incarnations as Cosmic Boar, as Man·Lion, as Rama and as Krishna, and thereafter they got back their place in Vaikuntha.

Those brought up in Hindu religious traditions accept these accounts as literal facts. Others may not. Such examples of Vidvesha Bhakti are exceptions and not the general rule. We never come across such examples in life, and however much the psychological principle involved may be acceptable, it is of no use in the practice of devotion. So Sandilya and Narada, the authorities on Bhakti, have not given importance to this type of attitude in formulating their theory of devotion.

It is to be noted that in Christian mythology also there is a
parallel to this, though it has no devotional implication. Satan
was one of the Archangels of God. He revolted against God and
lost his place, and became Satan, the great enemy of God, seduc-
ing His creatures. Satan is ever in confrontation with God, but
unlike Jaya and Vijaya, he has no contrition and is ultimately
condemned to eternal hell. One wonders how Christian thinkers
failed to recognize that one's antagonism to God involves
Remembrance of Him and should ultimately work out one's
salvation.

*Through the words of Sruti Devatas (Vedas conceived as
female deities singing the praise of Lord Krishna), all conflicting
forms of devotional attitudes, including those of confrontation and
sex love, are reconciled on the ground that they are all forms cf
Smarana or Remembrance. Their words are followed by Krishna's
words stating the principle involved :*

निभृतमरुन्मनोऽक्षदृढयोगयुजो हृदि यन्-
मुनय उपासते तदरयोऽपि ययुः स्मरणात् ।
स्त्रिय उरगेन्द्रभोगभुजदण्डविषक्तधियो
वयमपि ते समाः समदृशोंऽघ्रिसरोजसुधाः ॥
विषयान् ध्यायतश्चित्तं विषयेषु विषज्जते ।
मामनुस्मरतश्चेतो मय्येव प्रविलीयते ॥

(16-17) Through Remembrance Thy antagonists attained to
the same spiritual goal as the sages who had established complete
control over their vital forces, mind and senses, and meditated
on Thee in the heart. To Thee, we (the Sruti Devatas or Vedas
conceived as female deities) who commune with Thy presence in
everything alike, and the women (Gopikas of Vrindavana) who
longed for the embrace of Thy powerful and handsome arms, are of
equal worth. A mind that thinks intensely of sense objects becomes converted into the form and nature of those objects, and a
mind that thinks of Me attains union with Me. (10.87.23; 11.14.27)

NOTE: Yogic meditation, philosophical contemplation, antagonism and carnal affection are all equated in the above verses as means for the attainment of the Lord who responds to the followers of these paths in a manner appropriate to their respective attitudes. The intensity of their mood and the fact of the Divine being the object towards which their mind is directed, are the reasons for their attainment of union with the Lord.

The attainment of communion through confrontation (Vidvesha Bhakti) has already been discussed in the Notes on the earlier verse. The example of attainment through carnal affection referred to here is that of the famous Gopikas (milkmaids) of Vrindavana. There is much confused thinking regarding the attitude of the Gopikas. The difficulty in accepting the doctrine of communion through confrontation is often overlooked with ease, probably because of its impracticality and non-occurrence in actual life. But we cannot so easily dismiss the attitude of the Gopikas, which has been taken as the example of the highest form of Bhakti by great theorizers on the subject like Narada and Sandilya, and which forms the central theme of the teachings of great Vaishnava Acharyas like Chaitanya.

The doctrine, however, is complicated by many ethical problems arising from the fact that our accepted moral codes equate carnality and adultery with sin. So various attempts have been made to get over these difficulties by several theories, some of the most important of which are as follows: (1) The whole episode of Krishna and the Gopikas is symbolical and not factual. The Gopika stand for the soul (the Jivatman) and Krishna for the Supreme Soul (Paramatman), and the intense aspiration of the former for the latter is depicted through sex-love. The Jiva in this philosophy is taken as the Prakriti of the Lord and is therefore depicted as female. Hence historicity is denied to the descriptions. (2) The *Bhagavata* states that Krishna was only a boy of ten or eleven at the time. So the highly erotic descriptions of the relationship between him and the Gopikas, who are depicted as ladies of mature years, are only poetic exaggerations of some innocent pastoral sports of Krishna with boys and girls of the cowherd community among whom he spent his boyhood days. Here historicity is accepted, but the existence of any ethical problem is denied. (3) According to a third theory, while historicity is accepted, it is maintained that the Gopikas were devoid of bodily consciousness and that they met Krishna at a spiritual level. Therefore there is nothing carnal about the relationship. In support of this is pointed out the *Bhagavata* verse 10.33.38, which states that while the Gopikas were away engaged in Rasa Lila, their people found them at home also. This mystic fact is also hinted at in the statement at the beginning of the description of Rasa Lila, that Krishna took part in it assuming his Yoga Maya (10.29.1).

Now what does the *Bhagavata* itself say on the point? While it is true that the *Bhagavata* text holds forth hints justifying all the three explanations given above, the overwhelming evidence of language and description in the text declares unequivocally that the Gopika episode was a physical fact and that all aspects of love were involved in the relationship. Raja Parikshit, to whom the *Bhagavata* was revealed, takes it in that sense and questions Sri Suka whether there was any ethical justification at all for it.

Suka's famous reply, as given in the *Bhagavata*, is as follows: "Divine personages are found to override the rules of Dharma (ethics) and do actions of a shocking nature. But just as no impurity affects fire which consumes everything, nothing causes blemish to such persons of immense potency. But lesser men should not imitate them in these respects even in their minds. If they do so foolishly, they will perish, as one will perish if one drinks poison following the example of Rudra. The instructions of godly persons are valid; so are some of their actions too. A wise man will follow only such of their actions as are consistent with their words. It is admitted that for enlightened men without the ego sense, there is no selfish gain to be attained by their actions and no evil to be warded off by abstinence from them. What good or evil can then affect the supreme Lord Krishna who is the Master of all beings—gods, men, animals and the rest? By devotion to His holy feet the great sages derive that Yogic power by which they become free from the bondage of all actions. How can there be any bondage or sin in the Universal Being who has assumed a body of His own will, and by devotion to whom even great sages derive their spiritual excellence? He who permeates all beings, including the Gopikas and their husbands, and directs the minds and senses of every one,—even He out of sportive inten tion has assumed a body as Krishna. For bestowing His blessings on all beings He has assumed a body, and He sports with that body in ways that will interest and attract beings to Him. By Krishna's mystic power the inhabitants of Vraja found their women in their homes all the time, and had no occasion to be displeased with Krishna... ..... He who either hears or describes the sport of Krishna with the Gopikas with deep faith (in its sup- reme spiritual significance) obtains the highest devotion and is soon able to overcome lust, the universal disease of the human heart" (10.33.30-40).

From this it is clear that as Krishna faced Kamsa and Sisu- pala (examples of communion through confrontation) with weapons in hand and raised them to the highest spiritual glory by delivering deadly blows on them, He received the Gopikas, who came to Him with passionate love stimulated by His exquisite physical charm and the ravishing strains of His flute, just as an earthly lover receives his beloved, although mentally He was un- perturbed and ever-poised in His spiritual Essence. But what starts as a physical passion in the Gopikas gets transformed into a pure spiritual experience in the course of their association with Krishna. By the touch of Krishna, who, in the words of the Gita, is 'Brahman supreme, the most exalted state of Existence and the seat of all purity and holiness', the Kamukis (lustful females) and the Abhisarikas (the passionate women going in search of their lover) became converted into Premikas (persons endowed with rapturous and loving devotion), transcending body· consciousness like the Paramahamsas. If we remember this aspect of the Krishna-Gopi episode, we will find that Krishna needs no defence and we need not be apologetic about Him by taking refuge in allegorical interpretations. The allegory and the symbolism are there, but we should not use them to overlook or cover up the

Bhagavata doctrine that when the mind is firmly fixed on Him, whatever might be the motivating feeling or circumstance, He responds to the Jiva in a manner appropriate to the Jiva's attitude, and transforms him by His touch. As the verse under consideration states, the Yogis who concentrate their minds on Him as the indwelling Self, the philosophers who try to see Him as pervading everything, the Asuras who live in mortal dread of, and in confrontation with, Him, and the passionate women who seek physical union with Him in violation of all social and ethical sanctions—these are all alike to Him. The fact that the minds of all these are directed to Him with intensity, brings about their transformation when they receive His touch. In reading Krishna's life we should not forget that He was not an ordinary man, but that He was the Supreme Being manifest as man in order to reveal how the one Supreme Being becomes the many, and yet continues to be the one Perfect Being in spite of being the many.

The importance of Remembrance, even while engaged in worldly life, is stated in the words of the kings imprisoned by Jarasandha:

तं नः समादिशोपायं येन ते चरणाब्जयं : ।
स्मृतिर्यथा न विरमेदपि संसरतामिह ॥

(18) Teach us how, even when involved in Samsara (worldly life), we can keep up Thy Remembrance without break.

(10.73.15)

Sri Suka reports, as follows, the last prayer of the Gopikas to Sri Krishna to bless them with Remembrance even when they are engaged in worldly life:

आहुश्च ते नलिननाभ पदारविन्दं यांगेश्वरैर्हृदि विचिन्त्यमगाधबोधैः ।
संसारकूपपतित चरणावलम्बं गेहंजुषामपि मनस्युदियात्सदा नः ॥

(19) O Lord, may we, even when engrossed in worldly life, ever remember Thy holy feet on which Yogis of deep insight meditate in their hearts and which form the means for the uplift of those fallen in the pit of Samsara.   (10.82.49)

That such Remembrance can fill one's mind with a joy that makes one oblivious of all the little joys and sorrows of Samsara, is taught by Suka from the experience of the Vrishnis, the devoted followers of Sri Krishna :

शय्यासनाटनालाप-क्रीडास्नानाशनादिषु ।
न विदुः संतमात्मानं वृष्णयः कृष्णचेतसः ॥

(20) The Vrishnis, with their minds engrossed in Krishna, did not know their own individual existence when they engaged themselves in daily activities like resting in bed, walking about, talking, playing, bathing, eating and the like.   (10.90.46)

Sri Krishna says to Uddhava :

मय्यर्पितात्मनः सभ्य निरपेक्षस्य सर्वतः ।
मयात्मना सुखं यत्तत् कुतस्तद्विषयात्मनाम् ॥

अकिञ्चनस्य दान्तस्य शान्तस्य समचेतसः ।
मया सन्तुष्टमनसः सर्वाः सुखमया दिशः ॥

न पारमेष्ठ्यं न महेन्द्रधिष्ण्यं न सार्वभौमं न रसाधिपत्यम् ।
न योगसिद्धीरपुनर्भवं वा मय्यर्पितात्मेच्छति मद्विनान्यत् ॥

(21-23) O noble one, a person who has cut off his dependence on external things and dedicated his mind entirely to Me, attains to a state of bliss derived from Me, who am the soul of his soul. How can people, whose mind dwells on external objects, ever have that bliss? A person who has nothing as his own, whose mind and senses are under control, who is even-minded in all situations, and who finds full satisfaction in having communion with Me, feels happy wherever he is placed. One who has dedicated one's mind to Me entirely, wants nothing but Me—even if they are given the choice of the status of Brahma, the position of Indra, the office of an emperor, overlordship of Rasatala, the possession of Yogic powers, or the birthless state of liberation.   (11.14.12-14)

*Remembrance of the Lord, characterised by loving devotion
is practised even by sages who have attained to knowledge of
Non-duality :*

भजन्त्यथ त्वामत एव साधवो व्युदस्तमायागुणविभ्रमोदयम् ।
भवत्पदानुस्मरणाद्दते सर्वं निमित्तमन्यद्भगवन्न विद्महे ॥

(24) **Even after attaining knowledge of Thee as devoid of
the world of multiplicity which is manifested by the power of Thy
mysterious Maya, knowing ones continue to worship Thee with
loving devotion. For they cannot find, O Lord, any purpose
other than Remembrance of Thee in their life.** (4.20.29)

NOTE: This verse seems to echo the same philosophy as has
been propounded by Sri Ramakrishna in his doctrine of Vijnana
as distinguished from Jnana. Jnana is the process of negation
generally referred to as 'Neti Neti' (not this, not this), by which
the knowledge of the unity of existence is realized through the
sublation of multiplicity as illusory. This is referred to in the
verse as *Vyudastamāyāguṇavibhramodayam.* When multiplicity is
totally sublated, the Jnani attains to Nirvikalpa Samadhi, in which
he realizes the unity of the essence of his 'I sense' and of the
multiplicity experienced outside as its opposite, both dissolving in
the Absolute Consciousness, which is described as Nirguna (without modification) and Nishprapancha (without multiplicity or
acosmic). According to Sri Ramakrishna, in the case of ordinary
Jivas, when this kind of Samadhi is attained, the individuality of
the Jiva is lost for ever. In the absence of the ego-sense, personality has no support, and the body of the one immersed in such
perpetual Samadhi perishes in the course of twenty-one days.
But, says Sri Ramakrishna, in the case of rare persons – the
Incarnations and divinely commissioned personages – the 'I sense'
that has become one with the Absolute Consciousness is, *by the
Divine will,* restored after Samadhi, but in a transformed state.
In the state of ignorance before the intuition of unity, the ego
knows itself only in its worldly relationships—as one of a particular nationality, as the son of so and so, as occupying such and
such a position etc. This, according to Sri Ramakrishna, is the

Avidya-Aham (the 'I' of ignorance). As against this, the transformed and illumined 'I' (the 'I' of knowledge or Vidya-Aham)
realizes itself as intimately related with the Universal Self in some
form of loving relationship as son, friend, sweetheart etc. And
as regards the external world, what was experienced in the state
of 'ignorance' as mere multiplicity, is now understood as the One
manifesting as the many. In fact the Vijnani, as the person with
this illumined ego is called, experiences that the one Sat-chit-
ananda (Existence-Knowledge-Bliss) is manifesting Himself as
Iswara (God), Jivas (individual souls), and Jagat (universe) in a
sportive manner out of the abundance of His inherent Bliss.
The Vijnani lives as a playmate of God and as an expression of
His redeeming love. In him is expressed the most powerful form
of loving and ecstatic devotion called Mahabhava. For him God
is not power, as He is to an ignorant devotee, but Love, and he
himself becomes an expression of that Love through service. As
it is stated in the above verse, God-love is the only possible
occupation in life for the Vijnani. The *Srimad Bhagavata* verse
numbered 1.7.10 describes this condition as follows: 'Great sages,
even after attaining Mukti and engrossment in the Self, are still
found to practise motiveless devotion to the Lord. So very
wonderful are the excellences of Hari!'

In the next verse, Narada, a sage of this type, describes his
own condition.

*Sage Narada says how, after realizing the Lord, he lived in
Remembrance of Him and moved about propagating the gospel of
devotion :*

दृष्टं तवांघ्रियुगलं जनतापवर्गं ब्रह्मादिभिर्हृदि विचिन्त्यमगाधबोधैः ।
संसारकूपपतितोच्चरणावलम्बं ध्यायंश्चराम्यनुगृहाण यथा स्मृतिः स्यात्

(25) I have been blessed with the vision of Thy holy feet,
where devotees find freedom, on which even Brahma and others of
deep insight meditate, and which form the means for the uplift
of those who have fallen into the pit of Samsara. I shall travel
all over, meditating on Thy holy feet. I beseech that I may ever
have Thy Remembrance.   (10.69.18)

The topic of Smarana is concluded with the following words of Sri Krishna:

तस्मादसदभिध्यानं यथा खममनोरथम् ।
हित्वा मयि समाधत्स्व मनो मद्भावभावितम् ॥

(26) Therefore abandon all vain fancies about transitory worldly objects which are like the mental projections of dream, and fix your mind on Me, having purified it by devotion to Me.
(11.14.28)

NOTE : The comparison of worldly objects with dream is not done to equate them ontologically but is done in a valuational sense. The projection is not by the individual mind. Just as Swapna-Maya (dream power) of the individual projects his very transitory dream experiences, so the Yoga-Maya (the Divine creative power) of the Lord manifests this universe of multiplicity, including the individualities of the Jivas. Realizing this, the Jiva should not get entangled in that manifestation, which too is transitory like dream experiences, but should look towards his own Source, the Supreme Being or Iswara. The analogy of the dream also helps us to get a glimpse of the Divine mystery of creation.*

---

*In this Chapter, the following rearrangement of verses has been made for effecting a greater topical sequence; verse 22 in the original into 13 here; 20 into 14; 14 into 15; 21 into 16; 23 into 17; 15 into 18; 25 into 19; 16 into 20; 19 into 21; 17 into 22; 18 into 23; 13 into 24; 24 into 25.

STRAND 7

PADASEVA OR DIVINE SERVICE

[Introduction : The seventh section deals with Padaseva, the fourth of the nine devotional disciplines. The word literally means 'Serving', especially, 'Shampooing the feet'. Personal service of this type in a literal sense can be done by one to one's revered Teacher (Guru). Men in general can practise it in a symbolic way through the service of a consecrated image, which is identified with the Lord through faith, according to the devotional philosophy. It will thus be seen that this discipline, and also the two that follow, those of making offerings and prostrations, have a special significance to people who practise worship of God through consecrated images. It should be noted that image worship is one of the most effective disciplines in the cultivation of devotion. It is not only a means of concentration as widely believed, but is also a means to gain a sense of the concreteness of God and of having actually served and worshipped Him.

'Serving the feet of the Lord' can have also a wider significance. The *Purusha Sukta* speaks of the four Padas of the Lord, of which one alone is manifest as the worlds, while the others are transcendent. Here Pada means an 'aspect', and the service of the world, which is a manifestation of Him, becomes His service, when done with the correct devotional attitude. When we personalize the Deity and conceive of ourselves as His humble votaries, the Lord's feet gain a special significance to us. If we do all our work in a spirit of dedication to Him, we can speak of 'offering all our actions at the feet of the Lord'. When we surrender ourselves to Him, we can speak of 'surrendering ourselves at His feet'. So 'Service of His feet' can mean, in a wider sense, any act of dedication we do in His name. In a still wider sense it can mean 'service' in general, including service of His devotees and of His immanent presence in all beings. It is better to understand Padaseva in this wider sense than as mere 'Shampooing of the feet' of the Guru or holy men, as is generally understood in devotional circles. Devotional discipline is thereby given a wider social implication and is freed from the criticism that it makes man purely other-worldly. Besides, involvement in the good of the neighbour is the best safeguard against man developing self-centredness in his pursuit of mere individual salvation. For, self-centredness is the opposite of spirituality. We have added four verses to the original text, to make the selection more comprehensive.]

Prahlada on Divine service as the source of all happiness:

देवोऽसुरो मनुष्यो वा यक्षो गन्धर्व एव च ।
भजन्मुकुन्दचरणं स्वस्तिमान् स्याद्यथा वयम् ॥

(1) It is through the service of the feet of the Lord that all beings, be they Devas, Asuras, men, Yakshas, or Gandharvas, attain to peace and happiness. This is our experience.   (7.7.50)

Rema (or Lakshmi), the Consort of Vishnu and the Goddess of Prosperity on the same subject:

मत्प्राप्तये पद्मभवादयः प्रभो तप्यन्त उग्रं तप ऐन्द्रियेधियः ।
ऋते भवत्पादपरायणान्न मां विन्दन्त्यहं त्वद्धृदया यतोऽजित ॥

(2) Brahma and other Devas, attracted by a desire for material gains, perform terrible austerities and penances for the attainment of Me (the Mistress of all forms of prosperity). But, O Lord, unless they are devoted to Thy feet, they cannot win My favour, as My heart has been offered unto Thee.   (5.18.22)

NOTE: The meaning seems to be that even when men take to the worship of various Deities for worldly prosperity, they must remember that these Deities are all aspects of the one Supreme Being, without whom they have no power.

The supreme value of Padaseva is described in Brahma's words:

त्वय्यम्बुजाक्षाखिलसत्त्वधाम्नि समाधिनावेशितचेतसैके ।
त्वत्पादपोतेन महत्कृतेन कुर्वन्ति गोवत्सपदं भवाब्धिम् ॥

(3) Some great sages merge their minds in Thee, the home
of all beings, through concentration (and attain to liberation).
But there are others who, following the path of devotion exemplified by great devotees like Narada, use the service of Thy feet as
boat to cross the ocean of Samsara with utmost ease, as if it
were a puddle made by a calf's hoof.   (10.2.30)

*It is said in the Vedanta Sastra that liberation is obtained only
through Jnana (knowledge) generated by reflection on the great
Vedic sentence (Mahavakya). Then how is it stated here that by the
Padaseva of the Lord, Moksha can be obtained? The reply is given
in the words of Brahma:*

अथापि ते देव पदाम्बुजद्वय-प्रसादलेशानुगृहीत एव हि ।
जानाति तत्त्वं भगवन्महिम्नो न चान्य एकोऽपि चिरं विचिन्वन्॥

(4) O Lord, only those who have Thy grace, obtained
through devotion to Thy holy feet, can come to know the truth
about Thy infinite greatness—not others who search for a long
time and alone (through practice of Yoga and philosophic
reflection).   (10.14.29)

NOTE: This is another assertion of the superiority of the
path of devotion and Divine grace to other types of spiritual discipline. The *Bhagavata* maintains that to be fruitful, all forms of
spiritual discipline must be based on devotion and surrender to
the Supreme Being. It is only God's grace that can give illumination—not mere philosophic reflection of the Jnani or introverted
concentration of the Yogi. These can be successful only if they
are supported by devotion and self-surrender to God, whose grace
alone can ultimately uplift man from the pit of ignorance. Our
ignorance of our 'real' nature is not of our making. It must have
been due to another will. That will is God's. So His will or grace
alone can remove ignorance, and man's duty is to pray to Him
aud surrender to Him.

*It is generally contended in Vedanta, that knowledge of Truth
(Tattva-jnana) gives freedom from fear. But in truth it is God's
grace that generates Tattva-jnana and therefore He alone can offer*

freedom from fear. This is stated in the words of Devaki, the Mother of Krishna.

मर्त्यो मृत्युव्याळभीतः पलायन् लोकान् सर्वान् निर्भयं नाध्यगच्छत् ।
त्वत्पादाब्जं प्राप्य यदृच्छयाद्य खस्थः शेते मृत्युरसादपैति ॥

(5) Afraid of the serpent of Death, man runs about, as it were, through numerous transmigrations, in this and other spheres, seeking in vain for freedom from fear of death. O Thou Original Being! Having attained to Thy holy feet through some good fortune (resulting from past auspicious Karmas), he lies there in peace, and Death leaves him alone and departs.　(10.3.27)

NOTE: The truth of this will be realized when we remember that all efforts of living beings from the amoeba to the most civilized man, are for self-preservation—which means keeping away from destruction. Life is thus a constant flow of fear, and death which is the source of that fear, is itself called fear. It is stated that ultimately freedom from destruction, i.e. from fear, can be had only at the feet of God.

Prahlada on the same truth :

तस्माद्रजोरागविषादमन्यु-मानस्पृहाभयदैन्याधिमूलम् ।
हित्वा गृहं संसृतिचक्रवालं नृसिंहपादं भजताऽकुतोभयम् ॥

(6) Therefore abandon worldly life—the domain of repeated births and deaths and the source of passions, attachments, sorrow, anger, pride, desire, fear, misery, and worry—, and seek refuge at the feet of the Lord, the domain of fearlessness.　(5.18.14)

Why then are all not seeking refuge at the Lord's feet, but go after various forms of spiritual disciplines based only on self-effort? The answer is given in the words of Uddhava:

अथात आनन्ददुघं पदाम्बुजं हंसाः श्रयेरन्नरविन्दलोचन ।
सुखं तु विश्वेश्वर योगकर्मभि-स्त्वन्मायया ऽस्मी विहता न मानिनः ॥

(7) Therefore, O Lord of all the worlds! Wise men with true discrimination and understanding (Paramahamsas) take

shelter without any reservation at Thy holy feet, the seat of all
bliss. They are not afflicted by Thy great illusory power, Maya.
Unlike these, those who depend on Yoga and Karma, with pride
in their own power, fail to attain the spiritual summum bonum,
being overcome by the illusory power of Thy Maya.   (11.29.3)

NOTE: The idea is that the path of devotion and self-surrender, when genuinely motivated and practised, is free from the
vitiation of egotistic impulses, to which men depending merely on
self-effort, as in the case of pure Yogis and Karmis, are exposed.
This should not be interpreted as any discouragement of self-
effort. Practice of spiritual discipline should be only an expression
of one's ardour and intensity of aspiration. One should not have
behind the practice of such discipline, any idea that one can
either compel or purchase God through those disciplines. The
revelation of God is an act of grace which is bestowed only when
self-will is absolulely effaced. Spiritual practice should lead to the
effacement of self-will and egotism, and not contribute to their
growth, as it unfortunately happens in the case of many a votary
given to pure self-effort. A spiritual aspirant with great capacity
for work and concentration should, if he is a genuine aspirant,
feel that all his powers of self-effort come from God. He is then
safe. Thus devotion and self-surrender should accompany spiritual
effort in all its phases. In the absence of true devotion, Karma
and Yoga and philosophic reflection may themselves become
sources of bondage.

*When there are many ways of attaining salvation, why one
should take to Padaseva—the path of devotion and service—is explained in the words of sage Sanatkumara.*

कुच्छ्रो महानिह भवार्णवमप्रवेशां पड्वर्गनक्रमसुखेन तितीर्षयन्ति ।
तच्वं हरेभगवतो भजनीयमंघ्रि कृत्वोडुपं व्यसनमुत्तर दुस्तराणम् ॥

(8) The task of those who seek to cross the ocean of Samsara, rendered dangerous by the crocodiles constituted of the six
passions, is very difficult indeed, if it is undertaken without the
help of Iswara as the boat. Therefore, resort to the boat of the

worship of Sri Hari, the Supreme Lord, and cross this ocean of
misery which is difficult to cross by any other means.   (4.22.40)

NOTE: This is in criticism of those doctrines of salvation
which do not accept the idea of a Supreme Iswara, or do not
stress sufficiently His importance in the scheme of salvation.
Several schools of Buddhism, Sankhya and Yoga uphold such a
doctrine, in which God and His grace have no place. Even some
schools of Kevaladvaitins consider God only as a phenomenal
reality, and give Him only a very formal place in the scheme of
salvation. The *Bhagavata*, though Advaitic in its philosophy,
is uncompromisingly devotional in its outlook, and maintains
that God is the supreme factor in salvation and that without His
grace, a spiritual aspirant, standing solely on his own strength,
will surely be devoured by the alligators of passions in his fool-
hardy attempt to cross the ocean of life through mere self-effort.
For the *Bhagavata*, Iswara is not a lower Brahman, as some
Advaitins contend, but the very Non-dual Principle who in a very
real sense has manifested Himself as the world of Jivas and Jagat;
the only way of grasping His non-duality is through worship
and self-surrender, which in turn would elicit His grace, and
through this grace alone can the Jiva overcome Samsara and be a
participant in Divine Love.

*Advising Prachetas, Rudra speaks of the importance of cling-
ing to the Lord's feet :*

कस्त्वत्पदाब्जं विजहाति पण्डितो यस्तेऽवमानव्ययमानकेतनः ।
विशङ्क्याप्मद् गुरुरर्चति स्म यद्विनोपपत्ति मनबश्चतुर्देश ॥

(9) Whichsoever intelligent men, save those who want to
waste their lives by indulgence in blasphemy and in impious living,
would fail to cling to Thy lotus feet that are worshipped with un-
disturbed and unquestioning faith by our Guru (Brahma) as also
by the fourteen Manus ?   (4.24.67)

NOTE: The idea implied here seems to be that it is not
reason but passion that stands in the way of developing a strong
faith in God. The more a man is attracted by the life of the senses,

the less will be his proneness to have a vigorous and living faith in a Supreme Being.

The keen delight to be had in the service of the Lord's feet is highlighted in the words of Prithu :

यत्पादसेवाभिरुचिस्तपस्विना-महोषजन्मोपचितं मलं धियः ।
सद्यः क्षिणोत्यन्वहमेधती सती यथा पदाङ्गुष्ठविनिःसृता सरित् ॥

विनिर्धुताशेषमनोमलः पुमा-नसङ्गविज्ञानविशेषवीर्यवान् ।
यदंघ्रिमूले कृतकेतनः पुनः न संसृतिं क्लेशवहां प्रपद्यते ॥

(10-11) The delight in the service of His feet, growing day by day, washes off the agelong accumulations of impurities in the aspirant's mind, even as the waters of the Ganga, sprung from His toes, remove his sins (through his bodily contact with it). A devotee, cleansed of all mental impurities and endowed with the strength born of non-attachment and realization, establishes himself at the feet of God and is never affected by the miseries of the cycle of births and deaths.   (4.21.31-32)

If it is argued that it is only by Vedic Karma that purity of mind is attained, it is pointed out in Yama's words that it is not so :

कृष्णांघ्रिपद्ममधुलिण्न पुनर्विसृष्ट-
मायागुणेषु रमते वृजिनावहेषु ।
अन्यस्तु कामहत आत्मरजः प्रमार्ष्टु-
मीहेत कर्म यत एव रजः पुनः स्यात् ॥

(12) The devotee who, like the bee, has enjoyed the nectar of Sri Krishna's lotus feet, never again finds delight in the abandoned enjoyments of worldly life, which are nothing but an accumulation of sins. But there are others who, prompted by their own passionate nature, resort to ritualistic Karma under the guise of atoning for their sins, but who, in the process, generate and accumulate more sins.   (6.3.33)

NOTE: It is the uncompromising doctrine of the *Bhagavata* that genuine devotion is the best atonement for all sin and the most potent cause of all enlightenment. It is here contended, that Vedic ritualistic actions prescribed as expiation for sins are themselves born of the prompting of Rajas (passion) which is the source of all sin. But Nishkama-Karma, or action without desire, performed as an offering to God is not of this kind. It stands on a different footing. It is a part of devotional life, and should be distinguished from mere Vedic ritualistic Karma criticised above. Nishkama-Karma is performed to please God, and its sure fruit is the strengthening of our devotion to Him.

In Brahma's words the service of the Lord's feet is described as the highest good fortune that can befall a person:

तदस्तु मे नाथ स भूरिभागो भवेऽत्र वान्यत्र तु वा तिरश्चाम् ।
येनाहमेकोऽपि भवज्जनानां भूत्वा निषेवे तव पादपल्लवम् ॥

(13) O Lord, I shall consider it my greatest good fortune, if, in this life as Brahma or in any possible lower embodiment in future, I become one among Thy devotees and do service to Thy holy feet.
(10.14.30)

समाश्रिना ये पदपल्लवप्लवं महत्पदं पुण्ययशो मुरारेः ।
भवाम्बुधिर्वत्सपदं परं पदं पदं पदं यद्विपदां न तेषाम् ॥

(14) The lovely feet of the Lord, far-famed for holiness and affording shelter even to great sages, are to His votaries, who seek such shelter, a veritable ship that renders the great ocean of Samsara as easily negotiable as the puddle made by the hoof of a calf. The Lord's devotees verily attain to the supreme state from which there is no danger of return to Samsara. (10.14.58)

King Muchukunda on the danger of not seeking shelter at the feet of the Lord:

लब्ध्वा जनो दुर्लभमत्र मानुषं कथंचिदव्यंगमयत्नतोऽनघ ।
पादारविन्दं न भजत्यसन्मति-गृहान्धकूपे पतितो यथा पशुः ॥

(15) If a man, having by some good fortune got the rare embodiment in a healthy and perfect human body, fails to take
shelter at the lotus feet of the Lord, he will fall into the pit of
worldly life drawn by the attractions of the flecting sense-objects
and domestic affections, just as an animal falls into a well
(covered or camouflaged with attractive grass).   (10.51.47)

*Some hold that the performance of duty (Swadharma) is sufficient for one's spiritual welfare.   Why then should one at all do
the Padaseva of the Lord?   The answer is given in Prahlada's words:*

विप्राद्द्विषड्गुणयुतादरविन्दनाभ-पादारविंदविमुखाच्छ्वपचं वरिष्ठम् ।
मन्ये तदर्पितमनोवचनेहितार्थ-प्राणं पुनाति स कुलं न तु भूरिमानः ॥

(16) I consider a dog-eater (a low-born outcaste), who
none the less has dedicated his mind, speech, bodily activities,
wealth and senses to the Lord, as more worthy than a Brahmana
endowed with the twelve noble qualifications but averse to Thy
Holy feet. For, the former (by virtue of the holiness derived from
his dedication to Thy feet) purifies even his race, while the latter,
with his inordinate pride and egotism, cannot purify even
himself.   (7.9.10)

NOTE: The twelve virtues referred to above are given in the
previous verse of the *Bhagavata* text (7.9.9.). They are as follows:
wealth (Vitta), high birth (Abhijana), knowledge of scriptures
(Srutam), power of the senses (Ojas), impressiveness of personality (Tejas), grandeur (Pratapa), strength of body (Balam), capacity
for self-effort, (Pourusham), intelligence (Buddhi), and concentration (Yoga). A man possessed of all these qualifications will
be considered a distinguished person from the worldly point of
view. But according to this devotional scripture, he is a worthless
man, if he has no devotion to God.

Yama's condemnation of the non-devotional people:

तानानयध्वमसतो विमुखानन्मुकुन्द-पादारविन्दमकरन्दरसादजस्रम् ।
निष्किंचनैः परमहंसकुलै रसज्ञै-र्जुष्टात् गृहे निरयवर्त्मनि बद्धतृष्णान् ॥

(17) Fetch such wicked men as are steeped in worldliness, which is the veritable pathway to hell, and are averse to the nectar of the lotus-feet of the Lord, which the all-renouncing Paramahamsas, the true connoisseurs of spiritual values, always drink.

(6-3-28.)

NOTE: From the point of view of the path of devotion, no mental and intellectual endowments are of any good, unless they help to generate devotion to God. It is from this position that in verse 16, it is stated that even a highly talented and powerful person is inferior to a low-born man with genuine devotion to God. Here in verse 17 persons with high endowments, but devoid of devotion are positively classified as wicked. For, a person with ability and power, but devoid of devotion and universal love, is sure to use his capacities for self-aggrandisement alone.

Rudra speaks of the non-devotional as the 'living-dead':

देवदत्तमिमं लब्ध्वा नृलोकमजितेन्द्रियः ।
यो नाद्रियेत त्वत्पादौ स शोच्यो ह्यात्मवंचकः ॥

(18) If a man, having obtained this human embodiment, a veritable gift of God, fails to adore Thy feet owing to the pull of his uncontrolled senses, he is indeed cheating himself (or committing suicide). He is to be pitied.   (10.63.41)

NOTE: It is hinted here that what stands in the way of a man's accepting the existence of God, is not reason, as is often said, but his slavery to the senses. Sense-indulgences steep us in animality and make us impervious to devotional thoughts. When we are without the capacity for faith and worship, the highest faculties given to us, we can be said to be committing suicide.

The all-round greatness of those who serve the feet of the Lord, is praised in the words of Yudhishthira:

त्वत्पादुके अविरतं परि ये चरंति
ध्यायन्त्यभद्रनशने शुचयो गृणन्ति ।

विन्दन्ति ते कमलनाभ भवापवर्ग-
माशासते यदि त आशिष ईश नान्ये ॥

(19) They, who for the destruction of all sins, ever serve
Thy feet, and meditate on them, and speak and sing about them,
get purified and attain to liberation from Samsara.   If they pray
for other blessings of a worldly nature, they get them too, unlike
others who have a hankering for them.   (10.72.4)

*But such devotees never seek anything except the service of the
Lord's feet.   This is stated in the words of the Nagapatnis and King
Muchukunda:*

न नाकपृष्ठं न च सार्वभौमं न पारमेष्ठ्यं न रसाधिपत्यम् ।
न योगसिद्धीरपुनर्भवं वा वाञ्छन्ति यत्पादरजः प्रपन्नाः ॥
न कामयेऽन्यं तव पादसेवना-दकिञ्चनप्रार्थ्यतमाद् वरं विभो
आराध्य कस्त्वां ह्यपवर्गदं हरे वृणीत आर्यो वरमात्मबन्धनम् ॥

(20-21) Those who have taken refuge at the dust of Thy feet
do not desire for heaven, emperorship, creatorship, dominion
ever Rasa-Tala or Super-human Yogic power.   They do not desire
even Moksha.   O Lord, Thou all-pervading Being! I do not desire
for any boon other than the privilege of serving Thy feet, which
is the only blessing worthy of aspiration by men of renunciation.
There is really no other boon that I seek for.   Whoever endowed
with wisdom would, after worshipping Thee, the bestower of liberation, ask for boons which bring only bondage to the self?
                                          (1 '.16.37;10.51.56)

*In the words of Sri Krishna's wives addressed to queen Drau-
padi it is pointed out how devotees reject even Moksha, because,
being a state of oneness with the Lord, it does not give the privilege
of Divine service, to the devotee:*

न वयं साध्वि साम्राज्यं स्वाराज्यं भौज्यमप्युत ।
वैराज्यं पारमेष्ठ्यं वा आनन्त्यं वा हरेः पदम् ॥

कामयामह एतस्य श्रीमत्पादरजः श्रीयः ।
कुचकुंकुमगन्धाढ्यं मूर्ध्ना वोढुं गदाभृतः ॥

(22-23) O good lady, we have no desire for empire, or the
state of Indra, or the position of Brahma, or for a combination of
both these, or for the possession of multifarious Yogic powers, or
even for the state of eternal mergence in Hari (Moksha). What
we yearn for is the opportunity to wear always on our head the
dust of the feet of Sri Krishna fragrant with the sweet smell of
saffron that has fallen from the bosom of Sri Devi herself (as she
serves the Lord).   (10.83.41.42)

NOTE: Sri Krishna's wives say in the above verses that
service of the Lord is preferable to Moksha, which is the highest
state according to the Vedanta, and that there is no privilege open
to them greater than the opportunity for such service.   The dust
of the Lord's feet is said to be fragrant with the smell of saffron
fallen from the body of Sri Devi, the Divine consort of Vishnu,
in order to indicate that Sri, whom all beings from Brahma down
resort to for boons and even Moksha, is Herself serving the Lord
and considers the satisfaction arising from the service as superior
to everything else.   Thus according to the Bhakti Sastra, there is
no greater, or more desirable, state for the Jiva than service of
the Lord.

The same idea is emphasized in the words of Sri Suka:

को नु राजन्निन्द्रियवान् मुकुन्दचरणाम्बुजम् ।
न भजेत्सर्वतो मृत्यु-रुपास्यममरोत्तमैः ॥

(24) Seeing that life is surroundered on all sides by the
great Terror (Death), who, having with powers of observation and
reflection, would not worship the feet of Sri Hari, whom even the
immortal gods adore?   (11.2.2)

*The same idea is again emphasized in the words of Kavi, one of
the Navayogis:*

मन्येऽकुतश्चिद्भयमच्युतस्य पादाम्बुजोपासनमत्र नित्यम् ।
उद्विग्नबुद्धेरसदात्मभावाद् विश्वात्मना यत्र निवर्तते भीः ॥

(25) I consider that the worship of the feet of the Lord, the
Imperishable Being, is the means for man to get relief from constant fear of death arising from the identification of the perishable
body with the Atman. Through resignation at the feet of the
Lord, fear is overcome.   (11.2.33)

*The importance of devotion over Swadharma is stressed by
Narada:*

त्यक्त्वा स्वधर्मं चरणांबुजं हरे-भजन्नपक्कोऽथ पतेत्ततो यदि ।
यत्र क्व वाऽभद्रमभूदमुष्य किं को वाऽर्थ आप्तोऽभजतां स्वधर्मतः ॥

(26) A man who has abandoned Swadharma and taken to
the exclusive service of Sri Hari's feet may, out of his immaturity,
have a fall (or fail to achieve the goal before death). But what
evil can befall him thereby? And what high end can a performer
of Swadharma achieve, if he is devoid of devotion?   (1.5.17)

NOTE: In this verse we hear echoes of the controversy
between the Vedic ritualists and the devotional school of thought
called the Bhagavatas or Pancharatras. The performance of Swadharma consisted, according to the orthodox Vedists, in the
meticulous performance of daily rituals like Agnihotra, Sandhya
etc., and occasional rituals like Sraddha etc., as also the discharge
of social duties based on caste. These can be done even without
any genuine devotional element in them. The Bhagavatas, however, considered the practice of devotion to be a higher duty than
the performance of Vedic rituals. So in the place of Vedic rituals
they substitued the service of God in His image in temples or in
the homes. The old thinkers held that Swadharma saves one
from moral fall and degradation. But the Bhagavatas thought
that it is better to face this risk and practise devotion through
'hearing', 'praise', 'Padaseva' etc., than live a ritual-bound life.
If at all a Bhakta falls, he will be corrected by the power of
sincere devotion. Besides, in the next birth he can start from
where he left. In the *Bhagavad Gita*, which is also a text of the
Bhagavata School, a reconciliation is effected between the discharge
of Swadharma and devotion, by the theory that all one's actions
should be done as offering unto God.

In the words of Karabhajana, one of the Navayogis, it is pointed out with sufficient reason that no true devotee will really fall and be degraded:

खपादमूलं भजतः प्रियस्य त्यक्तान्यभावस्य हरिः परेशः ।
विकर्म यच्चोत्पतितं कथंचित् धुनोति सर्वं हृदि सन्निविष्टः ॥

(27) The supreme Lord Hari, dwelling in the heart of His dear devotee, effaces all the possible evil effects of any forbidden Karma that may accrue to him, provided the devotee has abandoned all other loves and allegiances, and worships Him and takes refuge at His feet.   (11.5.42)

NOTE: Speaking about the power of devotion to dispel every kind of obstruction in the path of the devotee, the *Bhagavata* text says in the verse earlier to the present one (11.5.41): 'A person who has surrendered himself entirely to the Lord, the one Being to whom such surrender is appropriate, and abandoned all sense of agency, is no longer a servant of, nor a debtor to, Devas or Rishis or manes or men or Bhutas.'

The above idea emphasized in the words of Bahulaswa:

को नु त्वच्चरणांभोज-मेवंविद् विसृजेत्पुमान् ।
निष्किचनानां शान्तानां मुनीनां यस्त्वमात्मदः ॥

(28) O Lord, it is Thy nature to offer Thyself to wise men who are free from passions and possessions. Whosoever knowing this will give up clinging to Thy holy feet?   (10.86.33)

That all evil from which man suffers is due to want of devotion to the feet of the Lord, is shown in the words of Brahma:

तावद्द्वयं द्रविणगेहसुहृन्निमित्तं शोकः स्पृहा परिभवो विपुलश्च लोभः ।
तावन्ममेत्यसदवग्रह आर्तिमूलं यावन्न तेऽङ्घ्रिमभयं प्रवृणीत लोकः ॥

(29) So long as man does not seek absolute shelter at Thy feet, the refuge from all fears, he will be dominated by the vile sense of 'I' and 'mine', which is the root cause of all suffering.

and as a consequence, he will be subject to grief, desire, defeat, and insatiable greed on account of wealth, home and friends.

(3.9.6)

Universal application of Bhakti in Kapila's words:

ज्ञानवैराग्ययुक्तेन भक्तियोगेन योगिनः ।
क्षेमाय पादमूलं मे प्रविशन्त्यकुतोभयम् ॥

(30) For the attainment of the spiritual *summum bонum,* Yogins serve My holy feet, the abode of fearless felicity, practising the discipline of Bhakti (devotion), accompanied with knowledge and dispassion.   (3.25.43)

The words of Kavi, one of the Navayogis, in praise of Padaseva:

इत्यच्युतांघ्रिं भजतोनुवृत्या भक्तिर्विरक्तिर्भगवत्प्रबोधः ।
भवन्ति वै भागवतस्य राजन् ततः परां शान्तिमुपैति साक्षात् ॥

(31) By this steady and continuous service of the feet of the Lord, an aspirant is blessed with devotion, dispassion and experience of God. He then attains to liberation, the state of Supreme Peace.   (11.2.43)

NOTE: It is the contention of the *Bhagavata* that devotion or service of the Lord is in itself a self-sufficient path for the attainment of the spiritual *summum bonum.* It is not merely a discipline for purification of mind, to be followed by the Jnana disciplines of Sravana (hearing of the Upanishads), Manana (cogitating on them) and Nididhyasana (concentrated contemplation on them). It is not merely an indirect aid to knowledge, but a direct means for attaining the spiritual *summum bonum.* The *Bhagavata* puts this view very effectively in 11.2.42. of the full text, as follows: 'A person who has surrendered himself to the Lord becomes endowed at the same time with devotion to Him, knowledge of Him, and dispassion for all other things unconnected with Him, just as a man eating a ball of rice feels simultaneously with every mouthful, enjoyable taste, a sense of the stomach getting full, and freedom from hunger'.

*The selection of verses under 'Padaseva' in the Bhakti Ratna-
vali stops with Verse 31. It will be seen that in these, 'Pada' is
treated as 'feet' of God, taking Him in a theological sense. But in
the Bhagavata and the Vedas, Pada has a wider meaning. It means
an aspect of Him or a manifestation of His. Thus it is said that of
His four 'Padas' one is manifest as this world of Becoming
(Prapancha) and the other three are transcendent. In this conception,
'Pada' becomes a manifested aspect of God, and that is for us
the whole world in which we find ourselves. So Padaseva can mean
the service of society or the world at large with the devotional
sense that it is an aspect of the Supreme Being. This interpretation
of Padaseva will make the Bhagavata Dharma a more comprehensive
discipline and synthesise it with man's social aspirations. With
this in view we have added below four more verses from the
Bhagavata, which are not included in the Bhakti Ratnavali.*

*A basis for the wider notion of Padaseva will be found in the
conception of God manifesting as the All. The experience of the
Navayogis (group of nine Yogis) in this respect is given below :*

त एते भगवद्रूपं विश्वं सदसदात्मकम् ।
आत्मनोऽव्यतिरेकेन पश्यन्तो व्यचरन्महीम् ॥

(32) **They (the group of nine Yogis) moved about, seeing
the whole universe in its subtle and gross aspects as the form of
the Lord, not different from the Lord Himself.**   (11.2.22)

*The same idea of the service of all beings being Padaseva, is
implied in the following description of the different types of
Bhagavatas (devotees) in the words of Hari, one of the Navayogis :*

सर्वभूतेषु यः पश्येद्भगवद्भावमात्मनः ।
भूतानि भगवत्यात्म-न्येष भागवतोत्तमः ॥
ईश्वरे तदधीनेषु बालिशेषु द्विषत्सु च ।
प्रेम मैत्री कृपोपेक्षा यः करोति सः मध्यमः ॥

आचार्यामेव हरये पूजां यः श्रद्धयेहते ।
न तद्भक्तेषु चान्येषु स भक्तः प्राकृतः स्मृतः ॥

(33-35) The perfect Bhagavata or devotee of the Lord
(Bhagavatottama) is one who sees the Atman in all creatures as
an expression of the Supreme Being, and all beings as dwelling in
the Bhagavan, the Supreme Spirit.   A mediocre Bhagavata is one
who entertains an attitude of adoring love towards God, of friend-
liness to His devotees, of kindness and sympathy to common
people, and of indifference to enemies and bad people.   And he is
the inferior type of Bhagavata who performs the worship of God in
mages with faith and devotion, but is totally indifferent to devotees
of God and other beings (on account of his incapacity to recognize
the Divinity manifesting through everything).   (11 2.45-47)

STRAND 8
ARCHANA OR WORSHIP

[Introduction: This section deals with Archana, or worship, the fifth of the devotional disciplines. Archana is also popularly known as Pooja. Pooja is a way of honouring God conceived in a personal sense with offerings of several pure ingredients according to rituals laid down in scriptures called Agamas, which are authoritative in this field. This is a devotional practice special to Hinduism, because it can be done only where worship of God in images or other similar symbols is in vogue, and Hinduism, with the exception of some forms of Buddhism, is the only religion which unreservedly accepts image worship and advocates it as a universally helpful, though not absolutely necessary, devotional discipline.

Semitic religions, especially Islam and, theoretically Christianity also, are hostile to this form of devotion. Their hostility seems to spring from a peculiarly unconscious assumption that God is an individual absolutely different from Nature, that there can therefore be no substitute for Him drawn from Nature in the shape of a symbol or image, and that any such worship, being, worship of something other than God, can be nothing better than adoration of stock and stone —a heinous sin and a prostitution of man's capacity for reverence and worship. As against this, the Hindu point of view is that Nature is only a manifestation of God who indwells it, that through every striking aspect of Nature the Indwelling Spirit can be communed with, and that above all, He manifests Himself, for blessing the adoring votaries, in consecrated images where His presence is invoked and worshipped with faith and reverence. It is derogatory to call such holy images idols, as is often done. They are manifestations of God in a way that even an ordinary man with faith may serve Him and be spiritually elevated. While prayer advocated by Semitic religions is addressed to an imaginary being, the worship of Divine Images gives a sense of realism and concreteness to the devotional practice of the Hindus.

The worship of images can become corrupted when an over-growth of soulless ritualism is allowed to smother the devotional sense. The essence of such worship is a live feeling that God is presenting Himself in the image. Rituals are only an aid, and not an end. Like any other code or procedure, they can help us to keep up the sense of vigilance and seriousness in the worshipper, besides providing a channel and a form for his devotional sentiment. But a worshipper should not forget that Bhakti, and not ritual, is the essence of Pooja. As the Bhagavan has stated in the Gita: 'If a devotee offers some Tulasi leaf, flower, fruit or water to Me, I accept that offering with great satisfaction, provided it is an offering of love and devotion'.

There have been, however, great devotees who have combined elaborate rituals and intense devotion in the practice of worship. The reader who is interested to have a peep into this aspect of devotion, may read the life of Swami Ramakrishnananda, one of the great disciples of Sri Ramakrishna. This kind of ecstatic Pooja is considered so important a form of devotion that the Narada Bhakti Sutras give 'attachment for, and absorption in, Pooja' as one of the definitions of Bhakti.

There is also a form of Pooja which transcends all rituals. It is called Seva or Service. Here rituals are discarded or reduced to a minimum, and the image is treated as a living being, near and dear to one, and served accordingly with bath, decoration, food, cloth etc., with great care and love. The devotional schools founded by Vallabhacharya and Sri Chaitanya are noted for this form of Pooja.

The high-water mark of Pooja is reached when the devotee begins to feel the presence of God everywhere and in everything. His whole life then becomes a service of the One through the All, and of the All through the One. The present section begins with a verse embodying this lofty conception of Pooja or Archana.

[We have added seven verses to the original text at the end of the section in order to make the selection more comprehensive.]

In Narada's words the relation between worship, God and service of the world is stated :

यथा तरोर्मूलनिषेचनेन तृप्यन्ति तत्स्कन्धभुजोपशाखाः ।
प्राणोपहाराच्च यथेन्द्रियाणां तथैव सर्वार्हणमच्युतेज्या ॥

(1) Just as by pouring water at the root of the tree, all its branches, leaves etc., are nourished, and just as food eaten to sustain vitality strengthens all the senses, so also adoration of Achyuta is the adoration of all Deities (or the whole universe).

(4.31.14)

NOTE : This verse is generally interpreted, restricting the meaning of the word Sarva, 'all', to the various Deities accepted in the Hindu scriptures. God has manifested as several Deities, but one need not go to worship them all. If we worship the one Supreme Being (Achyuta) all other beings are also simultaneously worshipped. But by extending the meaning of the word 'all' to 'all beings', who in fact are manifestations of God, we get a better meaning. In this sense worship of God in the image must symbolize for us the worship of Him in all beings, and as such, we should deal with all beings in our daily life with that reverential feeling, of which worship is an expression. Further implications are explained in the note to the next verse.

The real implication of worship is emphasised in the words of Brahma :

यथा हि स्कन्धशाखानां तरोर्मूलावसेचनम् ।
एवमाराधनं विष्णोः सर्वेषामात्मनश्च हि ॥

(2) What the watering of a tree at the root is to all the branches of the tree, that the worship of Vishnu is to all beings, including oneself.

(8.5.49)

NOTE : The real implication of the above two verses is this: In order to benefit the whole tree, water must fall at the root, even if it be falling through the leaves and branches. So also man may discharge his duties or go about helping his fellow beings, but if he does not have the feeling that he is thereby serving God who is the essence in man and the world, it will not lead to real good to others or to himself. If we do not have God in view, our work, both social and devotional, will become purely ego-centred and selfish, and to that extent, it will only harm and corrupt others as also ourselves. The verses also imply that if a person is really absorbed in God and is apparently doing nothing in the external world, he is still working for the greatest good of all. His thoughts and prayers are so concentrated and powerful that they have a beneficial impact on the whole world. · God is the root or soul of all this world of living and non-living beings, and these are related to Him as the branches are to the tree or as the organs are to the organism. So when a devotee is in intense communion with Him, he is in touch with all, and the spiritual and moral values he generates by his holy life exert their uplifting influence on all beings.

Rudra on worship being the supreme teaching of the scriptures:

क्रियाकलापैरिदमेव योगिनः श्रद्धान्विता साधु यजन्ति सिद्धये ।
भूतेन्द्रियान्तःकरणोपलक्षितं वेदे च तन्त्रे च त एव कोविदाः ॥

(3) The real masters of the Vedas and the Tantras are those Yogis who, prompted by great faith and sincerity, worship Thee with proper rites and ceremonies for the attainment of Moksha, knowing the object they worship to be Thyself, the Universal Being — the originator, the pervader, the sustainer, and the director of the totality and its parts, whose existence the whole manifested universe proclaims. (4.24.62)

NOTE : The ideas implied in the above verse are as follows: (1) The object of worship may be only the cult Deity or Ishta Devata. But the worshipper should overcome all narrow feelings by recognising the one God of all, the universal Iswara, in his object of worship as well as in the object of worship of others. (2) Ritualism or external worship, and knowledge or spiritual understanding, should go hand in hand if spiritual progress is to be made. Dry philosophical intellectualism on the one hand, and self-stifling and excessive ritualism on the other, are the Scylla and Charybdis to be avoided for a harmonious development of man's spiritual capacities. Worship through communion is the spiritual discipline of choice for the ordinary individuals. External worship of God in the image forms an important part of it. As explained in the Note on an earlier verse, such worship disciplines the mind and creates a sense of realism in worship. But it must be accompanied by knowledge and meditation. (3) The *Bhagavata*, seems to indicate that the conflict which existed at one time between Vedic thinkers and Pancharatrins (referred to here as followers of Tantra) can be resolved by the recognition that the one Universal Being is worshipped through all Deities and through all rituals. (4) Sincerity, spiritual motivation and the recognition that all Deities are expressions of the one Universal Being, are what make any ritual real worship.

Why man should worship the Lord as described above, is stated in the words of Munis:

चित्तस्योपशमोऽयं वै कविभिः शास्त्रचक्षुषा ।
दर्शितः सुगमो योगो धर्मश्चात्ममुदावहः ॥
अयं स्वस्त्ययनः पन्था द्विजातेगृहमेधिनः ।
यच्छ्रद्धयाप्तवित्तेन शुक्लेनेज्येत पूरुषम् ॥

(4-5) Householders should worship the Lord with the help of resources earned in righteous ways. This is the best means for the attainment of spiritual welfare. Wise men who know the scriptures have recognised this as the easiest way to spiritual communion, mental peace, and moral excellence leading to inward joy.   (10.84. 36-37)

The true meaning of worship is given in the words of Prahlada:

नैवात्मनः प्रभुरयं निजलाभपूर्णो मानं जनादविदुषः करुणो वृणीते ।
यद्यज्जनो भगवते विदधीत मानं तच्चात्मने प्रतिमुखस्य यथा मुखश्रीः

(6) **Being self-satisfied with His own inherent blissful nature, the Lord does not desire to be worshipped by ignorant people. If He accepts worship, it is only out of mercy to the worshipping devotee. Whatever honour man does to God by worship and praise, really benefits himself, just as the beauty that a face derives from decorations goes to its reflection in the mirror.**
                                                                    (7.9.11)

NOTE : It is said that just as a seed sown in good soil returns greatly augmented to the cultivator, so also what a worshipper offers to God comes back to him in an enhanced form. The example of the image of the face gives us the rationale behind worship. Man is an entity dependent on God, as a reflection is on its prototype. Worship and communion are ways by which he realises this dependence, and when a worshipper thus feels linked with Him through disciplines, he becomes a sharer of His glory. The object of all worship is thus communion and not giving material gifts to God. The beneficiary is not God but man. The decorations applied to the face (or the prototype standing for God) go to his reflection in the mirror i.e. to the Jiva who derives his existence from God.

As worship of God benefits oneself, it is pointed out through the words of Dhruva that ritualistic worship with desires for worldly enjoyments is meaningless :

नूनं विमुष्टमतयस्तव मायया ते
ये त्वां भवाप्ययविमोक्षणमन्यहेतोः ।
अर्चन्ति कल्पकतरुं कुणपोपभोग्य-
मिच्छन्ति यत्स्पर्शजं नरकेऽपि नृणाम् ॥

(7) **Those who worship Thee for perishable worldly satisfaction—Thee who art the all-powerful and all-loving master of creation, preservation, dissolution and redemption, must indeed have been deprived of their intellegence by Thy delusive power of Maya. For how else will they pray to Thee, a veritable Kalpataru (Heavenly Tree) that can yield any blessing sought by a votary, for these petty sensuous satisfactions pertaining to this**

corpse-like body, which could be had even in the hellish bodies of
animals?   (4.9.9)

*The important thing in worship is not richness of offerings but
devotion. This is stated in the words of Brahma :*

यत्पादयोरशठधीः सलिलं प्रदाय
दूर्वांकुरैरपि विधाय सतीं सपर्याम् ।
अप्युत्तमां गतिमसौ भजते त्रिलोकीं
दाश्वानविक्लवमनाः कथमार्तिमिच्छेत् ॥

(8) A man attains to liberation even by offering worship
unto Thee with mere water and Durva grass, actuated by true
faith and devotion. Why then should this evil befall him (Bali)
who with liberality offered Thee the three worlds?   (8.22.23)

NOTE :   The allusion here is to the Lord's Incarnation as
Vamana, the Dwarf.   Bali was a virtuous Asura king but was
vainglorious about his power and resources.   Mahavishnu
incarnated Himself as Vamana, the Dwarf, to restore the world
from Bali to Indra, and through that act, bestow spiritual wisdom
on Bali.   When the Vamana approached Bali as a Brahmacharin
(religious student) and asked for a gift of three feet of earth, the
latter expressed surprise at the pettiness of the gift asked for, of such a
great personage as himself, but at last offered to give it, as the
Vamana would ask for nothing more. Thereupon Vamana assumed
His cosmic form and measured all the worlds with His two feet,
and Bali had to offer his own head to place the third foot. Having
lost everything and being enslaved himself, Bali was tied up
with Varunapasa.   Brahma now came to the scene and pleaded
for Bali with the Lord Incarnate.   The verse selected above is
his plea.   In answer the Lord said that He was not punishing
but blessing Bali.   Those whom He really wanted to bless, He
would subject to trials by way of suffering, insult, deprivation
etc., in order to eliminate pride and egotism from them.   Bali
had stood this test well and his higher evolution was assured.
Worship and offering to God should not be made with pride and
a sense of ostentation at heart as was done by Bali.

Sri Krishna's words approving ritualistic worship if it is accompanied with devotion :

एवं क्रियायोगपथैः पुमान् वैदिकतान्तिकैः ।
अर्चन्नुभयतः सिद्धि मत्तो विन्दत्यभीप्सिताम् ॥

(9) **A person who worships Me thus according to the rituals prescribed in the Vedas and the Tantras attains to the fulfilment of all his wants here and hereafter.** (11.27.49)

NOTE : This passage occurs in the Bhagavata after a long description of the procedures of ritualistic worship of the Lord in an image, in a diagram, in the fire, in the sun and in a holy man. But the Lord insists that faith and devotion must be the core of all these rituals, and that even if the offering consists of water alone, He is pleased with it, provided it is offered with true devotion. This is the verdict of the *Bhagavad Gita* also. In the maze of rituals and procedures, it should never be forgotten that devotion is the essence of worship.

(The following seven verses are not given in the selection contained in the *Bhakti Ratnavali.* But the *Bhagavata* view of external worship as depicted in the above verses will be misunderstood unless it is studied in relation to the *Bhagavata* theory of worship of God in man. So the following supplementary verses are added here.)

Mere ritualistic worship without service of God in man is here decried by Kapila :

अहं सर्वेषु भूतेषु भूतात्मावस्थितः सदा ।
तमवज्ञाय मां मर्त्यः कुरुतेऽर्चाविडंबनम् ॥

यो मां सर्वेषु भूतेषु सन्तमात्मानमीश्वरम् ।
हित्वार्चां भजते मौढ्याद्भस्मन्येव जुहोति सः ॥

द्विषतः परकाये मां मानिनो भिन्नदर्शिनः ।
भूतेषु बद्धवैरस्य न मनः शान्तिमृच्छति ॥

अहमुच्चावचैर्द्रव्यैः क्रिययोत्पन्नयाऽनघे ।
नैव तृप्येऽर्चितोऽर्चायां भूतग्रामावमानिनः ॥

(10-13) I abide in all beings as their inmost self. Without recognising this, the mere worship of Me in images is only a semblance of worship. If one disregards Me present in all as their soul and Lord, and offers worship to images, such worship is as ineffective as sacrificial offering made in ashes. A man who thus makes a clear-cut difference between worship and his worldly activities, and lives a purely ego-centred life, will be enimical to other beings and be thus persecuting Me who resides in them. Such a person never attains to peace. If a man disregards and persecutes fellow beings, but worships Me in images with numerous rituals and rich offerings, I am not at all pleased with Him by such worship.   (3.29.21-24)

The proper place of ritualistic worship and of service of fellow beings in a scheme of int grated spiritual life is shown below :

अर्चादावर्चयेत्तावदीश्वरं मां स्वकर्मकृत् ।
यावन्न वेद स्वहृदि सर्वभूतेष्ववस्थितम् ॥
आत्मनश्च परस्यापि यः करोत्यन्तरोदरम् ।
तस्य भिन्नदृशो मृत्युर्विदधे भयमुल्बणम् ॥
अथ मां सर्वभूतेषु भूतात्मानं कृतालयम् ।
अर्हयेद्दानमानाभ्यां मैत्र्याऽभिन्नेन चक्षुषा ॥

(14-16) A man should, however, worship Me in images along with the discharge of his duties towards all beings, until he actually realises My presence in himself and in all beings. As long as a man is self-centred and makes an absolute difference between himself and others (without recognising their unity in Me, the inner pervader of them all), he will be subject to the great fear of death. So overcoming the differences of self-centred life, one should serve all beings with gifts, honour, and love, with the recognition that such service is really being done to Me who reside in all beings as their innermost soul.   (3.29. 25-27)

STRAND 9

VANDANA OR SALUTATION

[Introduction : Vandana, the sixth of the devotional disciplines, which forms the subject matter of this section, means 'salutation' in general, but 'bowing down in a devotional attitude' in this context. Like several of the earlier disciplines, this too is possible in a literal sense only before Divine images. It is however practised by Muslims and Christians also by kneeling down, even without the use of images. Perhaps when they do so, they imagine that God is before them. Hindus do Vandanam by bending low with folded hands or by prostration. In ritualistic worship prostration is always done at the beginning and at the end of worship. It signifies the devotee's sense of submission to Him and surrender to His will. But Vandana in a more comprehensive sense is an attitude in life, and consists in subordinating our ego-sense to Him and feeling that we are nothing and that He is everything. It also implies that one should have respect for all fellow beings, seeing that God resides in all. Now this genuine sense of reverential submission to the Divine, born out of keen awareness of His universal rulership and all-pervading presence, should be clearly distinguished from the pseudo-humility and self-depreciation that some people consider and practise as a part of their devotional life. The former is rooted in a sense of the dignity and worthiness of oneself and others in God, whereas the latter is a kind of unconscious hypocrisy at its best and a positive humbug at its worst. A true servant of God alone can evince a natural and dignified humility without any touch of ego in all his movements and relationships.]

Akrura on the value of Vandana:

ममाद्यमंगलं नष्टं फलवांश्चैव मे भवः ।
यन्नमस्ये भगवतो योगिध्येयाङ्घ्रिपङ्कजम् ॥

(1) Today all evil in life has been overcome; today my life in the world has become fruitful. For I have been able actually to prostrate at the feet of the Lord, which even Yogis could do only in their imagination at the time of contemplation. (10.38.6)

Brahma on Vandana as an attitude in life:

तच्चेऽनुकम्पां सुसमीक्षमाणो भुञ्जान एवात्मकृतं विपाकम् ।
हृद्वाग्वपुर्भि-र्विदधन्नमस्ते जीवेत यो मुक्तिपदे स दायभाक् ॥

(2) He who spends the span of his life in patient and constant expectation of Thy mercy, undergoing the consequences of his past actions, and ever prostrating himself to Thee in body, mind and speech—he becomes eligible for Moksha. (10.14.8)

Suta on the sanctifying effect of Vandana:

पतितः स्खलितो वार्तः क्षुधया विवशोऽगृणन् ।
हरये नभ इत्युच्चै-र्मुच्यते सर्वपातकात् ॥

(3) Even if one cries in fear or excitement, "Salutation to Hari!" when threatened with physical danger or overpowered by hunger and ailments— one is freed from sins. (12.12.46)

Kavi, one of the Navayogis, on this comprehensive meaning of Vandana:

खं वायुमग्निं सलिलं महीं च ज्योतींषि सत्त्वानि दिशो द्रुमादीन् ।
सरित्समुद्रांश्च हरेः शरीरं यत्किंच भूतं प्रणमेदनन्यः ॥

(4) One who adores Sri Hari as the All-Inclusive Absolute should salute the sky, air, fire, water, earth, shining celestial bodies, quarters, living beings, trees, rivers, oceans—in fact every manifested object— as constituting the body of Sri Hari.(11.2.41)

STRAND 10
DASYA OR SERVANTSHIP

[Introduction : Dasya, the seventh of the devotional disciplines, means cultivating the attitude of a servant of the Lord. This and the succeeding disciplines (Sakhya and Atmanivedana) have to be distinguished from the earlier ones, as they form the devotional attitudes that settle on one through long practice of the earlier ones. These Bhavas or devotional attitudes are of the very essence of the higher forms of Bhakti (Para-Bhakti), which are distinguished from the formal or ordinance-regulated Bhakti (Vaidhi Bhakti). In the stage of Vaidhi Bhakti it is incumbent that the devotee practises the earlier disciplines dealt with, but when devotion has become spontaneous, these disciplines cease to be disciplines, but become natural channels for the expression of the devotional sentiment.

In devotional literature these Bhavas are enumerated as follows: Santa (placid and philosophical), Dasya (servitude), Apatya (filial), Vatsalya (parental) Sakhya (companionship) and Madhurya (conjugal). All these Bhavas except the first (Santa) are intensely personal with powerful sentiments as the moving force. Santa is largely impersonal and philosophical and does not really come under the category of sentimental love. There is therefore a tendency on the part of the scholars of the devotional schools which exalt the personal relationship as the highest, to relegate Santa Bhava to an inferior level. This can be attributed only to a kind of narrowness. Intellectual love of God is a favourite idea of a great philosopher like Spinoza. A great thinker and scholar like Madhusudana, who was an ardent Advaitin but also an equally ardent devotee, considers Santa as Knowledge-oriented (Jnana-misra) devotion, sufficient to secure the spiritual *summum bonum* for the aspirant. Devotees who take to Santa are full of the spirit of renunciation born of a sense of the unworthiness and miserable nature of worldly existence and they seek refuge in God. They recognize a philosophical relationship between the

16

Jiva and God in place of a personal and sentimental one. It may be one of 'part and the whole', 'organ and organism' or 'reflection and its prototype.' As the knowledge of this relationship becomes vivid in their consciousness, they attain to supreme love based on that knowledge. They surrender themselves to the Lord (Atmanivedana) and obtain unity with Him.

It is unfair to consider Santa Bhava as in any way inferior to the personal Bhavas. It is of another type, being love stimulated by an intellectual apprehension rather than by a sense of human relationship. Madhusudhana has a significant verse in which he says: " 'I am His', 'He is mine', 'I am He'—refuge in God takes these three forms according to progress in the practice of spiritual disciplines." In the Santa type, the devotion perhaps passes from an awareness of 'I am His' to 'I am He' or absorption in God, without the intervening stage of 'He is mine', which forms the core of personal Bhavas. The Santa Bhava may, however, be mixed with Apatya and Dasya attitudes born of a sense of God's Fatherhood, Motherhood, or Lordship.

In the personal Bhavas the feeling that God is "one's own" dominates, and finds expression in a sense of intimate and personal, in the place of philosophical, relationship. Of these, to feel that God is one's father or mother, or master is natural to a devotee, and is all that is practicable for an ordinary aspirant following the path of devotion. But to feel that God is one's Child, or one's Companion, or one's Sweetheart, is so intimate a form of relationship that an ordinary devotee, who is dominated by a sense of Divine majesty, does not dare to cultivate it. Even the sense of Fatherhood, Motherhood and Lordship can be felt by him only in a philosophic sense and not in an intensely personal relationship. The attitude of Madhura (conjugal love) is considered the most intimate, involving in itself the essence of Dasya (servitude) Sakhya, (companionship), and perhaps Vatsalya (parental affection) too.

In the enumeration of the nine devotional disciplines, only Dasya (servitude) and Sakhya (companionship) are mentioned in the Text. Besides these, there is mention also of

Atmanivedana (self-dedication). Probably the other attitudes are considered as included in the last one.

In the present chapter Dasya Bhava is dealt with.

Durvasas on the greatness of being a servant of God:

यन्नामश्रुतिमात्रेण पुमान् भवति निर्मलः ।
तस्य तीर्थपदः किं वा दासानामवशिष्यते ॥

(1) He by uttering whose Name itself a person is purified, He whose feet form the abode of all holiness—to one who is the servant of Him—what is there that remains to be achieved!

(9.5.16)

In Brahma's words servitude to God means real freedom:

तावद्रागादयः स्तेना-स्तावत्कारागृहं गृहम् ।
तावान्मोहोऽङ्घ्रिनिगडो यावत्कृष्ण न ते जनाः ॥

(2) As long as a man has not dedicated himself to Thee as Thy servant, passions confront him as thieves; home confines him as a prison; and infatuation binds him as fetters. (10.14.36)

In Uddhava's words it is stated that servitude to God takes an aspirant to the spiritual summmum bonum :

किं चित्रमच्युत तवैतदशेषबन्धो दासेष्वनन्यशरणेषु यदात्मसात्त्वम् ।
योऽरोचयत्सह मृगैः स्वयमीश्वराणां श्रीमत्किरीटतट-पीडित-पादपीठः ॥

(3) Though all the gods were offering homage at Thy feet in readiness to serve Thee, Thou didst prefer to take animals (monkeys) as Thy allies (in Thy Incarnation as Rama). Immeasurable One and Friend of all! What wonder is there then in Thy looking upon as Thy own self, such devotees as have none else but Thee as their refuge! (11.29.4)

NOTE : In the previous verse of the *Bhagavata* it is stated that those who surrender themselves to Him overcome Maya easily unlike those who depend on Yoga and Karma—in other words, who try to succeed by their own effort. Here it is stated why they, the resigned ones, are able to overcome Maya. The Lord considers or makes them His own self, and because of their being thus one with Him, Maya has no more hold on them even as it has no hold on Him. Such is the greatness of the attitude of servitude to the Lord. Any one, however low, is acceptable to Him as servant. Even monkeys were accepted as allies by Him in His incarnation as Rama. This idea is confirmed by the following saying of Sri Ramakrishna: A servant serves a Master for long very faithfully. The Master is extremely pleased with him, and putting him on his own seat, says, 'You are my own self.' Advaitic consciousness is like that—a gift of God on His faithful and loving servant.

According to Kavi servitude to God means surrender of all one's actions to Him :

कायेन वाचा मनस्येन्द्रियैर्वा बुध्यात्मना वाऽनुसृतस्वभावात् ।
करोति यद्यत्सकलं परस्मै नारायणायेति समर्पयेत्तत् ॥

(4) **Whatever is done according to one's natural capacity by one's body, words, mind, senses, Buddhi, and the self—all that should be dedicated to Narayana, the Supreme Being.**

(11.2.36)

SAKHYA OR COMRADESHIP

[**Introduction:** Sakhya or comradeship with the Lord forms the topic of this section. Companionship is a very close relationship, wherein the degree of intimacy is greater than in servitude. The sense of God's power and glory is counterpoised by the sense of His being "one's own ", and the devotee·becomes equal with God without forgetting His greatness. It is this closeness and intimacy with God that the upholders of these forms of personal devotion point to as its superiority over intellectual love (Santa Bhakti). The subject matter has already been discussed in the Introduction to the earlier section.

The famous example of this relationship is that of the cowherds and cowherdesses of Vrindavana among whom Sri Krishna was brought up. The other attitudes of parental (Vatsalya) and conjugal (Madhura) love are also illustrated in Sri Krishna's life at Vrindavana. The Anthologist is very brief on Sakhya itself, and is silent on the others, probably because they are not separately enumerated in the ninefold discipline. It may also be that they are considered included in Sakhya, as it conveys the sense of that intimacy which forms the basis of both the others, Madhura Bhava can also come under this or the next heading, Atmanivedana or self-dedication to God. The philosophy of it has been discussed in detail in the General Introduction.]

Brahma, the creator, expresses his astonishment at the intimate companionship of the inhabitants of Vraja with Sri Krishna :

अहो भाग्यमहोभाग्यं नन्दगोपव्रजौकसाम् ।
यन्मित्रं परमानन्दं पूर्णं ब्रह्म सनातनम् ॥

(1) How fortunate are Nanda and the other inhabitants of Vraja! For they have got Sri Krishna—the eternal and undecaying Brahman, the embodiment of supreme Bliss—as their companion! (10.14.32)

NOTE: It is evident that in this one verse the whole episode
of Sri Krishna's life at Vrindavana is included. So ' companionship' here should be taken as including the parental and conjugal
relationships also, as the sense of intimacy is the basis of the other
relationships too.

*What companionship with God achieves, is put in the words
of Rishabha :*

एवं मनः कर्मवशं प्रयुंक्ते अविद्ययात्मन्युपधीयमाने ।
प्रीतिर्न यावन्मयि वासुदेवे न मुच्यते देहयोगेन तावत् ॥

(2) So long as the Atman is enshrouded in ignorance, its
association with the mind subjects the Atman to Karma and
consequently to repeated births and deaths. Until the aspirant
cultivates intimate love (Priti or Sakhya) for Vasudeva, he is not
released from the bondage of the body.   (5.5.6)

NOTE : Priti is the loving and joyous feeling one has in the
presence of an object that has deep and irresistible attraction for
one. People usually have this feeling towards their dear and
near ones and to worldly objects that give them pleasure or profit.
If one has Priti with regard to God, it becomes devotion of the
highest order. All the preparatory part of the ninefold devotional
discipline is meant to generate Priti in man for God. Priti grows
into Prema. Sakhya (comradeship), Vatsalya (parental affection)
and Madhura (conjugal love) are all aspects of Prema, and Priti
in different degrees is the experience they yield.

ATMASAMARPANA OR SELF-DEDICATION

[**Introduction**: The subject of this section is **Atmanivedana** or dedication of oneself to the Lord. This is the end of all devotional disciplines. The devotional attitudes mentioned earlier culminate in this. A dedicated devotee abandons all that he holds near, dear or precious, all considerations of security, status, honour, pride of possesion — in fact every kind of worldly value — for the sake of God, and finds self-fulfilment in contemplation on, and service of, Him.

He seeks nothing from God, and gives everything that is his unto Him. Ever filled with a sense of the Lord's universal rulership and His all-prevading presence, he is free from all fear, worry, jealousy and antagonism. He rises above the sense of agentship and enjoyership, and rests in God in peace. Every form of Bhakti culminates in this attainment, but the *Bhagavata* and the Bhakt scriptures in general hold forth the examples of the Gopikas as the most conspicuous instance of self-dedication and surrender. In this selection not many verses are devoted to the Gopikas except what lie scattered here and there. But in the General Introduction, the reader will get an elaborate discussion of it. Unlike devotees in general, they did not, it is true, pass through the earlier phases of devotional discipline. Being fortunate enough to be the contemporaries of Sri Krishna, the Lord Incarnate, their purification was effected by direct contact with him. Their mind got fixed on him in passionate personal love as their beloved, and they had the bliss of communion with him. But then they were separated from him when he left Gokula for Mathura, from where he sent them the message: "Separation only strengthens love. Soon will you attain to the joy of Brahman which will make you experience separation and union as equally bissful" (*Narayaneeyam*). When they met him again at Samanta Panchaka some years after, they were found to have developed that depth of love through that tormenting yet delightful pangs of separation.

On that occasion, Krishna gives them full enlightenment that would enable them to realize his presence in everything and everywhere. He conveys to them the following as his last message: "Devotion to Me is the only means for attaining to bliss undecaying. It is fortunate that you have developed attachment to Me which is the means for attaining to Me. Just as all objects of the world have their beginning and their end in the five Elements, and are also covered and infilled by these Elements, in the same way understand Me to be the basis and substance pervading all the worlds, living and non-living. The living beings only experience objects, but those objects do not rest in them but in the Elements constituting them. It is, however, in and through Me, supreme and imperishable Being, that both these—the experiencing Jivas and the experienced objects constituted of Elements—have their entity and subsistence." (Bh. 10.82.45-47) With this enlightenment given by the blessing of Krishna, the Gopikas found themselves to be ever in His blessed presence, irrespective of proximity in a physcial sense. Thus Atmanivedana or self-dedication as an expression of personal love and intimacy with the Divine, brought also enlightenment to the Gopikas.]

Sri Kirshna on Atmanivedana as the crown of spiritual life:

मर्त्यों यदा त्यक्तसमस्तकर्मा निवेदितात्मा विचिकीर्षितो मे ।
तदाऽमृतत्वं प्रतिपद्यमानो मयात्मभूयाय च कल्पते वै ॥

(1) When a man has abandoned all self-centred efforts and has dedicated himself entirely to Me, then he becomes the special object of My grace. Freed from the round of births and deaths, he becomes one with My being.   (11.29.34)

The superiority of self-dedication to all disciplines is stated in the words of Prahlada.

धर्मार्थकाम इति योभिहितस्त्रिवर्ग
ईक्षा त्रयी नयदमौ विविधा च वार्ता ।

मन्ये तदेतदखिलं निगमस्य सत्यं
खात्मार्पणं खसुहृदः परमस्य पुंसः ॥

(2) The Vedas do indeed deal with the three worldly values
of morality, wealth and pleasure—with philosophy and ethics,
with sacrifical rites, with statecraft and with various accomplish-
ments useful to man. But I regard that the dedication of oneself
to the Supreme Being, the Friend and Well-wisher of all, is their
real teaching.   (7.6.26)

SARANAGATI OR
TAKING REFUGE IN THE LORD

[Introduction: The nine disciplines of Bhakti have been treated in the previous chapters. In this section Saranagati or "Taking Refuge in the Lord" is explained. It is difficult to distinguish it in effect from Self-dedication (Atmanivedana) treated in the previous section. Probably the following distinction may be made: Self-dedication may be described as the effect that gradually comes on a soul that has practised for long the devotional disciplines mentioned earlier. It may be described as the ripe fruit of devotional discipline. What is described here as 'taking refuge in the Lord' is also involved in it. But 'taking refuge' may also be the result of a sudden conversion due to an oppressive sense of the wretchedness of worldly life, of a sense of sin, or of imminent danger of disease and death. Under such circumstances even an unprepared soul may throw himself helplessly at the feet of God and seek refuge in Him. The devotional doctrine has a place for such devotees also. So the *Gita* says : "Even if a man is a confirmed sinner, he must be considered a good man, provided he resigns himself to Me as his sole refuge. For he has taken the right resolve. Soon will he become righteous and attain to peace. No devotee of Mine is ever lost." In the *Bhagavata* itself there is the account of Ajamila who took the name of Narayana in dreadful fear when face to face with death, and he was saved. In verses 19—35 of the fifth Strand of this Anthology, reference will be found to the Ajamila episode with detailed explanation of how a sinner becomes a devotee. Narayana Bhattatiri, the author of the *Narayaneeyam*, is a famous example of one who took shelter with the Lord owing to the torments of an incurable ailment and became a great devotee in his later life. Girish Chandra Gosh, a talented artiste-disciple of Sri Ramakrishna, though without any spiritual discipline, took absolute shelter under the Great Master and became a transformed man.

There are several such examples of men who under physical or mental suffering of an irremediable nature lose hope in life and resign themselves completely to the Lord, though they are without any practice of devotional discipline earlier. If the resignation is complete and irrevocably wholehearted, the person becomes a great devotee, in spite of his past background. Such devotees are *saranagatas* (refugees) *par excellence*. The doctrine of Prapatti in Sri Ramanuja's system of Sri Vaishnavism comes under this teaching.]

How surrender frees one from all Rinas (debts), is stated in the words of Karabhaja :

देवर्षिभूतासनृणां पितृणां न किङ्करो नायमृणी च राजन् ।
सर्वात्मना यः शरणं शरण्यं गतो मुकुन्दं परिहत्य कर्तम् ॥

(1) **A person who has unreservedly taken refuge in the Lord, giving up all ideas of agentship, is no longer a servant of the Devas, Rishis, Bhutas, living beings or Pitrs, and (for this reason) is no longer a debtor to them.** (11.5.41)

NOTE: According to Hindu scriptures man is by nature heir to five debts. These are: debt to Devas or celestials; debt to Rishis or the founding Fathers of a culture; debt to Pitrs or forefathers; debt to fellow human beings; and debt to Bhutas or sub-human beings. These debts are repaid by what are called Panchamahayajnas (the fivefold sacrifice)—to Devas by worship; to Rishis by study of scripture; to Pitrs by performing obsequies like Tarpana and Sraddha and leaving a son to continue these performances; to fellow men by hospitality and charity: and to Bhutas by giving them food and shelter. If a man takes complete refuge in God and has nothing in this world to call his own, he is free from all these debts, even if he has not discharged them earlier.

Maitreya on the supreme value of self-surrender :

किं दुरापादनं तेषां पुंसामुद्दामचेतसाम् ।
यैराश्रितस्तीर्थपद-चरणो व्यसनात्ययः ॥

(2) What is there unattainable to such high-minded souls as have resigned themselves to the holy feet of the Lord, the panacea for every kind of misery here and hereafter?   (3.23.42)

The effects of self-surrender are further elaborated in the words of Maitreya :

शारीरा मानसा दिव्या वैयासे ये च मानुषाः ।
भौतिकाश्च कथं क्लेशा बाधन्ते हरिसंश्रयम् ॥

(3) O Vidura, a man who has surrendered himself to Sri Hari is not afflicted with sufferings arising from sources like his own body and mind, from divine and human agencies, or from inclemencies of Nature.   (3.23.37)

The potency of surrender is further described in the words of Rudra.

यत्र निर्विष्टशरणं कृतान्तो नाभिमन्यते ।
विश्वं विध्वंसयन् शौर्य-वीर्यविस्फूर्चितभ्रवा ॥

(4) One who has surrendered oneself at the feet of the Lord never comes within the sphere of Yama, the god of death, whose angry face cows down the whole world by the power and energy emanating from it.   (4.24.56)

Self-surrender is due only to the Supreme Being:

अविस्मितं तं परिपूर्णकामं स्वेनैव लाभेन समं प्रशान्तम् ।
विनोपसर्पत्यपरं हि बालिशः श्वलांगुलेनातितितर्ति सिंधुम् ॥

(5) There is none who surpasses Him in greatness and could therefore cause Him surprise. He is absorbed in the bliss of His all-comprehending self and seeks satisfaction from nothing external. He is unaffected by change and he is all peace. The man who abandons Him and seeks shelter in another (for over-coming Samsara) is silly like one trying to cross the ocean with the support of a dog's tail.   (6.9.22)

Prahlada on how the Lord alone is man's ultimate shelter.

बालस्य नेह शरणं पितरौ नृसिंह नार्तस्य चागदमुदन्वति मज्जतो नौः
तमस्य तत्प्रतिविधिर्य इहांजसेष्ट-स्त्वावद्विभोतनुभृतां त्वदपेक्षितानाम् ॥

(6)   In this world there are ready remedies given for sorrows and sufferings.   But they often fail, or their effects are of short duration in the case of those who have been abandoned by Thee. For it is seen that a father may fail to give shelter to a child, a medicine can fail to cure an ailment, and a boat may fail to save a man drowing in the sea.   He whom Thou hast forsaken has no shelter.   (7.9.19)

NOTE :   The idea is that God alone is the ultimate support for man.   What we call worldly supports, are relative and are dependent on His will.   They may succeed or fail according to His will, of which we have no fore-knowledge.   A devotee who is resigned must have this background of thought in all his undertaking.

Akrura on why man should take shelter in the Lord alone :

कः पंडितः त्वदपरं शरणं समीयाद्-
भक्तप्रियाद्ऋतगिरः सुहृदः कृतज्ञात् ।
सर्वान् ददाति सुहृदो भजतोऽभिकामा-
नात्मानमप्युपचयापचयौ न यस्य ॥

(7)   Which intelligent man would seek shelter in any one other than Thee, the lover of devotees, the truthful, the benevolent, the grateful?   Thou bestowest all the heart's desires of Thy intimate devotees who serve Thee—nay, Thou even givest Thyself unto them.   There is no ebb and flow in Thy love.   (10.48.26)

Uddhava on the glory of taking refuge in the Lord :

अहो बकी यं स्तनकालकूटं जिघांसयाऽपाययदप्यसाध्वी ।
लेमे गतिं धास्थुचितां ततोऽन्यं किं वा दयालुं शरणं व्रजेम ॥

(8)   The wicked demoness Pootana applied the infant Krishna to her breast poisoned with Kalakuta with a view to killing him. But she got in return from Him Mukti (liberation)—a reward befitting a mother.   In whom except so merciful a Lord shall we take refuge ?   (3.2.23)

NOTE: The reference is to Pootana, the female emissary of Kamsa, who came as a wet nurse to poison the infant Krishna. The infant Lord, when applied to the breast, suckled away the very life of the demoness. Physically she died, but having contacted the Lord in the capacity of a wet nurse, she was blessed with the highest spiritual elevation, befitting the Lord's mother herself. Thus all acts of Krishna, even the infliction of death on his so-called enemies, were only to bless them.

Uddhava on resignation as the supreme panacea for the ills of life :

तापत्रयेणाभिहतस्य घोरे संतप्यमानस्य भवाध्वनीश ।
पश्यामि नान्यच्छरणं तवांघ्रि-द्वन्द्वातपत्रा-दमृताभिवर्षात् ॥

(9)   For the man scorched on the roads of life by the heat of threefold misery, I do not find any shelter other than Thy lotus feet, which protect one like an umberella and cool like a rain of ambrosia. (11, 19. 9)

NOTE: The miseries of life are classed into three categories – Adhyatmika (mental or psychological) Adhibhautika (physical, including sickness, poverty, violence from others etc.), and Adhidaivika (caused by non-human agencies like natural cataclysms etc.)

The compilation from the Bhagavata ends with a verse of King Muchukunda on resignation :

चिरमिह वृजिनार्तस्तप्यमानोऽनुतापै-
रवितृषषडमित्रोऽलब्धशान्तिः कथंचित् ।
शरणद समुपेतस्त्वत्पदाब्जं परातम्-
भ्रभयमृतमशोकं पाहि माऽपन्नमीश ॥

(10) O Thou Supreme Self and the Refuge of all! Long
have I been afflicted and deprived of all peace by the six insatiable
enemies in the shape of my senses, by my sinful Karmas, and by
the evil tendencies born of them. Save me, O Lord, from the
besetting danger from these—me who have sought shelter at Thy
feet where there is no fear and no sorrow, and where truth abides.
                                                        (10.51.58)

*The following three verses, with which the work concludes, are
the composition of Vishnu Puri himself, conveying his thankfulness
to the Lord, and offering the work to Sri Hari and all His
devotees:*

एवं श्री श्रीरमण भवता यत्समुत्तेजितोऽहं
चांचल्ये वा सकलविषये सारनिर्द्धारणे वा ।
आत्मप्रज्ञाविभवसदृशैस्तत्र यत्नैर्मेमेतैः
साकं भक्तैरगतिसुगते पुष्टिमेहि त्वमेव ॥

साधूनां स्वत एव संमतिरिह स्यादेव भक्त्यर्थिना-
मालोक्य ग्रथनश्रमं च विदुषामस्मिन् भवेदादरः ।
ये केचित्परकृत्युपश्रुतिपरास्तानर्थ्ये मत्कृतिं
भूयो वीक्ष्य वदन्त्ववद्यमिह चेत्सा वासना स्थास्यति ॥

एषस्यामहमल्पबुद्धिविभवोऽप्येकोऽपि कोऽपि ध्रुवम्
मध्ये भक्तजनस्य मत्कृतिरियं न स्याद्वज्ञास्पदम् ।
किं विद्याः शरधाः किमुज्ज्वलकुलाः किं पौरुषं किं गुणा-
स्तत्किं सुंदरमादरेण रसिकैर्नाऽपीयते तन्मधु ॥

(11) O Lord of Sri, this literary effort of mine, into which I
have put whatever intellectual capacity I have—whether it be of
the nature of wanton childishness or of deep and mature understanding— is entirely due to Thy prompting. O Refuge of helpless people! May Thou, with Thy devotees, be pleased to accept
it as an offering.

(12)   Good men who aspire for devotion are likely to welcome this work. Learned men may also show it much consideration, seeing the great effort I have made in the selection and arrangement of the verses (topically and with sequence). As for those who always criticise other people's literary efforts, I pray, let them read this work over again, and then point out its defects, if their fault-finding tendency remains at all by that time! (For, reading it several times will generate devotion in them and efface their fault-finding tendency.)

(13)   I may be a man of little intelligence, alone, without any following, and unknown in distant places. Yet this Anthology of mine will not have to face disdain among men who are in quest of devotion. For look at the bees! What learning, what splendour of lineage, what power of personality, what noble virtues do they possess! Yet do not even refined connoisseurs welcome and drink with relish the sweet honey the bees collect!

|| श्रीकृष्णार्पणमस्तु ||
In dedication to Sri Krishna